For any of us to be fully conscious
intellectually we should not only be able
to detect the world views of others
but be aware of our own—
why it is ours and why
in light of so many options
we think it is true.

Other Books by James W. Sire

How to Read Slowly
Scripture Twisting
Beginning with God
Meeting Jesus

THE UNIVERSE NEXT DOOR

JAMES W. SIRE

A BASIC
WORLD
VIEW
CATALOG

**Updated &
Expanded Edition**

INTERVARSITY PRESS
DOWNERS GROVE, ILLINOIS 60515

Second edition © 1988 by James W. Sire. First edition © 1976 by InterVarsity Christian Fellowship of the United States of America.

InterVarsity Press is the book-publishing division of InterVarsity Christian Fellowship, a student movement active on campus at hundreds of universities, colleges and schools of nursing. For information about local and regional activities, write Public Relations Dept., InterVarsity Christian Fellowship, 6400 Schroeder Rd., P.O. Box 7895, Madison, WI 53707-7895.

Distributed in Canada through InterVarsity Press, 860 Denison St., Unit 3, Markham, Ontario L3R 4H1, Canada.

All Scripture quotations, unless otherwise indicated, are from the Revised Standard Version of the Bible, copyrighted 1946, 1952, 1971 by the Division of Christian Education of the National Council of the Churches of Christ in the U.S.A., and are used by permission. All rights reserved. Quotations from the Upanishads are reprinted from pages 83-84 and 117 of The Upanishads, translated by Juan Mascaró (Penguin Classics, 1965). Reprinted by permission of Penguin Books Ltd.

Cover illustration: Jerry Tiritilli

ISBN 0-8308-1220-2

Printed in the United States of America

Library of Congress Cataloging in Publication Data

Sire, James W.
    The universe next door / James W. Sire.—2nd ed., updated and
expanded.
        p.   cm.
    Bibliography: p.
    Includes index.
    ISBN 0-8308-1220-2
      1. Ideology.   2. Theism.   3. Naturalism.   4. Nihilism (Philosophy)
    5.   New Age movement.   I. Title.
    B823.3.S56 1988
    110—dc19   88-8852
                                        CIP

17   16   15   14   13   12   11   10   9   8   7   6   5   4   3   2   1
99   98   97   96   95   94   93   92   91   90   89   88

To Marjorie, Carol, Eugene and Carol,
Richard and Kay Dee, and Ann—
whose worlds on worlds
compose my familiar and expanding universe

Preface to the Second Edition

The continued interest of readers in this book which I wrote over twelve years ago continues to surprise and please me. Each year it has been finding its way into the hands of many students at the behest of professors in courses as widely divergent as apologetics, history, English literature, introduction to religion, introduction to philosophy and even one on the human dimensions of science. Such a range of interests suggests that one of the assumptions on which the book is based is indeed true: the most fundamental issues we as human beings need to consider have no departmental boundaries. What is prime reality? Is it God or the cosmos? What is a human being? What happens at death? How should we then live? These questions are as relevant to literature as to psychology, to religion as to science.

In a very important sense how these questions have been answered has not changed at all over the past decade. There are only a few ways that they can be answered, and little "advance" or "progress" in answering them is even possible. Still, one set of answers—that is, one world view—has been developing. In the first edition I wrote that "we are experiencing . . . the birth pangs of a new world view, . . . [one] not completely formed." Now the baby has been born and is screaming rather loudly for attention. What I called the new consciousness in 1976 is now known as the New Age. Twelve years ago its major exponent was Carlos Castaneda, no longer much in the news; today its foremost public exponent is Shirley MacLaine. In light of these developments I have extensively revised chapter eight and retitled it "The New Age."

A second major revision will be found in chapter four and is a response to reviews of the first edition. Few American reviewers found anything major missing. But several reviewers outside the United States asked, "Where is Marxism, one of today's most significant world views?" Actually, I had mentioned Marxism briefly as a subspecies of naturalism. These reviewers, however, took Marxism as important enough to deserve independent treatment. I think they are right, and I have added a special section in this edition. Since I do not consider my own understanding of Marxism to be adequate for the task, I am deeply grateful that my good friend C. Stephen Evans, associate professor of philosophy at St. Olaf College, kindly consented to write that section for me. It is found on pages 75-82.

A third less substantial revision is an added section on secular humanism. Too many reviewers did not notice that in describing naturalism I was at the same time describing the basic tenets of this world view as well. I have now made the connection explicit.

Finally, I have tried to polish the book throughout, updating bibliographical references, correcting verbal infelicities, and generally bringing the book into the context of the late 1980s. I have, for example, added to the chapter on nihilism allusions to Douglas Adams's *Hitchhiker's Guide to the Galaxy* space-science trilogy in four volumes and taken account of some of the cultural analyses published since 1976.

I have not, however, made all the additions and corrections reviewers and readers have suggested. For example, some have suggested that I shortchanged the lifestyle dimensions of each world view; after all, we indicate by our actions as much what we really think and are as we do by our stated views. I accept this criticism and am sorry I could not take the time and space to at least sketch what is needed. The task must be left to others.

On one issue I remain constant: I am convinced that for any of us to be fully conscious intellectually we should not only be able to detect the world views of others but be aware of our own—why it is ours and why in light of so many options we think it is true. I can only hope that this book becomes a steppingstone for others toward their own self-conscious development and justification of their own world view.

In addition to the many acknowledgments contained in the footnotes, I would especially like to thank Mr. C. Stephen Board, general manager of Harold Shaw Publishers, who many years ago invited me to present much of this material in lecture form at the Christian Study Project sponsored by the InterVarsity Christian Fellowship and held at Cedar Campus in Michigan. He and Mr. Thomas Trevethan, also on the staff of that program, have given excellent counsel in the development of the material and in the continued critique of my world-view thinking since the first publication of this book.

Other friends who have read the manuscript and helped polish some of the rough edges are Dr. C. Stephen Evans, Dr. Os Guinness, Dr. Charles Hampton and Dr. Keith Yandell. To them and to the editor of this edition, Mr. James Hoover, go my sincere appreciation. Finally, I would like to acknowledge the feedback from many students who have weathered world-view criticism in my classes and lectures.

Responsibility for the continued infelicities and the downright errors in this book is, alas, my own.

James W. Sire
November 1987

1
A World of Difference

But often, in the world's most crowded streets,
But often, in the din of strife,
There rises an unspeakable desire
After the knowledge of our buried life:
A thirst to spend our fire and restless force
In tracking out our true, original course;
A longing to inquire
Into the mystery of this heart which beats
So wild, so deep in us—to know
Whence our lives come and where they go.
Matthew Arnold
"The Buried Life"

In the late nineteenth century Stephen Crane captured our plight as we in the late twentieth century face the universe.

A man said to the universe:
"Sir, I exist."
"However," replied the universe,
"The fact has not created in me
A sense of obligation."[1]

How different this is from the words of the ancient psalmist who looked around himself and up to God and wrote:

O LORD, our Lord,
how majestic is thy name in all the earth!
Thou whose glory above the heavens is chanted
by the mouth of babes and infants,

thou hast founded a bulwark because of thy foes,
   to still the enemy and the avenger.
When I look at thy heavens, the work of thy fingers,
   the moon and the stars which thou hast established;
what is man that thou art mindful of him,
   and the son of man that thou dost care for him?
Yet thou hast made him little less than God,
   and dost crown him with glory and honor.
Thou hast given him dominion over the works of thy hands;
   thou hast put all things under his feet,
all sheep and oxen,
   and also the beasts of the field,
the birds of the air, and the fish of the sea,
   whatever passes along the paths of the sea.
O LORD, our Lord,
   how majestic is thy name in all the earth! (Ps 8)

There is a world of difference between the world views of these two poems. Indeed, they propose alternative universes. Yet both poems reverberate in the minds and souls of people today. Many who stand with Stephen Crane have more than a memory of the psalmist's great and glorious assurance of God's hand in the cosmos and his love for his people. They long for what they no longer can truly accept. The gap left by the loss of a center to life is like the chasm in the heart of a child whose father has died. How those who no longer believe in God wish something could fill this void!

And many who yet stand with the psalmist and whose faith in the Lord God is vital and brimming still feel the tug of Crane's poem. Yes, that is exactly how it is to lose God. Yes, that is just what those who do not have faith in the infinite-personal Lord of the Universe must feel—alienation, loneliness, even despair.

We recall the struggles of faith in our nineteenth-century forebears and know that for many faith was the loser. As Tennyson wrote in response to the death of his close friend,

> Behold, we know not anything;
>   I can but trust that good shall fall
>   At last—far off—at last, to all
> And every winter change to spring.
>
> So runs my dream; but what am I?
>   An infant crying in the night;
>   An infant crying for the light;
> And with no language but a cry.[2]

With Tennyson faith eventually won out, but the struggle was years in being resolved.

The struggle to discover our own faith, our own world view, our beliefs about reality is what this book is all about. Formally stated, the purposes of this book are (1) to outline the basic world views that underlie the way we in the Western world think about ourselves, other people, the natural world, and God or ultimate reality; (2) to trace historically how these world views have developed from a breakdown in the theistic world view, moving in turn into deism, naturalism, nihilism, existentialism, Eastern mysticism and the new consciousness of the New Age; and (3) to encourage us all to think in terms of world views, that is, with a consciousness of not only our own way of thought but also that of other people, so that we can first understand and then genuinely communicate with others in our pluralistic society.

That is a large order. In fact it sounds very much like the project of a lifetime. My hope is that it will be just that for many who read this book and take seriously its implications. What is written here is only an introduction to what might well become a way of life.

In writing this book I have found it especially difficult to know what to include and what to leave out. But, because I see the whole book as an introduction, I have tried rigorously to be brief—to get to the heart of each world view, suggest its strengths and weaknesses, and move to the next. I have, however, indulged my own interest by including textual and bibliographical footnotes that will, I trust, lead readers into greater depths than the chapters themselves. Those who wish first to get at what I take to be the heart of the matter can safely ignore them. But those who wish to go it on their own (may their name be legion!) may find the footnotes helpful in suggesting further reading and further questions for investigation.

What Is a World View?

Despite the fact that such philosophical names as Plato, Aristotle, Sartre, Camus and Nietzsche will appear on these pages, this book is not a work of professional philosophy. And though we will refer time and again to concepts made famous by the apostle Paul, Augustine, Aquinas and Calvin, this is not a work of theology. Rather, it is a book of world views—in some ways more basic, more foundational, than formal studies in either philosophy or theology. Or, to put it yet another way, it is a book of universes fashioned by words and concepts that work together to provide a more or less coherent frame of reference for all thought and action.[3]

Few people have anything approaching an articulate philosophy—at least as epitomized by the great philosophers. Even fewer, I suspect, have a carefully constructed theology. But everyone has a world view. Whenever any of us thinks about anything—from a casual thought (Where did I leave my watch?) to a profound question (Who am I?)—we are operating within such a framework. In fact, only the assumption of a world view—however basic or simple—allows us to think at all.

What, then, is this thing called a world view that is so important to all of us? I've never even heard of one. How could I have one? That may well be the response of many people. One is reminded of M. Jourdain in

Moliere's *The Bourgeois Gentleman* who suddenly discovered he had been speaking prose for forty years without knowing it. But to discover one's own world view is much more valuable. In fact, it is a significant step toward self-awareness, self-knowledge and self-understanding.

So what is a world view? Essentially this: A world view is a set of presuppositions (assumptions which may be true, partially true or entirely false) which we hold (consciously or subconsciously, consistently or inconsistently) about the basic make-up of our world.

The first thing every one of us recognizes before we even begin to think at all is that something exists. In other words, all world views assume that something is there rather than that nothing is there. This assumption is so primary most of us don't even know we are assuming it.[4] We take it as too obvious to mention. Of course, something is there!

Indeed, it is. And that's just the point. If we do not recognize that, we get nowhere. Still, as with many other simple "facts" that stare us in the face, the significance may be tremendous. In this case the apprehension that something is there is the beginning of conscious life, as well as of two branches of philosophy: *metaphysics* (the study of being) and *epistemology* (the study of knowing).

What we discover quickly, however, is that once we have recognized *that* something is there, we have not necessarily recognized *what* that something is. And here is where world views begin to diverge. Some people assume (with or without thinking about it) that the only basic substance that exists is *matter*. For them, everything is ultimately one thing. Others agree that everything is ultimately one thing, but assume that that one thing is Spirit or Soul or some such nonmaterial substance.

But we must not get lost in examples. We are now concerned with the definition of a world view. A world view is composed of a number of basic presuppositions, more or less consistent with each other, more or less consciously held, more or less true. They are generally unquestioned by each of us; rarely, if ever, mentioned by our friends; and only brought to mind when we are challenged by a foreigner from another ideological universe.

Seven Basic Questions

Another way to get at what a world view is is to see it as our essential, rock-bottom answers to the following seven questions:

1. What is prime reality—the really real? To this we might answer: God, or the gods, or the material cosmos.

2. What is the nature of external reality, that is, the world around us? Here our answers point to whether we see the world as created or autonomous, as chaotic or orderly, as matter or spirit, or whether we emphasize our subjective, personal relationship to the world or its objectivity apart from us.

3. What is a human being? To this we might answer: a highly complex machine, a sleeping god, a person made in the image of God, a "naked ape."

4. What happens to a person at death? Here we might reply personal extinction or transformation to a higher state or departure to a shadowy existence on "the other side."

5. Why is it possible to know anything at all? Sample answers include the idea that we are made in the image of an all-knowing God or that consciousness and rationality developed under the contingencies of survival in a long process of evolution.

6. How do we know what is right and wrong? Again, perhaps we are made in the image of a God whose character is good, or right and wrong are determined by human choice alone, or the notions simply developed under an impetus toward cultural or physical survival.

7. What is the meaning of human history? To this we might answer: to realize the purposes of God or the gods, to make a paradise on earth, to prepare a people for a life in community with a loving and holy God, or something else.

Within various basic world views other issues often arise. For example: Who is in charge of this world—God or humans or no one at all? Are we as human beings determined or free? Are we alone the maker of values? Is God really good? Is God personal or impersonal? Or does he exist at all?

When stated in such a sequence, these questions boggle the mind. Either the answers are obvious to us and we wonder why anyone would bother to ask such questions, or else we wonder how any of them can be answered with any certainty. If we feel the answers are too obvious to consider, then we have a world view but we have no idea that many others do not share it. We should realize that we live in a pluralistic world. What is obvious to us may be "a lie from hell" to our neighbor next door. If we do not recognize that, we are certainly naive and provincial, and we have much to learn about living in today's world. Alternatively, if we feel that none of the questions can be answered without cheating or committing intellectual suicide, we have already adopted a sort of world view—a form of skepticism which in its extreme form leads to nihilism.

The fact is that we cannot avoid assuming some answers to such questions. We will adopt either one stance or another; refusing to adopt an explicit world view will turn out to be itself a world view or at least a philosophic position. In short, we are caught. So long as we live, we will live either the examined or the unexamined life. It is the assumption of this book that the examined life is better.

So the following chapters—each of which examines a major world view—are designed to illuminate the possibilities. We will examine the answers each world view gives to the seven basic questions. This will give us a consistent approach to each one, help us see their similarities and differences, and suggest how each might be evaluated within its own frame of reference as well as from the standpoint of other competing world views.

The world view I have adopted will be detected early in the course of the argument. But to waylay any guessing I will declare now that it is the subject of the next chapter. Nonetheless, the book is not a revelation of my world view but an exposition and critique of the options. If in the course of this examination readers find, modify or make more explicit their own individual world view, a major goal of this book will have been reached.

There are many verbal or conceptual universes. Some have been around a long time; others are just now forming. Which is your universe? Which are the universes next door?

2
A Universe Charged with the Grandeur of God: Christian Theism

The world is charged with the grandeur of God.
   It will flame out, like shining from shook foil;
   It gathers to a greatness, like the ooze of oil
Crushed. Why do men then now not reck his rod?
Gerard Manley Hopkins
"God's Grandeur"

In the Western world, up to the end of the seventeenth century, the theistic world view was clearly dominant. Intellectual squabbles—and there were as many then as now—were mostly family squabbles. Dominicans might disagree with Jesuits, Jesuits with Anglicans, Anglicans with Presbyterians ad infinitum, but all these parties subscribed to the same set of basic presuppositions. The Triune personal God of the Bible existed; he had revealed himself to us and could be known; the universe was his creation; human beings were his special creation. If battles were fought, the lines were drawn within the circle of theism.

How, for example, do we know God? By reason, by revelation, by faith, by contemplation, by proxy, by direct access? This battle was fought on many fronts over a dozen centuries and is still an issue with those remaining on the theistic field. Or take another issue: Is the basic stuff of the universe matter only, form only or a combination?

Theists have differed on this too. What role does human freedom play in a universe where God is sovereign? Again, a family squabble.

During the period from the early Middle Ages to the end of the seventeenth century, very few challenged the existence of God or held that ultimate reality was impersonal or that death meant individual extinction. The reason is obvious. Christianity had so penetrated the Western world that, whether people believed in Christ or acted as Christians should, they all lived in a context of ideas influenced and informed by the Christian faith. Even those who rejected the faith often lived in the fear of hellfire or the pangs of purgatory. Bad people may have rejected Christian goodness, but they knew themselves to be bad by basically Christian standards—crudely understood, no doubt, but Christian in essence. The theistic presuppositions which lay behind their values came with their mother's milk.

This, of course, is no longer true. Being born in the Western world now guarantees nothing. World views have proliferated. Walk on the street of any major city in Europe or North America, and the next person you meet could adhere to any one of a dozen distinctly different patterns of understanding what life is all about. It is getting so that little seems bizarre to us, making it more and more difficult for talk-show hosts to get good ratings by shocking their television audiences.

Consider the problem of growing up today. Baby Jane, a twentieth-century child of the Western world, often gets reality defined in two widely divergent forms—her mother's and her father's. Then if the family breaks apart, the court may enter with a third definition of human reality. This poses a distinct problem in deciding what the true shape of the world actually is.

Baby John, a child of the seventeenth century, however, was cradled in a cultural consensus that gave a sense of place. The world around was really there—created to be there by God. As God's vice regent, young John sensed being given dominion over the world. He was required to worship God, but God was eminently worthy of worship. He was required to obey God, but then obedience to God was true freedom since that was what people were made for. Besides, God's yoke was easy and his burden light. Furthermore, God's rules were seen as primarily moral, and people were free to be creative over the external universe, free to learn its secrets, free to shape and fashion it as God's stewards cultivating God's garden and offering up their work as true worship before a God who honors his creation with freedom and dignity.

There was a basis for both meaning and morality and also for the question of identity. The apostles of absurdity were yet to arrive. Even Shakespeare's King Lear (perhaps the English Renaissance's most "troubled" hero) does not end in total despair. And Shakespeare's later plays suggest that he too had passed well beyond the moment of despair and found the world to be ultimately meaningful.

It is fitting, therefore, that we begin a study of world views with theism. It is the foundational view, the one from which all others, developing between 1700 and 1900, essentially derive. It would be possible to go behind theism to Greco-Roman classicism, but even this, as it was reborn in the Renaissance, was seen almost solely within the framework of theism.[1] So it is time we treated theism directly.

Basic Christian Theism

As the core of each chapter I will try to express the essence of each world view in a minimum number of succinct propositions. Each world view considers the following basic issues: the nature and character of God or ultimate reality, the nature of the universe, the nature of humanity, the question of what happens to a person at death, the basis of human knowing, the basis of ethics and the meaning of history.[2] In the case of theism the prime proposition concerns the nature of God. Since this first proposition is so important, we will spend more time with it than with any other.

1. God is infinite and personal (Triune), transcendent and immanent, omniscient, sovereign and good.[3]

Let's break this proposition down into its parts.

God is infinite. This means that he is beyond scope, beyond measure, as far as we are concerned. No other being in the universe can challenge him in his nature. All else is secondary. He has no twin but is alone the be-all and end-all of existence. He is, in fact, the only self-existent being.[4] As the Lord God spoke to Moses out of the burning bush, "I AM WHO I AM" (Ex 3:14). He *is* in a way that none else is. As Moses proclaimed, "Hear, O Israel: The LORD our God is one LORD" (Deut 6:4). So God is the one prime existent, the one prime reality and, as we shall develop later, the one source of all other reality.

God is personal. This means God is not mere force or energy or existent "substance." God is *He;* that is, God has personality. Personality requires two basic characteristics: (1) self-reflection and (2) self-determination. In other words, God is personal in that he knows himself to be (he is self-conscious) and he possesses the characteristics of self-determination (he "thinks" and "acts").

One implication of the personality of God is that he is like us. In a way, this puts the cart before the horse. Actually, we are like him, but it is helpful to put it the other way around at least for a brief comment. He is like us. That means there is *someone* ultimate who is there to ground our highest aspirations, *our* most precious possession—personality. But more on this under proposition 3.

Another implication of the personality of God is that God is not simple unity, an integer. He has attributes, characteristics. He is a unity, yes, but a unity of complexity.

Actually, in Christian theism (not Judaism) *God is not only personal, but Triune.* That is, "within the one essence of the Godhead we have to distinguish three 'persons' who are neither three gods on the one side, not three parts or modes of God on the other, but coequally and coeternally God."[5] The Trinity is certainly a great mystery, and we cannot even begin to elucidate it now. What is important here is to note that the Trinity confirms the communal, "personal" nature of ultimate being. God is not only there—an actually existent being—he is personal and we can relate to him in a personal way. To know God, therefore, means knowing more than that he exists. It means knowing him as we know a brother or, better, our own father.

God is transcendent. This means God is beyond us and our world. He is *otherly.* Look at a stone: God is not it; God is beyond it. Look at a man: God is not he; God is beyond him. Yet God is not so beyond that he bears no relation to us and our world. It is likewise true that *God is immanent,* and this means that he is with us. Look at a stone: God is present. Look at a person: God is present. Is this, then, a contradiction? Is theism nonsense at this point? I think not.

My daughter Carol, when she was five years old, taught me a lot here. She and her mother were in the kitchen, and her mother was teaching her about God's being everywhere. So Carol asked, "Is God in the living room?"

"Yes," her mother replied.

"Is he in the kitchen?"

"Yes," she said.

"Am I stepping on God?"

Suddenly my wife was speechless. But look at the point that was raised. Is God *here* in the same way a stone or a chair or a kitchen is here? No, not quite. God is immanent, here, everywhere, in a sense completely in line with his transcendence. For God is not *matter* as you and I, but Spirit. And yet he is here. A text from the New Testament book of Hebrews states it this way: Jesus Christ is said to be "upholding the universe by his word of power" (Heb 1:3). That is, God is beyond all, yet in all and sustaining all.

God is omniscient. This means that God is all-knowing. He is the alpha and the omega and knows the beginning from the end (Rev

22:13). He is the ultimate source of all knowledge and all intelligence. He is *He Who Knows.* The author of Psalm 139 expresses beautifully his amazement at God's being everywhere, pre-empting him—knowing him even as he was being formed in his mother's womb.

God is sovereign. This is really a further ramification of God's infiniteness, but it expresses more fully his concern to rule, to pay attention, as it were, to all the actions of his universe. It expresses the fact that nothing is beyond God's ultimate interest, control and authority.

God is good. This is the prime statement about God's character. From it flow all others. To be good means to *be* good. God *is* goodness. That is, *what* he is is good. There is no sense in which goodness surpasses God or God surpasses goodness. As being is the essence of his nature, goodness is the essence of his character.

God's goodness is expressed in two ways, through holiness and through love. Holiness emphasizes his absolute righteousness which brooks no shadow of evil. As the apostle John says, "God is light and in him is no darkness at all" (1 Jn 1:5). God's holiness is his separateness from all that smacks of evil. But God's goodness is also expressed as love. In fact, John says "God is love" (1 Jn 4:16), and this leads God to self-sacrifice and the full extension of his favor to his people, called in the Hebrew Scriptures the "sheep of his pasture" (Ps 103:3).

God's goodness means then, first, that there is an absolute standard of righteousness (it is found in God's character) and, second, that there is hope for humanity (because God is love and will not abandon his creation). These twin observations will become especially significant as we trace the results of rejecting the theistic world view.

2. God created the cosmos ex nihilo to operate with a uniformity of natural causes in an open system.

God created the cosmos ex nihilo. God is *He Who Is,* and thus he is the source of all else. Still, it is important to understand that God is not the source of the cosmos in that he made it out of himself. Rather, God spoke it into existence. It came into being by his word: "God said,

'Let there be light'; and there was light" (Gen 1:3). Theologians thus say God "created" (Gen 1:1) the cosmos ex nihilo—out of nothing, not out of himself or some pre-existent chaos (for if it were really "pre-existent," it would be as eternal as God).

Second, God created the cosmos as *a uniformity of natural causes in an open system*. This phrase is a useful piece of shorthand for two key conceptions.[6] First, it signifies that the cosmos was not created to be chaotic. Isaiah states this magnificently:

For thus says the LORD,
who created the heavens
 (he is God!),
who formed the earth and made it
 (he established it;
he did not create it a chaos,
 he formed it to be inhabited!):
"I am the LORD, and there is no other.
I did not speak in secret,
 in a land of darkness;
I did not say to the offspring of Jacob,
 'Seek me in chaos.'
I the LORD speak the truth,
 I declare what is right." (Is 45:18-19)

The universe is orderly, and God does not present us with confusion but with clarity. The nature of God's universe and God's character are, thus, closely related. This world is as it is at least in part because God is who he is. We will see later how the Fall qualifies this observation. Here it is sufficient to note that there is an orderliness, a regularity to the universe. We can expect the earth to turn so the sun will "rise" every day.

But another important notion is buried in this shorthand phrase. The system is *open*, and that means it is not programmed. God is constantly involved in the unfolding pattern of the ongoing operation of the universe. And so are we as human beings! The course of the world's operation is open to reordering by either. So we find it dramatically reordered in the Fall. Adam and Eve made a choice which had tremendous significance. But God made another choice in redeeming people through Christ.

The world's operation is also reordered by our continued activity after the Fall. Each action of each of us, each decision to pursue one course rather than another, changes or rather "produces" the future. By dumping pollutants into fresh streams, we kill fish and alter the way we can feed ourselves in years to come. By "cleaning up" our streams, we again alter our future and so forth. If the universe were not orderly, our decisions would have no effect. If the course of events were determined, our decisions would have no significance. So theism declares that the universe is orderly but not determined. The implications of this become clearer as we discuss humanity's place in the cosmos.

3. Human beings are created in the image of God and thus possess personality, self-transcendence, intelligence, morality, gregariousness and creativity.

The key phrase here is the *image of God,* a conception highlighted by the fact that it occurs three times in the short space of two verses in Genesis:

> Then God said, "Let us make man in our image, after our likeness; and let them have dominion over the fish of the sea, and over the birds of the air, and over the cattle, and over all the earth, and over every creeping thing that creeps upon the earth. So God created man in his own image, in the image of God he created him; male and female he created them. (Gen 1:26-27; compare Gen 5:3 and 9:6)

That people are made in the image of God means they are like God. We have already noted that God is like us. But the Scriptures really say it the other way. *We are like God* puts the emphasis where it belongs—on the primacy of God.

We are personal because God is personal. That is, we know our-selves to be (we are self-conscious), and we make decisions uncoerced (we possess self-determination). In other words, we are capable of acting on our own. We do not merely react to our environment but can act according to our own character, our own nature.

No two people are alike, we say. And this is not just because no two people have shared exactly the same heredity and environment, but because each of us possesses a unique character out of which we think, desire, weigh consequences, refuse to weigh consequences, in-dulge, refuse to indulge—in short, choose to act.

In this, each person reflects (as an image) the transcendence of God over his universe. God is totally unconstrained by his environment. God is limited (we might say) only by his character. God, being good, cannot lie, be deceived, act with evil intent and so forth. But nothing external to God can possibly constrain him. If he chooses to restore a broken universe, it is because he "wants" to, because, for example, he loves it and wants the best for it. But he is free to do as he wills, and his will is in control of his character *(Who* He Is).

So we participate *in part* in a transcendence over our environment. Except at the very extremities of existence—in sickness or physical deprivation (utter starvation, cooped up in darkness for days on end, for example)—a person is not forced to any necessary reaction.

Step on my toe. Must I curse? I may. Must I forgive you? I may. Must I yell? I may. Must I smile? I may. What I do will reflect my character, but it is the "I" that will act and not just react like a bell ringing when a button is pushed.

In short, people have personality and are capable of transcending the cosmos in which they are placed in the sense that they can know something of that cosmos and can act significantly to change the course of both human and cosmic events. This is another way of saying that the cosmic system, as God has created it, is *open* to reordering by human beings.

Personality is the chief thing about us as human beings as, I think it is fair to say, it is the chief thing about God who is infinite both in his personality and in his being. Our personality is grounded in the personality of God. That is, we find our true home in God and in being in close relationship with him. "There is a Godshaped vacuum in the heart of every man," wrote Pascal. "Our hearts are restless till they rest in thee," wrote Augustine.

How does God fulfill our ultimate longing? He does so in many ways: by being the perfect fit for our very nature, by satisfying our longing for interpersonal relationship, by being in his omniscience the end to our search for knowledge, by being in his infinite being the refuge from all fear, by being in his holiness the righteous ground of our quest for justice, by being in his infinite love the cause of our hope for salvation, by being in his infinite creativity both the source of our creative imagination and the ultimate beauty we seek to reflect as we ourselves create.

We can summarize this conception of human nature by saying that, like God, we have *personality, self-transcendence, intelligence* (the capacity for reason and knowledge), *morality* (the capacity for recognizing and understanding good and evil), *gregariousness* or social capacity (our characteristic and fundamental desire and need for human companionship—community—especially represented by the "male" and "female" aspect) and *creativity* (the ability to imagine new things or to endow old things with human significance).

We will discuss the root of human intelligence below. Here I want to comment on human creativity—a characteristic often lost sight of in popular theism. Human creativity is borne as a reflection of the infinite creativity of God himself. Sir Philip Sidney (1554-1586) once wrote about the poet who, "lifted up with the vigor of his own invention, doth grow, in effect, into another nature, in making things either better than nature bringeth forth, or quite anew, forms such as never were in nature, . . . freely ranging within the zodiac of his own wit." To honor human creativity, Sidney argued, is to honor God, for God is the "heavenly Maker of that maker."[7] Artists operating within the theistic world view have a solid basis for their work. Nothing is more freeing for artists than to realize that because they are like God they can really invent. Artistic inventiveness is a reflection of God's unbounded capacity to create.

In Christian theism human beings are indeed dignified. In the psalmist's words, they are a "little less than God," for God himself has made them that way and has crowned them "with glory and honor" (Ps 8:5). Human dignity is in one way not our own; contrary to Protagoras, man is not the measure. Human dignity is derived from God. But though it is derived, people do possess it, even if as a gift. Helmut Thielicke says it well: "[Man's] greatness rests solely on the fact that God in his incomprehensible goodness has bestowed his love upon him. God does not love us because we are so valuable; we are valuable because God loves us."[8]

So human dignity has two sides. As human beings we are dignified, but we are not to be proud of it, for it is a dignity borne as a reflection of the Ultimately Dignified. Yet it *is* a reflection. So people who are theists see themselves as a sort of midpoint—above the rest of creation (for God has given them dominion over it—Gen 1:28-30 and Ps 8:6-8) and below God (for people are not autonomous, not on their own).

This is then the ideal balanced human status. It was in failing to remain in that balance that our troubles arose, and the story of how that happened is very much a part of Christian theism. But before we see what tipped the balanced state of humanity, we need to understand a further implication of being created in the image of God.

4. Human beings can know both the world around them and God himself because God has built into them the capacity to do so and because he takes an active role in communicating with them.

The foundation of human knowledge is the character of God as creator. We are made in his image (Gen 1:27). As he is the all-knowing knower of all things, so we can be the sometimes-knowing knowers of some things. The Gospel of John puts the concept this way:

In the beginning was the Word, and the Word was with God, and the Word was God. He was in the beginning with God; all things were made through him, and without him was not anything made that was made. In him was life, and the life was the light of men. (Jn 1:1-4)

The Word (in Greek, *Logos,* from which our word *logic* comes) is eternal, an aspect of God himself.[9] That is, logicality, intelligence, rationality, meaning are all inherent in God. Out of this intelligence the world, the universe, came to be. And, therefore, because of this source the universe has structure, order and meaning.

Moreover, this Word, this inherent intelligence, is the "light of men," light being in John a symbol for both moral capacity and intelligence. Verse 9 adds that the Word, "the true light . . . enlightens every man." God's own intelligence is thus the basis of human intelligence. Knowledge is, therefore, possible because there is something to be known (God and his creation) and someone to know (the omniscient God and human beings made in his image).[10]

Of course, God himself is forever so beyond us that we cannot have anything approaching total comprehension of him. In fact, if God desired, he could remain forever hidden. But God wants us to know him, and he takes the initiative in this transfer of knowledge.

In theological terms this initiative is called revelation. God reveals, or discloses, himself to us in two basic ways: (1) by general revelation and (2) by special revelation. In general revelation God speaks through the created order of the universe. The apostle Paul wrote, "For what can be known about God is plain to them [all people], because God has shown it to them. Ever since the creation of the world his invisible nature, namely, his eternal power and deity, has been clearly perceived in the things that have been made" (Rom 1:19-20). Centuries before that the psalmist wrote,

The heavens are telling the glory of God;
and the firmament proclaims his handiwork.
Day to day pours forth speech,
and night to night declares knowledge. (Ps 19:1-2)

In other words, God's existence and his nature as Creator and powerful sustainer of the universe is revealed in God's prime "handiwork," his universe. As we contemplate the magnitude of this—its orderliness and its beauty—we can learn much about God. When we turn from the universe at large to look at humanity, we see something more, for human beings add the dimension of personality. God, therefore, must be at least as personal as we are.

Thus far can general revelation go, but little further. As Aquinas said, we can know that God exists through general revelation, but we could never know that God is Triune except for special revelation.

Special revelation is God's disclosure of himself in extranatural ways. Not only has he revealed himself by appearing in spectacular forms such as a bush that burns but is not consumed, but he also has spoken to people in their own language. To Moses he defined himself as "I AM WHO I AM" and identified himself as the same God who had acted before on behalf of the Hebrew people. He called himself the God of Abraham, Isaac and Jacob (Ex 3:1-17). In fact, in this passage God carried on a dialog with Moses in which genuine two-way communication took place. This is one way special revelation occurred.

Later God gave Moses the Ten Commandments and revealed a long code of laws by which the Hebrews were to be ruled. Later yet God revealed himself to prophets from a number of walks of life. His word came to them, and they recorded it for posterity. The New Testament writer of the letter to the Hebrews summed it up this way: "In many and various ways God spoke of old to our fathers by the prophets" (Heb 1:1). In any case, the revelations to Moses, David and the various prophets were by God's command written and kept to be read over and over to the people (Deut 6:4-8; Ps 119). The cumulative writings grew to become the Old Testament, which was affirmed by Jesus himself as an accurate and authoritative revelation of God.[11]

The writer of the letter to the Hebrews did not end with the summary of God's past revelation. He went on to say, "But in these last days he has spoken to us by a Son, whom he appointed the heir of all things. . . . He reflects the glory of God and bears the very stamp of his nature" (Heb 1:2-3). Jesus Christ is God's ultimate special revelation. Because Jesus Christ was very God of very God, he showed us what God is like more fully than can any other form of revelation. Because Jesus was also completely human, he spoke more clearly to us than can any other form of revelation.

Again the opening of the Gospel of John is relevant. "The Word became flesh and dwelt among us, full of grace and truth" (Jn 1:14). That is, the Word is Jesus Christ. "We have beheld his glory," John continues, "glory as of the only Son from the Father." Jesus has made God known to us in very fleshly terms.

The main point for us is that theism declares that God can and has clearly communicated with us. Because of this we can know much about who God is and what he desires for us. That is true for people at all times and all places, but it is especially true before the Fall, to which we now turn.

5. Human beings were created good, but through the Fall the image of God became defaced, though not so ruined as not to be capable of restoration; through the work of Christ God redeemed humanity and began the process of restoring people to goodness, though any given person may choose to reject that redemption.

Human "history" can be subsumed under four words—*creation, Fall, redemption, glorification*. We have just seen the essential human characteristics. To these we must add that human beings and all the rest of creation were created good. As Genesis records, "And God saw everything that he had made, and behold, it was very good" (Gen 1:31). Because God by his character set the standards of righteousness, human goodness consisted in being what God wanted people to be—beings made in the image of God and acting out that nature in their daily life. The tragedy is that we did not stay as we were created.

As we have seen, human beings were created with the capacity for self-determination. God gave them the freedom to remain or not to remain in the close relationship of image to original. As Genesis 3 reports, the original pair, Adam and Eve, chose to disobey their Creator at the only point where the Creator put down limitations. This is the essence of the story of the Fall. Adam and Eve chose to eat the fruit God had forbidden them to eat, and hence they violated the personal relationship they had with their Creator.

In this manner people of all eras have attempted to set themselves up as autonomous beings, arbiters of their own way of life. They have chosen to act as if they had an existence independent from God. But that is precisely what they do not have, for they owe everything—both their origin and their continued existence—to God.

The result of this act of rebellion was death for Adam and Eve. And their death has involved for subsequent generations long centuries of personal, social and natural turmoil. In brief summary, we can say that the image of God in man was defaced in all its aspects. In *personality*, we lost our capacity to know ourselves accurately and to determine our own course of action freely in response to our intelligence.

Our *self-transcendence* was impaired by the alienation we experienced in relation to God, for as Adam and Eve turned from God, God let them go. And as humankind slipped from close fellowship with the ultimately transcendent one, so they lost their ability to stand over against the external universe, understand it, judge it accurately and thus make truly "free" decisions. Rather, humanity became more a servant to nature than to God. And our status as God's vice regent over nature (an aspect of the image of God) was reversed.

Human *intelligence* also became impaired. Now we can no longer gain a fully accurate knowledge of the world around us, nor are we able to reason without constantly falling into error. *Morally,* we became less able to discern good and evil. *Socially,* we began to exploit other people. *Creatively,* our imagination became separated from reality; imagination became illusion, and artists who created gods in their own image led humanity further and further from its origin. The vacuum in each human soul created by this string of consequences is ominous indeed. (The fullest biblical expression of these ideas is Romans 1—2.)

Theologians have summed it up this way: we have become alienated from God, from others, from nature and even from ourselves. This is the essence of *fallen* humanity.[12]

But humanity is redeemable and has been redeemed. The story of creation and Fall is told in three chapters of Genesis. The story of redemption takes the rest of the Scriptures. The Bible records God's love for us in searching us out, finding us in our lost, alienated condition and redeeming us by the sacrifice of his own Son, Jesus Christ, the Second Person of the Trinity. God, in unmerited favor and great grace, has granted us the possibility of a new life, a life involving substantial healing of our alienation and restoration to fellowship with God.

That God has provided a way back for us does not mean we play no role. Adam and Eve were not forced to fall. We are not forced to return. While it is not the purpose of this description of theism to take sides in a famous family squabble within Christian theism (predestination vs. free will), we must note that Christians disagree on precisely what role God takes and what role he leaves us. Still, most would agree that God is the primary agent in salvation. Our role is to respond by repentance for our wrong attitudes and acts, to accept God's provisions and to follow Christ as Lord as well as Savior.

Redeemed humanity is humanity on the way to the restoration of the defaced image of God—in other words, substantial healing in every area—personality, self-transcendence, intelligence, morality, social capacity and creativity. *Glorified* humanity is humanity totally healed and at peace with God, and individuals at peace with others and themselves. But this happens only on the other side of death and the bodily resurrection, the importance of which is stressed by Paul in 1 Corinthians 15. Individual people are so important that they retain a uniqueness—a personal and individual existence forever. Glorified humanity is humanity transformed into a purified personality in fellowship with God and God's people. In short, in theism human beings are seen as significant because they are essentially godlike and though fallen can be restored to original dignity.

6. For each person death is either the gate to life with God and his people or the gate to eternal separation from the only thing that will ultimately fulfill human aspirations.

The meaning of death is really part of proposition 5, but it is singled out here because the various attitudes to death are so important in every world view. What happens when a person dies? Put it personally, for this aspect of one's world view is indeed most personal. Do I disappear—personal extinction? Do I hibernate and return in a different form—reincarnation? Do I continue in a transformed existence in heaven or hell?

Christian theism clearly teaches the last of these. At death people are transformed. Either they enter an existence with God and his people—a *glorified* existence—or they enter an existence forever separated from God, holding their uniqueness in awful loneliness apart from precisely that which would fulfill them.

And that is the essence of hell. G. K. Chesterton once remarked that hell is a monument to human freedom, and, we might add, human dignity. Hell is God's tribute to the freedom he gave each of us to choose whom we would serve; it is a recognition that our decisions have a significance that extends far down into the reaches of forever-ness.[13]

Those, however, who respond to God's offer of salvation people the plains of eternity as glorious creatures of God—completed, fulfilled, but not sated, engaged in the ever-enjoyable communion of the saints. The Scriptures give little detail about this existence, but its glimpses of heaven in Revelation 4—5 and 21, for example, create a longing Christians expect to be fulfilled beyond their fondest desires.

7. *Ethics is transcendent and is based on the character of God as good (holy and loving).*

This proposition has already been considered as an implication of proposition 1. God is the source of the moral world as well as the physical world. God is the good and expresses this in the laws and moral principles he has revealed in Scripture.

Made in God's image, we are essentially moral beings, and thus we cannot refuse to bring moral categories to bear on our actions. Of course, our sense of morality has been flawed by the Fall, and now we only brokenly reflect the truly good. Yet even in our moral rela-tivity, we cannot get rid of the sense that some things are "right" or "natural" and others not. For years homosexuality was considered immoral by most of society. Now a large number of people challenge this. But they do so not on the basis that no moral categories exist but that this one area—homosexuality—really ought to have been on the other side of the line dividing the moral from the immoral. Homo-sexuals do not usually condone incest! So the fact that people differ in their moral judgments does nothing to alter the fact that we con-tinue to make, to live by and to violate moral judgments. Everyone lives in a moral universe and virtually everyone—if they reflect on it—recognizes this and would have it no other way.

Theism, however, teaches that not only is there a moral universe but there is an absolute standard by which all moral judgments are measured. God himself—his character of goodness (holiness and love)—is the standard. Furthermore, Christians and Jews hold that God has revealed his standard in the various laws and principles expressed in the Bible. The Ten Commandments, the Sermon on the Mount, the apostle Paul's ethical teaching—in these and many other ways God has expressed his character to us. There is thus a standard of right and wrong, and people who want to know it can know it.

The fullest embodiment of the good, however, is Jesus Christ. He is the complete man, humanity as God would have it be. Paul calls him the second Adam (1 Cor 15:45-49). And in Jesus we see the good life incarnate. Jesus' good life was supremely revealed in his death—an act of infinite love, for as Paul says, "One will hardly die for a righteous man. . . . But God shows his love for us in that while we were yet sinners Christ died for us" (Rom 5:7-8). And the apostle John echoes, "In this is love, not that we loved God but that he loved us and sent his Son to be the expiation for our sins" (1 Jn 4:10).

So ethics, while very much a human domain, is ultimately the business of God. We are not the measure of morality. God is.

8. History is linear, a meaningful sequence of events leading to the fulfillment of God's purposes for humanity.

History is linear means that the actions of people—as confusing and chaotic as they appear—are nonetheless part of a meaningful sequence that has a beginning, a middle and an end. History is not reversible, not repeatable, not cyclic; history is not meaningless. Rather, history is teleological, going somewhere, directed toward a known end. The God who knows the end from the beginning is aware of and sovereign over all human action.

Several basic turning points in the course of history are singled out for special attention by biblical writers, and these form the background for the theistic understanding of human beings in time. These turning points include the creation, the Fall, the revelation of God to the Hebrews (which includes the calling of Abraham from Ur to

Canaan, the exodus from Egypt, the giving of the Law, the witness of the prophets), the Incarnation, the life of Jesus, the Crucifixion and Resurrection, Pentecost, the spread of the good news via the church, the Second Coming of Christ and the Judgment. This is a slightly more detailed list of events paralleling the pattern of human life: creation, Fall, redemption, glorification.

Looked at in this way, history itself is a form of revelation. That is, not only does God reveal himself in history *(here, there, then)*, but the very sequence of events is revelation. One can say, therefore, that history (especially as localized in the Jewish people) is the record of the involvement and concern of God in human events. History is the divine purpose of God in concrete form.

This pattern is, of course, dependent on the Christian tradition. It does not at first appear to take into account people other than Jews and Christians. Yet the Old Testament has much to say about nations surrounding Israel and about Godfearers (non-Jewish people who adopted Jewish beliefs and were considered a part of God's promise). And the New Testament stresses even more the international dimension of God's purposes and his reign.

The *revelation* of God's design took place primarily through one people—the Jews. And while we may say with William Ewer, "How odd/Of God/To choose/The Jews," we need not think that doing so indicates favoritism on God's part. Peter once said, "God shows no partiality, but in every nation anyone who fears him and does what is right is acceptable to him" (Acts 10:34).

Theists look forward, then, to history being closed by judgment and a new age inaugurated beyond time. But prior to that new age, time is irreversible and history is localized in space. This conception needs to be stressed since it differs dramatically from the typically Eastern notion. To much of the East time is an illusion; history is eternally cyclic. Reincarnation brings a soul back into time again and again; progress in the soul's journey is long, arduous, perhaps eternal. But in Christian theism, "It is appointed for men to die once, and after that comes judgment" (Heb 9:27). A person's choices have meaning to him, to others and to God. History is the result of those choices which, under the sovereignty of God, bring about God's purposes for this world.

In short, the most important aspect of the theistic concept of history is that history has meaning because God—the Logos (meaning itself)—is behind all events, not only "upholding the universe by his word of power" (Heb. 1:3), but, "in everything . . . [working] for good with those who love him, who are called according to his purpose" (Rom 8:28). Behind the apparent chaos of events stands the loving God sufficient for all.

The Grandeur of God

It should by now be obvious that Christian theism is primarily dependent on its concept of God, for theism holds that everything stems from him. Nothing is prior to God or equal to him. He is *He Who Is.* Thus theism has a basis for metaphysics. Since *He Who Is* also has a worthy character and is thus The Worthy One, theism has a basis for ethics. Since *He Who Is* also is *He Who Knows,* theism has a basis for epistemology. In other words, theism is a complete world view.

So the greatness of God is the central tenet of Christian theism. When a person recognizes this and consciously accepts and acts on it, this central conception is the rock, the transcendent reference point, that gives life meaning and makes the joys and sorrows of daily existence on planet earth significant moments in an unfolding drama in which one expects to participate forever, not always with sorrows but someday with joy alone. Even now, though, the world is, as Gerard Manley Hopkins once wrote, "charged with the grandeur of God."[14] That there are "God adumbrations in many daily forms" signals to us that God is not just in his heaven but with us—sustaining us, loving us and caring for us.[15] Fully cognizant Christian theists, therefore, do not just believe and proclaim their view as true. Their first act is toward God—a response of love, obedience and praise to the Lord of the Universe—their maker, sustainer, and, through Jesus Christ, redeemer and friend.

3
The Clockwork Universe: Deism

Say first, of God above or man below,
What can we reason but from what we know?
Of man what see we but his station here
From which to reason, or to which refer?
Through worlds unnumbered though the God be known,
'Tis ours to trace him only in our own.
Alexander Pope
Essay on Man

If theism lasted so long, what could possibly have happened to undermine it? If it satisfactorily answered all our basic questions, provided a refuge for our fears and hope for our future, why did anything else come along? Answers to these questions can be given on many levels. The fact is that many forces operated to shatter the basic intellectual unity of the West.

Deism developed, some say, as an attempt to bring unity out of a chaos of theological and philosophical discussion which in the seventeenth century became bogged down in interminable quarrels over what began to seem even to the disputants like trivial questions. Perhaps Milton had such questions in mind when he envisioned the fallen angels making an epic game of philosophical theology:

Others apart sat on a Hill retir'd

In thoughts more elevate, and reason'd high

Of Providence, Foreknowledge, Will and Fate,

Fixt Fate, Free will, Foreknowledge absolute,

And found no end, in wandering mazes lost.[1]

After decades of wearying discussion, Lutheran, Puritan and Anglican divines might well wish to look again at points of agreement. Deism, to some extent, is a response to this, though the direction such agreement took put deism rather beyond the limits of traditional Christianity.

Another factor in the development of deism is a shift in the location of the authority for knowledge about the divine. It went from the special revelation found in Scripture to the presence of Reason, "the candle of God," in the human mind or to intuition, "the inner light." Why should such a shift in authority take place?

One of the reasons is especially ironic. It is linked with an implication of theism which, when it was discovered, was very successfully developed. Through the Middle Ages, due in part to the rather Platonic theory of knowledge that was held, the attention of theistic scholars and intellectuals was directed toward God. The idea was that knowers in some sense "become" what they know. And since one should become in some sense "good" and "holy," one should therefore study God.

Theology was thus considered the queen of the *sciences* (which at that time simply meant knowledge), for theology was the science of God. If people studied animals or plants or minerals (zoology, biology, chemistry and physics), they were lowering themselves. This hierarchical view of reality is really more Platonic than theistic or Christian because it picks up from Plato the notion that matter is somehow, if not evil, then at least irrational and certainly not good. Matter is something to be transcended, not to be understood.

But, as more biblically oriented minds began to recognize, this is God's world—all of it. And, though it is a fallen world, it has been created by God and has value. It is indeed worth knowing and understanding. Furthermore, God is a rational God, and his universe is thus rational, orderly, knowable. Operating on this basis, scientists began investigating the *form* of the universe. A picture of God's world began to emerge. It was like a huge, well-ordered mechanism, a giant clockwork, whose gears and levers meshed with perfect mechanical precision. Such a picture seemed both to arise from scientific inquiry and to prompt more inquiry and stimulate more discovery about the make-up of the universe. In other words, science as we now know it was born and was amazingly successful.

In Bacon's words, knowledge became power, power to manipulate and bring creation more fully under human dominion. J. Bronowski echoes this view in modern parlance: "I define science as the organization of our knowledge in such a way that it commands more of the hidden potential in nature."[2] If this way of obtaining knowledge about the universe was so successful, why not apply this same method to knowledge about God?

In Christian theism, of course, such a method was already given a role to play, for God was said to reveal himself in nature. The depth of content, however, that was conveyed in such general revelation was considered limited. Much more was made known about God in special revelation. But deism denies that God can be known by revelation, by special acts of God's self-expression in, for example, Scripture or the Incarnation. Having cast out Aristotle as an authority in matters of science, deism now casts out Scripture as an authority in theology and allows only the application of "human" reason. As Peter Medawar says, "The 17th-century doctrine of the *necessity* of reason was slowly giving way to a belief in the *sufficiency* of reason."[3] Deism thus sees God only in "Nature" by which was meant the *system* of the universe. And since the system of the universe is seen as a giant clockwork, God is seen as the clockmaker.

In some ways, we can say that limiting knowledge about God to general revelation is like finding that eating eggs for breakfast makes the morning go well and then eating *only* eggs for breakfast (and maybe lunch and dinner too) for the rest of one's life (which now unwittingly becomes rather shortened!). To be sure theism assumes that we can know something about God from nature. But it also holds that there is much *more to know* than can be known that way and that there are *other ways to know*.

Basic Deism

As Frederick Copleston explains, deism historically is not really a "school" of thought. In the late seventeenth and in the eighteenth century more than a few thinkers came to be called deists or called themselves deists. These men held a number of related views, but not all held every doctrine in common. John Locke, for example, did not reject the idea of revelation, but he did insist that human reason was to be used to judge it.[4] Some deists, like Voltaire, were hostile to Christianity; some, like Locke, were not. Some believed in the immortality of the soul; some did not. Some believed God left his creation to function on its own; some believed in providence. Some believed in a personal God; others did not. So deists were much less united on basic issues than were theists.[5]

Still, it is helpful to think of deism as a system and to state that system in a relatively extreme form. In that way we will be able to grasp the implications the various "reductions" of theism were beginning to have in the eighteenth century. Naturalism, as we shall see, pushes these implications even further.

1. A transcendent God, as a First Cause, created the universe but then left it to run on its own. God is thus not immanent, not fully personal, not sovereign over human affairs, not providential.

As in theism, the most important proposition regards the existence and character of God. Essentially, deism "reduces" the number of features God is said to display. He is a transcendent force or energy, a Prime Mover or First Cause, a beginning to the otherwise infinite regress of past causes. But he is really not a *he*, though the personal pronoun remains in the language used about him. Certainly, he does not *care* for his creation; he does not *love* it. He has no "personal" relation to it at all.

A modern deist of sorts, Buckminster Fuller, expressed his faith this way: "I have faith in the integrity of the anticipatory intellectual wisdom which we may call 'God.' "[6] But Fuller's God is not a person to be worshiped, merely an intellect or force to be recognized.

To the deist, then, God is distant, foreign, alien. The lonely state this leaves humanity in was, however, not seemingly felt by early deists. Almost two centuries passed before this implication was played out on the field of human emotions.

2. The cosmos God created is determined because it is created as a uniformity of cause and effect in a closed system; no miracle is possible.

The system of the universe is closed in two senses. First, it is closed to God's reordering, for he is not "interested" in it. He merely brought it to be. Therefore, no miracles or events which reveal any special interests of God are possible. Any tampering or apparent tampering with the machinery of the universe would suggest that God had made a mistake in the original plan and that would be beneath the dignity of an all-competent deity.

Second, the universe is closed to human reordering because it is locked up in a clocklike fashion. To be able to reorder the system, any human being alone or with others would have to be able to transcend it, get out of the chain of cause and effect. But this we cannot do. We should note, however, that this second implication is not much emphasized by deists. Most continue to assume, as we all do apart from reflection, that we can act to change our environment.

3. Human beings, though personal, are a part of the clockwork of the universe.

To be sure, deists do not deny that humans are personal. Each of us has self-consciousness and, at least on first glance, self-determination. But these have to be seen in the light of human dimensions only. That is, as human beings we have no essential relation to God—as image to original—and thus we have no way to transcend the system in which we find ourselves.

Bishop Fénelon (1651-1715), criticizing the deists of his day, wrote, "They credit themselves with acknowledging God as the creator whose wisdom is evident in his works; but according to them, God would be neither good nor wise if he had given man free will—that is, the power to sin, to turn away from his final goal, to reverse the order and be forever lost."[7] Fénelon put his finger on a major problem within deism: Human beings have lost their ability to act significantly. If we cannot "reverse the order," then we cannot be significant. We can only be puppets. If an individual has personality, it must then be a type which does not include the element of self-determination.

Deists, of course, recognize that human beings have *intelligence* (to be sure, they emphasize human reason), a sense of *morality* (deists are very interested in ethics), a capacity for *community* and for *creativity*. But all these, while built into us as a created beings, are not grounded in God's character. They have a sort of autonomous nature just like the rest of the stuff of the universe. Human beings *are* what they are; they have little hope of becoming anything different or anything more.

4. The cosmos, this world, is understood to be in its normal state; it is not fallen or abnormal. We can know the universe, and we can determine what God is like by studying it.

Because the universe is essentially as God created it, and because people have the intellectual capacity to understand the world around them, they can learn about God from a study of his universe. The Scriptures, as we saw above, give a basis for it, for the psalmist wrote, "The heavens are telling the glory of God; and the firmament proclaims his handiwork" (Ps 19:1). Of course, theists too maintain that

God has revealed himself in nature. But for a theist God has also revealed himself in words—in propositional, verbalized revelation to his prophets and the various biblical writers. And, theists maintain, God has also revealed himself in his Son, Jesus—the "Word became flesh" (Jn. 1:14). But for deists God does not communicate with people. No special revelation is necessary, and none has occurred.

Émile Bréhier, a historian of philosophy, sums up well the difference between deism and theism:

> We see clearly that a new conception of man, wholly incompatible with the Christian faith, had been introduced: God the architect who produced and maintained a marvelous order in the universe had been discovered in nature, and there was no longer a place for the God of the Christian drama, the God who bestowed upon Adam "the power to sin and to *reverse the order.*" God was in nature and no longer in history; he was in the wonders analyzed by naturalists and biologists and no longer in the human conscience, with feelings of sin, disgrace, or grace that accompanied his presence; he had left man in charge of his own destiny.[7]

The God who was discovered by the deists was an architect, but not a lover or a judge or anything personal. He was not one who acted in history. He simply had left the world alone. But humanity, while in one sense the maker of its own destiny, was yet locked into the closed system. Human *freedom from* God was not a *freedom to* anything; in fact, it was not a freedom at all.

One tension in deism is found at the opening of Alexander Pope's *Essay on Man* (1733). Pope writes,

> Say first, of God above or man below,
> What can we reason but from what we know?
> Of man what see we but his station here
> From which to reason, or to which refer?
> Through worlds unnumbered though the God be known,
> 'Tis ours to trace him only in our own.[9]

These six lines state that we can know God only through studying the world around us. This is deism's bow to empiricism. We learn from data and proceed from the specific to the general. Nothing is revealed to us outside that which we experience. Then Pope continues,

He who through vast immensity can pierce,
See worlds on worlds compose one universe,
Observe how system into system runs,
What other planets circle other suns,
What varied being peoples ev'ry star,
May tell why heav'n has made us as we are.
But of this frame the bearings and the ties,
The strong connections, nice dependencies,
Gradations just, has thy pervading soul
Looked through? or can a part contain the whole?[10]

Pope assumes here a knowledge of God and of nature that is not capable of being known by experience. He even admits this, as he challenges us as readers on whether we really have "looked through" the universe and seen its clockwork. But if we haven't seen it, then presumably neither has Pope. How then does Pope know it is a vast all-ordered clockwork?

One can't have it both ways. Either (1) all knowledge comes from experience and we, not being infinite, cannot know the system as a whole, or (2) some knowledge comes from another source—for example, from innate ideas built into us or from revelation from the outside. But Pope, like most deists, discounts revelation. And in this "essay" at least he never states or suggests the possibility of innate ideas.

So we have a tension in Pope's epistemology. And it was just such tensions that made deism a very unstable world view.

5. Ethics is limited to general revelation; because the universe is normal, it reveals what is right.

Another implication of seeing God only in a natural world which one views as unfallen is that God, being the omnipotent Creator, becomes responsible for everything as it is. This world must then reflect either what God wants or what he is like. Ethically this leads to the position expressed by Alexander Pope:

All nature is but art, unknown to thee;
All chance, direction which thou canst not see;
All discord, harmony not understood;
All partial evil, universal good;
And, spite of pride, in erring reason's spite,
One truth is clear, WHATEVER IS, IS RIGHT.[11]

This position really ends in destroying ethics. If whatever is, is right, then there is no evil. Good becomes indistinguishable from evil. As Baudelaire said, "If God exists, he must be the devil." Or, worse luck, there must be no *good* at all. For without the ability to distinguish, there can be neither one nor the other, neither good nor evil. Ethics disappears.

Yet, as we have seen, we human beings continue to make ethical distinctions. Somewhere every one of us distinguishes between good and bad, right and wrong. Deistic ethics do not fit us in our actual human dimensions. At this point deism becomes an impracticable world view, for no one can live by it.

No doubt not all deists saw (or now see) that their assumptions entail Pope's conclusions. Some felt, in fact, that Jesus' ethical teachings were really natural law expressed in words. And, of course, the Sermon on the Mount does not contain anything like the proposition "Whatever is, is right"! A deeper study of the deists would, I believe, lead to the conclusion that they simply were inconsistent and did not recognize it.

Alexander Pope himself is inconsistent, for while he held that whatever is, is right, he also berated humanity for pride (which, if it is, must be right!).

In pride, in reas'ning pride our error lies;

All quit their sphere and rush into the skies.
Pride still aiming at blessed abodes;
Men would be angels, angels would be gods. . . .
And who but wishes to invert the laws
Of order sins against th' Eternal Cause.[12]

For a person to think of himself more highly than he ought was pride. Pride was wrong, even a *sin*. Yet note—a sin not against a personal God but against the "Eternal Cause," against a philosophic abstraction. Even the word *sin* takes on a new color in such a context. More important, however, the whole notion of sin must disappear if one holds on other grounds that whatever is, is right.

As interested as the deists were in preserving the ethical content of Christianity, they were unable to find a suitable basis for it. Because of such tensions and inconsistencies deism had a relatively short life as a major world view, though there are still those today who would claim to be deists.

6. History is linear, for the course of the cosmos was determined at creation.

Deists themselves seem little interested in history, because as Bréhier has pointed out, they sought knowledge of God primarily in nature. The course of Jewish history as recorded in the Bible is most useful not as a record of God's acts in history but as illustrations of divine law from which ethical principles can be derived. John Toland (1670-1722), for example, argued that Christianity was as old as creation; the gospel was a "republication" of the religion of nature. With a view like that the specific acts of history are not very important. The stress is on general rules. As Pope says, "The first Almighty Cause/ Acts not by partial but by gen'ral laws."[13] God is quite uninterested in individual men and women or even whole peoples. Besides, the universe is closed, not open to his reordering at all.

An Unstable Compound

Deism did not prove to be a very stable world view. Historically it held sway over the intellectual world of France and England briefly from the late seventeenth into the first half of the eighteenth century. Preceded by theism, it was followed by naturalism.

What made deism so ephemeral? We have already touched on the major reasons: the inconsistencies within the world view itself and the impracticability of some of its principles. These internal inconsistencies, which were soon to become obvious, include the following: (1) In ethics, the assumption of an unfallen, normal universe tended (in the likes of Alexander Pope, for example) to imply that whatever is, is right. If whatever is, is right, then no place is left for a distinctive content to ethics. But deists were very interested in ethics, that being the one division of Christian teaching that was most acceptable. (2) In epistemology, the attempt to argue from particular to universal ended in failure, for it would take an infinite mind to hold the details necessary for an accurate generalization. No human mind was infinite. Hence, certain knowledge of universals was impossible, and thoughtful people were left with a relativity of knowledge they found hard to accept.[14] (3) In relation to human nature, one could not maintain significance and personality in the face of a universe closed to reordering. Human significance and mechanical determinism are impossible bedfellows.

Today, we could find even more aspects of deism to question. Scientists have largely abandoned thinking of the universe as a giant clock. Electrons (not to mention other even more baffling subatomic particles) do not behave like minute pieces of machinery. If the universe is a mechanism, it is far more complex than was then thought, and God must be quite different from a mere "architect" or "clockmaker." Furthermore, the human personality is a "fact" of the universe. If God made that, must he not be personal?

So historically deism is a transitional world view, and yet it is not dead. It lives on in some scientists and a few humanists in academic centers across the world. I have personally known people who claimed to be deists, and I suspect that there are many who are deists unconsciously. Scientists, like Albert Einstein for example, who "see" a higher power at work in or behind the universe and who want to maintain reason in a created world can be considered deists at heart, though no doubt many would not wish to claim anything sounding quite so much like a philosophy of life.[15]

4
The Silence of Finite Space: Naturalism

Without warning, David was visited by an exact vision of death: a long hole in the ground, no wider than your body, down which you were drawn while the white faces recede. You try to reach them but your arms are pinned. Shovels pour dirt in your face. There you will be forever, in an upright position, blind and silent, and in time no one will remember you, and you will never be called. As strata of rock shift, your fingers elongate, and your teeth are distended sideways in a great underground grimace indistinguishable from a strip of chalk. And the earth tumbles on, and the sun expires, an unaltering darkness reigns where once there were stars.
John Updike
"Pigeon Feathers"

Deism is the isthmus between two great continents—theism and naturalism. To get from the first to the second, deism is the natural route. Though perhaps without deism, naturalism would not come about so readily, deism is only a passing phase, almost an intellectual curiosity. Naturalism, on the other hand, is serious business.

In intellectual terms the route is this: In theism God is the infinite-personal Creator and Sustainer of the cosmos. In deism God is "reduced"; he begins to lose his personality, though he remains Creator and (by implication) sustainer of the cosmos. In naturalism God is further "reduced"; he loses his very existence.

Swing figures in this shift from theism to naturalism are legion, especially between 1600 and 1750. René Descartes (1596-1650), a theist by conscious confession, set the stage by conceiving of the universe as a giant mechanism of "matter" which people comprehended by "mind." He thus split reality into two kinds of being in such a way that ever since then the Western world has found it hard to see itself as an integrated whole. The naturalists, taking one route to unification, made mind a subcategory of mechanistic matter.

John Locke (1632-1714), a theist for the most part, believed in a personal God who revealed himself to us but thought that our God-given reason was the judge of what was to be taken as true from the "revelation" in the Bible. The naturalists removed the "God-given" from this conception and made "reason" the sole criterion for truth.

One of the most interesting figures in this shift, however, was Julien Offray de La Mettrie (1709-51). In his own day La Mettrie was generally considered an atheist, but he himself says, "Not that I call in question the existence of a supreme being; on the contrary it seems to me that the greatest degree of probability is in favor of this belief." Nonetheless, he continues, "It is a theoretic truth with little practical value."[1] The reason he can conclude that God's existence is of so little practical value is that the God who exists is *only* the maker of the universe. He is not personally interested in it nor in being worshiped by anyone in it. So God's existence can be effectively discounted as being of any importance.[2]

It is precisely this feeling, this conclusion, which marks the transition to naturalism. La Mettrie is a theoretical deist but a practical naturalist. It was easy for subsequent generations to make their theory consistent with La Mettrie's practice so that naturalism was both believed and acted on.[3]

Basic Naturalism

This brings us, then, to the first proposition defining naturalism.

 1. Matter exists eternally and is all there is. God does not exist.

As in theism and deism, the prime proposition concerns the nature of basic existence. In the former two the nature of God is the key factor. In naturalism it is the nature of the cosmos which is primary, for now, with an eternal creator-God out of the picture, the cosmos itself becomes eternal—always there though not necessarily in its present form, in fact, *certainly* not in its present form.[4] Carl Sagan, astrophysicist and popularizer of science, has said it as clearly as possible: "The Cosmos is all that is or ever was or ever will be."[5]

Nothing comes from nothing. Something is. Therefore something always was. But that something, say the naturalists, is not a transcendent creator but the matter of the cosmos itself. In some form all the matter of the universe has always been.

The word *matter* is to be understood in a rather general way, for since the eighteenth century, science has refined its understanding. In the eighteenth century, scientists had yet to discover either the complexity of matter or its close relationship with energy. They conceived of reality as made up of irreducible "units" existing in mechanical, spatial relationship with each other, a relationship being investigated and unveiled by chemistry and physics and expressible in inexorable "laws." Later scientists were to discover that nature is not so neat or, at least, so simple. There seem to be no irreducible "units" as such, and physical laws have only mathematical expression. Certainty about what nature is, or is likely to be discovered to be, has vanished.

Still, the proposition expressed above unites naturalists. The cosmos is not composed of two things—matter and mind, or matter and spirit. As La Mettrie says, "In the whole universe there is but a single substance with various modifications."[6] The cosmos is ultimately one thing, without any relation to a Being beyond; there is no "god," no "creator."

2. The cosmos exists as a uniformity of cause and effect in a closed system.

This proposition is similar to proposition 2 in deism. The difference is that the universe may or may not be conceived of as a machine or clockwork. Modern scientists have found the relations between the various elements of reality to be far more complex, if not more mysterious, than the clockwork image can account for.

Nonetheless, the universe is a *closed* system. It is not open to reordering from the outside—either by a transcendent Being (for there is none) or, as we shall discuss later at length, by self-transcendent or autonomous human beings (for they are a part of the uniformity). Émile Bréhier, describing this view, says, "Order in nature is but one rigorously necessary arrangement of its parts, founded on the essence of things; for example, the beautiful regularity of the seasons is not the effect of a divine plan but the result of gravitation."[7]

The Humanist Manifesto II (1973), which expresses the views of those who call themselves "secular humanists," puts it this way: "We find insufficient evidence for belief in the existence of a supernatural."[8] Without God or the supernatural, of course, nothing can happen except within the realm of things themselves. Writing in *The Columbia History of the World* (1972), Rhodes W. Fairbridge says flatly, "We reject the miraculous."[9] Such a statement, coming as it does from a professor of geology at Columbia University, is to be expected.

What is surprising is to find a seminary professor, David Jobling, saying much the same thing: "We [that is, modern people] see the universe as a continuity of space, time, and matter, held together, as it were, from within. . . . God is not 'outside' time and space, nor does he stand apart from matter, communicating with the 'spiritual' part of man. . . . We must find some way of facing the fact that Jesus Christ is the product of the same evolutionary process as the rest of us."[10]

Jobling is attempting to understand Christianity within the naturalistic world view. Certainly, after God is put strictly inside the system—the uniform, closed system of cause and effect—he has been denied sovereignty and much else which Christians have traditionally believed to be true about him. The point here, however, is that naturalism is a pervasive world view and is to be found in the most unlikely places.

What are the central features of this *closed* system? It might first appear that naturalists, affirming the "continuity of space, time, and matter, held together . . . from within," would be determinists, asserting that the closed system holds together by an inexorable, unbreakable linkage of cause and effect. Most naturalists are indeed determinists, though many would argue that this does not remove our sense of free will or our responsibility for our actions. Is such a freedom really consistent with the conception of a closed system? To answer we must first look more closely at the naturalist's conception of human beings.

3. Human beings are complex "machines"; personality is an interrelation of chemical and physical properties we do not yet fully understand.

While Descartes recognized that human beings were part machine, he also thought they were part mind; and mind was a different substance. A great majority of naturalists, however, see mind as a function of machine. La Mettrie was one of the first to put it bluntly: "Let us conclude boldly then that man is a machine, and that in the whole universe there is but a single substance with various modifications."[11] Putting it even more crudely, Pierre Jean Georges Cabanis (1757-1808) wrote that "the brain secretes thought as the liver secretes bile."[12]

William Barrett, in a fascinating intellectual history of the gradual loss of the notion of the soul or the self in Western thought from Descartes to the present, writes:

> Thus we get in La Mettrie . . . those quaint illustrations of the human body as a system of imaginary gears, cogs, and ratchets. Man, the microcosm, is just another machine within the universal machine that is the cosmos. We smile at these illustrations as quaint and crude, but secretly we may still nourish the notion that they are after all in the right direction, though a little premature. With the advent of the computer, however, this temptation toward mechanism becomes more irresistible, for here we no longer have an obsolete machine of wheels and pulleys but one that seems able to reproduce the processes of the human mind. Can machines think? now becomes a leading question for our time.[13]

In any case, the point is that as human beings we are simply a part of the cosmos. In the cosmos there is one substance—matter. We are that and only that. The laws applying to matter apply to us. We do not transcend the universe in any way.

Of course, we are very complex machines, and our mechanism is not yet fully understood. Thus people continue to amaze us and upset our expectations. Still, any mystery that surrounds our understanding is a result, not of genuine mystery, but of mechanical complexity.[14]

It might be concluded that humanity is not distinct from other objects in the universe, that it is merely one kind of object among many. But naturalists insist this is not so. Julian Huxley, for example, says we are unique among animals because we alone are capable of conceptual thought, employ speech, possess a cumulative tradition (culture) and have had a unique method of evolution.[15] To this most naturalists would add our moral capacity, a topic we will take up separately. All of these characteristics are open and generally obvious. None of them imply any transcendent power or demand any extra-material basis, say the naturalists.

Ernest Nagel points out the necessity of not stressing the human "continuity" with the nonhuman elements of our make-up: "Without denying that even the most distinctive human traits are dependent on things which are nonhuman, a mature naturalism attempts to assess man's nature in the light of *his* actions and achievements, *his* aspirations and capacities, *his* limitations and tragic failures, and *his* splendid works of ingenuity and imagination."[16] By stressing our *humanness* (our distinctness from the rest of the cosmos), a naturalist finds a basis for value, for, it is held, intelligence, cultural sophistication, a sense of right and wrong are not only human distinctives but are what make us valuable. This we will see developed further under proposition 6 below.

Finally, while some naturalists are strict determinists with regard to all events in the universe, including human action, thus denying any sense of free will, many naturalists hold that we are free to fashion our own destiny, at least in part. Some, for example, hold that while a closed universe implies determinism, determinism is still compatible with human freedom, or at least a sense of freedom. We can do many things which we want to do; we are not always constrained to act against our wants. I could, for example, stop writing this book if I wanted to. I don't want to.

This, so many naturalists hold, leaves open the possibility for significant human action, and it provides a basis for morality. For unless we are free to do other than we do, we cannot be held responsible for what we do. The coherence of this view has been challenged, however, and is one of the soft spots in the naturalist's system of thought, as we will see in the following chapter.

4. Death is extinction of personality and individuality.

This is, perhaps, the "hardest" proposition of naturalism for people to accept, yet it is absolutely demanded by the naturalists' conception of the universe. Men and women are made up of matter and nothing else. When that matter which goes to make up an individual is disorganized at death, then that person disappears.

The Humanist Manifesto II states, "As far as we know, the total personality is a function of the biological organism transacting in a social and cultural context. There is no credible evidence that life survives the death of the body."[17] Bertrand Russell writes, "No fire, no heroism, no intensity of thought and feeling, can preserve an individual life beyond the grave."[18] And A. J. Ayer says, "I take it . . . to be fact that one's existence ends at death."[19] In a more general sense mankind is likewise seen to be transitory. "Human destiny," Ernest Nagel confesses, "[is] an episode between two oblivions."[20]

Such statements are clear and unambiguous. The concept may trigger immense psychological problems, but there is no disputing its precision. The only "immortality," as The Humanist Manifesto II puts it, is to "continue to exist in our progeny and in the way that our lives have influenced others in our culture."[21] In his short story "Pigeon Feathers" John Updike gives this notion a beautifully human dimension as he portrays the young boy David reflecting on his minister's description of heaven as being "like Abraham Lincoln's goodness living after him."[22] Like the seminary professor quoted above, David's pastor is no longer a theist but is simply trying to provide "spiritual" counsel within the framework of naturalism.

5. History is a linear stream of events linked by cause and effect but without an overarching purpose.

First, the word *history*, as used in this proposition, includes both natural history and human history, for naturalists see them as a continuity. The origin of the human family is in nature. We arose out of it and, most likely, will return to it (not just individually but as a species).

Natural history begins with the origin of the universe which, despite the variations among naturalists, is said to be eternal. Most scientists will only say that some incredibly long time ago a process took place among the stuff of the cosmos which ultimately resulted in the formation of the universe we now inhabit and are conscious of. But exactly how this came to be, few are willing to say. Professor Lodewijk Woltjer, astronomer at Columbia University, speaks for many: "The origin of what is—man, the earth, the universe—is shrouded in a mystery we are no closer to solving than was the chronicler of Genesis."[23] A number of theories to explain the process have been advanced, but none have really won the day. Still, among naturalists, the premise always is that the process was self-activating. It was not set in motion by a Prime Mover—God or otherwise.

How human beings came to be is generally held to be more certain than how the universe came to be. The theory of evolution, long toyed with by naturalists, was given a "mechanism" by Darwin and has won the day. There is hardly a public school text that does not proclaim the theory as fact. We should be careful, however, not to assume that

evolution is strictly a naturalist theory. Many theists are also evolution-
ists.[24]

For a theist, the infinite-personal God is seen to be in charge of all
natural processes. If the biological order has evolved it has done so
by conforming to God's design; it is teleological, directed toward an
end personally willed by God. For a naturalist, the process is on its
own. G. G. Simpson puts this so well he is worth quoting at some
length:

> Organic evolution is a process entirely materialistic in its origin
> and operation. . . . Life is materialistic in nature, but it has prop-
> erties unique to itself which reside in its organization, not in its
> materials or mechanics. Man arose as a result of the operation of
> organic evolution and his being and activities are also materialistic,
> but the human species has properties unique to itself among all
> forms of life, superadded to the properties unique to life among
> all forms of matter and of action. Man's intellectual, social, and
> spiritual natures are exceptional among animals in degree, but they
> arose by organic evolution.[25]

This passage is significant for its clear affirmation of both human
continuity with the rest of the cosmos and special uniqueness. Yet lest
we conclude that our uniqueness, our position as nature's highest
creation, was designed by some teleological principle operative in the
universe, Simpson adds, "Man was certainly not the goal of evolution,
which evidently had no goal."[26]

In some ways the theory of evolution raises as many questions as
it solves, for while it offers an explanation for *what* has happened over
the eons of time, it does not explain *why*. The notion of a Purposer
is not allowed by naturalists. Rather, as Jacques Monod says, man's
"number came up in the Monte Carlo game," a game of pure
chance.[27] Any intentionality is ruled out as a possibility from the beginning.

In any case, naturalists insist that with the dawn of humanity, evolution suddenly took on a new dimension, for human beings are self-conscious—probably the only self-conscious beings in the universe.[28] Further, as humans we are free consciously to consider, decide and act. Thus, while evolution considered strictly on the biological level continues to be unconscious and accidental, human actions are not. They are not just a part of the "natural" environment. They are human history.

In other words, when human beings appear, meaningful history, human history—the events of self-conscious, self-determining men and women—appears. But like evolution which has no inherent goal, history has no inherent goal. History is what we make it to be. Human events have only the meaning people give them when they choose them or when they look back on them.

History proceeds in a straight line, as in theism (not in a cycle as in Eastern pantheism), but history has no predetermined goal. Rather than culminating in a Second Coming of the God-man, it is simply going to "last" as long as conscious human beings last. When we go, human history disappears, and natural history goes on its way alone.

6. Ethics is related only to human beings.

Ethical considerations did not play a central role in the rise of naturalism. Naturalism rather came as a logical extension of certain metaphysical notions—notions about the nature of the external world. Most early naturalists continued to hold ethical views similar to those in the surrounding culture, views which in general were indistinguishable from popular Christianity. There was a respect for individual dignity, an affirmation of love, a commitment to truth and basic honesty. Jesus was seen as a teacher of high ethical values.

Though it is becoming less and less so, it is still true to some measure today. With a few recent twists—for example, a permissive attitude to premarital and extramarital sex, a positive response to euthanasia, abortion and the individual's right to suicide—the ethical norms of The Humanist Manifesto II are similar to traditional morality. Theists and naturalists can often live side by side in communal harmony on ethical matters. There have always been disagreements between them. These disagreements will, I believe, increase as humanism shifts further and further from its memory of Christian ethics.[29] But whatever the disagreements (or agreements) on ethical norms, the *basis* for these norms is radically different.

For a theist, God is the foundation of values. For a naturalist, values are manmade. The naturalist's notion follows logically from the previous propositions. If there was no consciousness prior to humans, then there was no prior sense of right and wrong. Furthermore, if there were no ability to do other than what one does, any sense of right and wrong would have no practical value. So for ethics to be possible, there must be both consciousness and self-determination. In short, there must be personality.

Naturalists say both consciousness and self-determination came with the appearance of human beings, and so ethics too came then too. No ethical system can be derived solely from the nature of "things" outside human consciousness. In other words, no Natural Law is inscribed in the cosmos. Even La Mettrie, who fudged a bit when he wrote "Nature created us all [man and beast] solely to be happy," betraying his deistic roots, was a confirmed naturalist in ethics: "You see that natural law is *nothing but* an intimate feeling which belongs to the imagination like all other feelings, thought included."[30] La Mettrie, of course, conceived of the imagination in a totally mechanistic fashion so that ethics became for him simply people following out the pattern imbedded in them as creatures. Certainly there is nothing whatever transcendent about morality.

The Humanist Manifesto II states the locus of naturalistic ethics in no uncertain terms: "We affirm that moral values derive their source from human experience. Ethics is *autonomous* and *situational,* needing no theological or ideological sanction. Ethics stems from human need and interest. To deny this distorts the whole basis of life. Human life has meaning because we create and develop our futures."[31] Most conscious naturalists would probably agree with this statement. But exactly how value is created out of the human situation is just as much up for grabs as is the way we ought to understand the origin of the universe.

The major question is this: How does *ought* derive from *is?* Traditional ethics, that is, the ethics of Christian theism, affirms the transcendent origin of ethics and locates in the infinite-personal God the measure of the good. Good is what God is, and this has been revealed in many and diverse ways, most fully in the life, teachings and death of Jesus Christ.

Naturalists, however, have no such appeal, nor do they wish to make one. Ethics is solely a human domain. So the question: How does one get from the fact of self-consciousness and self-determination, the realm of *is* and *can,* to the realm of what *ought* to be or be done?

One observation naturalists make is that all people have a sense of moral values. These derive, G. G. Simpson says, from intuition ("the feeling of rightness, without objective inquiry into the reasons for this feeling and without possible test as to the truth or falseness of the premises involved"), from authority and from convention. No one grows up without picking up values from the environment, and, while a person may reject these and pay the consequences of ostracism or martyrdom, seldom does anyone succeed in inventing values totally divorced from culture.

Of course, values differ from culture to culture, and none seems absolutely universal. So Simpson argues for an ethic based on objective inquiry and finds it in a harmonious adjustment of people to each other and their environment.[32] Whatever promotes such harmony is good; what does not is bad.

John Platt, in an article which attempts to construct an ethic for B. F. Skinner's behaviorism, writes,

Happiness is having short-run reinforcers congruent with medium-run and long-run ones, and wisdom is knowing how to achieve this. And ethical behavior results when short-run personal reinforcers are congruent with long-run group reinforcers. This makes it easy to "be good," or more exactly to "behave well."[33]

The upshot of this is a definition of good action as group-approved, survival-promoting action. Both Simpson and Platt opt for the continuance of human life as the value above all values. Survival is thus basic, but it is *human survival* which is affirmed as primary.

Both Simpson and Platt are scientists with a consciousness of their responsibility to be fully human and thus to integrate their scientific knowledge and their moral values. From the side of the humanities comes Walter Lippmann. In *A Preface to Morals* (1929) Lippmann assumes the naturalists' stance with regard to the origin and purposelessness of the universe. His tack is to construct an ethic on the basis of what he takes to be the central agreement of the "great religious teachers." For Lippmann, the good turns out to be something which has been recognized so far only by the elite, a "voluntary aristocracy of the spirit."[34] His argument is that this elitist ethic is now becoming mandatory for all people if they are to survive the twentieth-century crisis of values.

The good itself consists of disinterestedness—a way of alleviating the "disorders and frustrations" of the modern world, now that the "acids of modernity" have eaten away the traditional basis for ethical behavior. It is difficult to summarize the content Lippmann pours into the word *disinterested*. The final third of his book is addressed to doing that. But it helps to notice that his ethic turns out to be based on a personal commitment of each individual who would be moral, and that it is totally divorced from the world of facts—the nature of things in general:

A religion which rests upon particular conclusions in astronomy, biology and history may be fatally injured by the discovery of new

truths. But the religion of the spirit does not depend upon creeds
and cosmologies; it has no vested interest in any particular truth.
It is concerned not with the organization of matter, but with the
quality of human desire.[35]

Lippmann's language must be carefully understood. By *religion* he
means morality or moral impulse. By *spirit* he means the moral faculty
in human beings, that which exalts people above animals and above
others whose "religion" is merely "popular." The language of theism
is being employed, but its content is purely naturalistic.

In any case, what remains of ethics is an affirmation of a high
vision of right in the face of a universe which is merely there and has
no value in itself. Ethics thus are personal and chosen. Lippmann is
not, to my knowledge, generally associated with the existentialists, but,
as we shall see in chapter six, his version of naturalistic ethics is
ultimately theirs.

Naturalists have tried to construct ethical systems in a wide variety
of ways. Even Christian theists must admit that many of the naturalists'
ethical insights are valid. Indeed theists should not be surprised by
the fact that we can learn moral truths by observing human nature
and behavior, for if women and men are made in the image of God
and if that image is not totally destroyed by the Fall, then they should
yet reflect—even if dimly—something of the goodness of God.

Naturalism in Practice: Secular Humanism

Two forms of naturalism deserve special mention. The first is *secular
humanism*, a term that has come to be both used and abused by
adherents and critics alike. Some clarification of terms is in order
here.

First, secular humanism is one form of humanism in general, but
not the only form. Humanism itself is the overall attitude that human
beings are of special value; their aspirations, their thoughts, their
yearnings are significant. There is as well an emphasis on the value

of the individual person.

Ever since the Renaissance thoughtful people of various convictions have called themselves and been called *humanists,* among them many Christians. John Calvin (1509-64), Desiderius Erasmus (1456?-1536), Edmund Spenser (1552?-99), William Shakespeare (1564-1616), John Milton (1608-74), all of whom wrote from a Christian theistic world view, were humanists, what are sometimes today called *Christian humanists.* The reason for this designation is that they emphasized human dignity, not as over against God but as deriving from the image of God in each person. Today there are many thoughtful Christians who so want to preserve the word *humanism* from being associated with purely secular forms that they signed a Christian Humanist Manifesto (1982) declaring that Christians have always affirmed the value of human beings.[36]

Secular humanism is another specific form of humanism. Its tenets are best expressed in Humanist Manifesto II, drafted by Paul Kurtz, professor of philosophy at the State University of New York at Buffalo.[37] Secular humanism is a form of humanism, one completely framed within a naturalistic world view. It is fair to say, I believe, that most who would feel comfortable with the label of secular humanist would find their views reflected in Propositions 1-6 above. Secular humanists, in other words, are simply naturalists, though not all naturalists are secular humanists.

Naturalism in Practice: Marxism*

Perhaps the most significant form of naturalism in today's world is Marxism. While not capturing the popular imagination in the United States, it is very influential in other parts of the world.

It is difficult to define or analyze Marxism briefly, for there are many different types of "Marxists."[38] One good way of thinking about

---

*This section was written by C. Stephen Evans, associate professor of philosophy, St. Olaf College.

Marxism, however, is to think of it as another type of humanism. Although some secular humanists are Marxists or at least sympathetic to Marxism, most are not. "We are committed to an open and democratic society," says the Humanist Manifesto II, implicitly rejecting Marxism.[39] Nonetheless, while Marxist humanism has characteristic themes of its own, Marxism and secular humanism, as forms of naturalism, share many assumptions.

All forms of Marxism trace back to the writings of Karl Marx (1818-83), and Marx is best seen as a kind of humanist. In one of his earliest essays, he says clearly that "man is the supreme being for man."[40] From this humanist theme Marx deduces his revolutionary imperative to "overthrow all those conditions in which man is an abased, enslaved, abandoned, contemptible being."[41]

Marx arrived at his humanism through an encounter with two important nineteenth-century philosophers: Georg Wilhelm Friedrich Hegel (1770-1830) and Ludwig Feuerbach (1804-72). Hegel's philosophy was a form of idealism, which taught that God or "absolute spirit" was not a being distinct from the world, but was a reality which was progressively realizing itself in the concrete world. For Hegel this process was *dialectical* in nature; that is, it proceeded through conflicts in which each realization of spirit calls forth its own antagonist or "negation." Out of this conflict a still higher realization of spirit emerges, which in turn calls forth its negation, and so on. For Hegel the highest vehicle for the expression of spirit was human society, particularly the modern societies which were coming to fruition in the capitalistic states of nineteenth-century western Europe.

His philosophy was therefore a highly sophisticated philosophy of history. It proposed as the reason for our sojourn on earth that we were realizing the ends of God conceived as "absolute spirit."

Feuerbach was a materialist who was famous for asserting that human beings "are what they eat" and that religion was a human invention. As Feuerbach saw it, God is a projection of human potentiality,

an expression of our own unrealized ideals. Religion functions per-
niciously, since as soon as we invent God we devote ourselves to
pleasing our own imaginary construction instead of working to overcome the shortcomings which led to the invention in the first place.
Feuerbach extended his critique of religion to Hegel's philosophical
idealism, seeing in Hegel's concept of "spirit" yet another human
projection, a slightly secularized version of the Christian God.

Marx accepted Feuerbach's critique of religion wholeheartedly, and
atheism remains a part of most forms of Marxism to this day. However, he was struck by the fact that if Feuerbach's criticism of Hegel
was right, then Hegel's philosophy may still contain truth. If Hegel's
concept of spirit is simply a misleading projection of our human reality, then the dialectical process Hegel described may be real, just as
a film when projected may give an accurate picture of the reality
which was filmed. It is only necessary to "turn Hegel right side up"
by translating Hegel's idealistic talk of spirit into materialistic talk of
concrete human beings. Once we realize that in Hegel we are seeing
a projection or "film," we can interpret his view in a way that makes
it true. History *has* proceeded through conflict in which the contending parties create their own antagonists, and this series of historical
conflicts is "going somewhere." The goal of history is a perfect or
ideal human society, but it is misleading and confusing to call such
a society "spirit."

Marx's world view can be alternately described as *dialectical materialism* or as *historical materialism*. It is a dialectical materialism in that the
universe is seen as a process in which progress comes about through
the conflict of opposing forces. It is historical materialism in that the
emphasis in Marx is not on matter as a static physical reality, but on
human history. Marx's naturalism is a naturalism which sees nature
as a dynamic process with unrealized potentialities. For Marx nature
is best understood as history.

Marx does call himself a "materialist," and in some sense he certainly is a materialist, since he would hardly have accepted the idea that human beings or the universe have any supernatural origin. Despite this fact, Marx hardly ever talks about "matter." For Marx, materialism is primarily a doctrine about human history. It means that economic factors are the primary determinants of that history. Since human beings are material, their lives must be understood in terms of the need to work to satisfy their material needs. History is the history of human beings' struggle to grow food, make shelters and clothes, and provide themselves with tools to do these things more efficiently.

Marx's overall vision of history goes something like this: History begins with relatively small human communities which are organized in family-like tribes. Private property is unknown; a kind of primitive or natural communism holds in which individuals identify with the community as a whole. However, these early communistic societies are indeed primitive, lacking any technological innovations to assist them in the material struggle to survive and provide for their needs. As society develops technology, gradually a division of labor occurs. Some people in society control the tools or resources which society depends on; this gives them the power to exploit others. Thus out of division of labor and consequent control over the means of production emerge social classes.

For Marx social classes are the dialectical antagonists which Hegel had confusedly identified with spiritual realities. History for Marx is the history of class struggle. Since the demise of primitive societies, societies have always been dominated by one class or classes, the group which controls the means of production. The process by which the material goods society requires are created is the key to understanding society. This process is termed by Marxists the "base" of society. A particular system for producing material goods, such as feudal agriculture or modern industrial capitalism, produces a particular class structure. On that class structure depends in turn what Marx calls the "superstructure" of society: art, religion, philosophy, morality and, most importantly, political institutions.

Social changes occur when one system of production gives rise to a new system. The new economic "base" comes into being within the womb of the old "superstructure." The dominant social classes of the old order of course try to maintain their power as long as possible, relying on the state to maintain their position. Eventually, however, the new economic system, and the emerging class, become too powerful. The result is a revolution in which the old superstructure is swept away in favor of a new order which better reflects the underlying economic order.

The history of capitalism illustrates these truths clearly, according to Marx. Medieval feudal societies created modern industrial society, which is its dialectical opposite. For a long time, the feudal aristocracy tried to hold onto its power, but in the French revolution, Marx saw the triumph of the new middle class, who controlled the means of production in capitalist society. However, the same dialectical forces which led to capitalism will also destroy it. Capitalism requires a large body of propertyless workers, the proletariat, to exploit.

As Marx saw it, the economic dynamics of capitalism will necessarily lead to a society in which the proletariat are more and more numerous, and more and more exploited. Capitalist societies become more and more productive, but wealth becomes more and more narrowly distributed. Eventually the concentration of wealth leads to a society in which more is produced than can be purchased; overproduction leads to unemployment and more suffering. At last the proletariat will be forced to revolt.

For Marx the revolt of the proletariat will be different from any previous revolution. In the past, one social class overthrew a rival oppressing class and became in its turn the oppressor. The proletariat will, however, be the majority, not a minority. They have no vested interest in the old order of things, so it will be in their own best interests to abolish the whole system of class oppression. The material abundance created by modern technology makes this a real possibility for the first time in human history, since without such abundance, struggle, competition and oppression would inevitably break out in new forms.

The new classless society which will emerge will make possible what Marxists used to call the "new socialist man," now referred to in less sexist terms as the "new socialist individual." People will be less individualistic and competitive, more apt to find fulfillment in working for the good of others. The "alienation" of all previous societies will be overcome, and a new and higher form of human life will emerge. This vision in many ways parallels the Christian vision of the coming of the kingdom of God, and it is therefore easy to see why some have characterized Marxism as a Christian heresy. Marxists themselves claim that their humanism and socialism is no idle dream. It is rooted in actual historical forces, and Marx claimed that his socialism was scientific in character, not merely utopian.

The vision of Marxism is appealing. Marx had a deep understanding of the human need for genuine community and for fulfillment in work. He was sensitive not merely to the problem of poverty, but to the loss of dignity which occurs when human beings are seen merely as cogs in a vast industrial machine. He looked for a society in which people would creatively express themselves in their work, and see in their work an opportunity to help others as well as themselves.

However, there are also hard questions which Marx does not convincingly answer. One crucial concern is his faith that human history is moving toward an ideal society. Having abandoned any religious belief in providence, as well as Hegel's belief in absolute spirit as underlying history, Marx has no real basis for this expectation. He bases his own hope on empirical study of history, particularly his analysis of economic forces. However, many of Marx's predictions, such as his claim that workers in advanced capitalist countries will become increasingly impoverished, have been far off the mark, and one may question whether any social scientist can accurately predict the future.

A second problem for Marx concerns our motivation for working toward this future society, especially when we recognize that this society is by no means inevitable. Why should I work for a better society and try to end social exploitation? Marx rejects any moral values as a basis for such motivation. As a naturalist, he views morality as simply a product of human culture. There are no transcendent values which can be used as a basis for critically evaluating culture. Yet Marx himself often seems full of moral indignation as he looks at the excesses of capitalism. What is the basis for Marx's condemnation of capitalism if such moral notions as "justice" and "fairness" are just ideological inventions?

Two final grave problems for Marx lie in his vision of human nature and his analysis of the fundamental human problem. For Marx human beings are fundamentally self-creating; we create ourselves through our work. When our work or life-activity is alienated, we are alienated, and when our work has become truly human, we will be human as well. Greed, competition and envy all arise because of social divisions and poverty; an ideal society will eliminate these evils.

The question is whether Marx's view of human nature and analysis of the human problem go deep enough. Is it really plausible to think that selfishness and greed are solely a product of scarcity and class division? Is it really possible to make human beings fundamentally good if we have the right environment for them? The experience of professedly socialist societies would seem to teach that humans are very inventive in finding ways to manipulate any system for their own benefit. Perhaps the problem with human nature lies deeper than Marx thought. And this problem may expose a problem with his view of human beings: Are we purely material beings?

Marx was certainly right to emphasize work and economic factors as crucially important in shaping human society, but isn't there more to human life than economics? Certainly many young people in the most economically advanced countries struggle with finding meaning and purpose for their lives. Marxism, like all forms of naturalism, has a difficult time providing such meaning and purpose for human beings.

The Persistence of Naturalism

Unlike deism, naturalism has had great staying power. Born in the eighteenth century, it came of age in the nineteenth and grew to maturity in the twentieth. While signs of age are now appearing, naturalism is still very much alive. It dominates the universities, colleges and high schools. It provides the framework for most scientific study. It poses the backdrop against which the humanities continue to struggle for human value, as writers, poets, painters and artists in general shudder under its implications. No rival world view has yet been able to topple it, though it is fair to say that the twentieth century has provided some powerful options and theism is experiencing somewhat of a rebirth at all levels of society.

What makes naturalism so persistent? There are two basic answers. First, it gives the impression of being honest and objective. One is asked to accept only what appears to be based on facts and on the assured results of scientific investigation or scholarship. Second, to a vast number of people it appears to be coherent. To them the implications of its premises are largely worked out and found acceptable. Naturalism assumes no god, no spirit, no life beyond the grave. It sees human beings as the makers of value. While it disallows that we are the center of the universe by virtue of design, it allows us to place ourselves there and to make of ourselves and for ourselves something of value. As Simpson says, "Man *is* the highest animal. The fact that he alone is capable of making such a judgment is in itself part of the evidence that this decision is correct."[42] It is up to us then to work out the implications of our special place in nature, controlling and altering, as we find it possible, our own evolution.[43]

All of this is attractive. If naturalism were really as described, it should, perhaps, be called not only attractive or persistent but true. We could then proceed to tout its virtues and turn the argument of this book into a tract for our times.

But long before the twentieth century got under way, cracks began appearing in the edifice. Theistic critics always found fault with it. They could never abandon their conviction that an infinite-personal God is behind the universe. Their criticism might be discounted as unenlightened or merely conservative, as if they were afraid to launch out into the uncharted waters of new truth. But more was afoot than this. As we shall see in more detail in the following chapter, within the camp of the naturalists themselves came rumblings of discontent. The facts on which naturalism was based—the nature of the external universe, its closed continuity of cause and effect—were not at issue. The problem was in the area of coherence. Did naturalism give an adequate reason for us to consider ourselves valuable? Unique, maybe. But gorillas are unique. So is every category of nature. Value was the first troublesome issue. Could a being thrown up by chance be worthy?

Second, could a being whose origins were so "iffy" trust his or her own capacity to know? Put it personally: If my mind is coterminous with my brain, if "I" am only a thinking machine, how can I trust my thought? If consciousness is an epiphenomenon of matter, perhaps the appearance of human freedom which lays the basis for morality is an epiphenomenon of either chance or inexorable law. Perhaps chance or the nature of things only built into me the "feeling" that I am free but actually I am not.

These and similar questions do not arise from outside the naturalist world view. They are inherent in it. The fears that these questions raised in some minds lead directly to nihilism, which I am tempted to call a world view but which is actually a denial of all world views.

5
Zero Point:
Nihilism

If I should cast off this tattered coat,
And go free into the mighty sky;
If I should find nothing there
But a vast blue,
Echoless, ignorant—
What then?
Stephen Crane
The Black Riders and Other Lines

Nihilism is more a feeling than a philosophy. Strictly speaking, nihilism is not a philosophy at all. It is a denial of philosophy, a denial of the possibility of knowledge, a denial that anything is valuable. If it proceeds to the absolute denial of everything, it even denies the reality of existence itself. In other words, nihilism is the negation of everything—knowledge, ethics, beauty, reality. In nihilism no statement has validity; nothing has meaning. Everything is gratuitous, de trop, that is, just there.

Those who have been untouched by the feelings of despair, anxiety and ennui associated with nihilism may find it hard to imagine that nihilism could be a seriously held "world view." But it is, and it is well for everyone who wants to understand the twentieth century to experience, if only vicariously, something of nihilism as a stance toward human existence.

Modern art galleries are full of its products—if one can speak of something (art objects) coming from nothing (artists who, if they exist, deny the ultimate value of their existence). As we shall see later, no art is ultimately nihilistic, but some does attempt to embody many of nihilism's characteristics. Marcel Duchamp's "Fountain," an ordinary urinal purchased on the common market, signed with a fictional name and labeled "Fountain," will do for a start. Samuel Beckett's plays, notably *End Game* and *Waiting for Godot,* are prime examples in drama. But Beckett's nihilistic art perhaps reached its climax in *Breath,* a 35-second play that has no human actors. The props are a pile of rubbish on the stage, lit by a light which begins dim, brightens (but never fully) and then recedes to dimness. There are no words, only a "recorded" cry opening the play, an inhaled breath, an exhaled breath and an identical "recorded" cry closing the play. For Beckett life is such a "breath."

Douglas Adams in his four cosmic science-fiction novels pictures for us the situation for those who seek in computer science an answer to human meaning. In *The Hitchhiker's Guide to the Galaxy, The Restaurant at the End of the Universe, Life, the Universe and Everything* and *So Long and Thanks for All the Fish,* Adams tells the story of the universe from the point of view of four time travelers who hitchhike back and forth across intergalactic time and space, from creation in the Big Bang to the final destruction of the universe.[1] During the course of this history a race of hyperintelligent pan-dimensional beings (mice, actually) build a giant computer ("the size of a small city") to answer "The Ultimate Question of Life, the Universe and Everything." This computer, which they call Deep Thought spends seven-and-a-half million years on the calculation.[2]

> For seven and a half million years, Deep Thought computed and calculated, and in the end announced that the answer was in fact Forty-two—and so another, even bigger, computer had to be built to find out what the actual question was.

And this computer, which was called the Earth, was so large that it was frequently mistaken for a planet—especially by the strange apelike beings who roamed its surface, totally unaware that they were simply part of a gigantic computer program.

And this is very odd, because without that fairly simple and obvious piece of knowledge, nothing that ever happened on the Earth could possibly make the slightest bit of sense.

Sadly, however, just before the critical moment of readout, the Earth was unexpectedly demolished by the Vogons to make way—so they claimed—for a new hyperspace bypass, and so all hope of discovering a meaning for life was lost for ever.

Or so it would seem.[3]

By the end of the second novel, the time travelers discover that the "question itself" (The Ultimate Question of Life, the Universe and Everything) is: What is six times nine?[4] So, they discover, both the question and the answer are inane. Not only is forty-two a meaningless answer to the question on a human level (the level of purpose and meaning), it is bad mathematics. The most rational discipline in the university has been reduced to absurdity.

By the end of the third novel, we have an explanation for why the question and the answer do not seem to fit each other. Prak, the character who is supposed to know the ultimate, says this: "I'm afraid . . . that the Question and the Answer are mutually exclusive. Knowledge of one logically precludes knowledge of the other. It is impossible that both can ever be known about the same Universe."[5] (Physics students will detect here a play on Heisenberg's uncertainty principle where the position and momentum of an electron can both be known but not with precision at the same time.)

So: We can either have the Answers—like forty-two—which don't mean anything without the Questions. Or we can have the Questions (which give direction to our *quest*). But we can't have both. That is, we cannot satisfy our longing for ultimate meaning.

To read Samuel Beckett, Franz Kafka, Eugene Ionesco, Joseph Heller and Kurt Vonnegut, Jr., and, more recently, Douglas Adams is to begin to feel—if one does not already do so in our depressing age—the pangs of human emptiness, of life which is without value, without purpose, without meaning.

But how does one get from naturalism to nihilism? Wasn't naturalism the enlightened readout of the assured results of science and open intellectual inquiry? As a world view did it not account for human beings, their uniqueness among the things of the cosmos? Did it not show human dignity and value? As the highest of beings, the only self- conscious, self-determined beings in the universe, men and women are rulers of all—free to value what they will, free even to control the future of their own evolution. What more could one wish?

Most naturalists are satisfied to end their inquiry right here. They do in fact wish no more. For them, there is no route to nihilism.

But for a growing number of people the results of reason are not so assured, the *closed* nature of the universe is perceived to be confining, the notion of death as extinction is psychologically disturbing, their position as the highest beings in the universe is seen either as an alienation from the universe or as a union with it such that they are no more valuable than a pebble on the beach. In fact, pebbles "live" longer! What have served as bridges between a naturalism that affirms the value of human life and a naturalism that does not? Just how did nihilism come about?

Nihilism came about, not because the theists and deists picked away at naturalism from the outside. Nihilism is the natural child of naturalism.

The First Bridge: Necessity and Chance
The first and most basic reason for nihilism is found in the direct logical implications of naturalism's primary propositions. Notice what happens to the concept of human nature when one takes seriously

the notions that (1) matter is all there is and it is eternal and that (2) the cosmos operates with a uniformity of cause and effect in a *closed* system. These mean that a human being is a part of the system. Naturalists go along with this, of course, as we saw in proposition 3: *Human beings are complex machines whose personality is a function of highly complex chemical and physical properties not yet understood.* But many naturalists still try to hold on to human freedom within the closed system.

The argument goes like this. Every event in the universe is caused by a previous state of affairs, including the genetic make-up, the environmental situation of each person and even that person's wants and desires. But each person is free to express those wants and desires. If I want a sandwich and a deli is around the corner, I can choose to have a sandwich. If I want to steal the sandwich when the owner isn't looking, I can do that. Nothing constrains my choice. My actions are self-determined.

Thus human beings who are obviously self-conscious and, it would appear, self-determined can act significantly and be held responsible for their actions. I can be arrested for stealing the sandwich and reasonably required to pay the penalty.

But are things so simple? Many think not. The issue of human freedom goes deeper than the naturalist sees. To be sure I can do anything I want, but what I want is the result of past states of affairs over which ultimately I had no control. I did not freely select my particular genetic make-up or my original family environment. By the time I asked if I was free to act freely, I was so molded by nature and nurture that the very fact that the question occurred to me was determined. That is, my self itself was determined by outside forces. I can indeed ask such questions, I can act according to my wants and desires, and I can appear to myself to be free, but it is appearance only.

The problem is that if the universe is truly closed, then its activity can only be governed from within. Any force which acts to change the cosmos on whatever level (microcosmic, human, macrocosmic) is a part of the cosmos. There would thus seem to be *only* one explanation for change: The present state of affairs must govern the future state. In other words, the present must cause the future which in turn must cause the next future and so on.

The objection that in an Einsteinian universe of time-relativity simultaneity is impossible to define and causal links are impossible to prove is beside the point. We are not talking here about how the events are linked together, only that they are linked. Events occur because other events have occurred. All activity in the universe is connected this way. We cannot, perhaps, know what the links are, but the premise of a closed universe forces us to conclude that they must exist.

Moreover, there is evidence that such links exist, for patterns of events are perceivable, and some events can be predicted from the standpoint of earth time with almost absolute precision, for example, precisely when and where the next eclipse will take place. For every eclipse in the next fifteen centuries the exact shadow can be predicted and tracked in space and time across the earth. Most events cannot be so predicted, but the presumption is that that is because all the variables and their interrelations are not known. Some events are more predictable than others, but none is *uncertain*. Each event must come to be.

In a closed universe the possibility that some things need not be, that others are possible, is not possible. For the only way change can come is by a force moving to make that change, and the only way that that force can come is if it is moved by another force, ad infinitum. There is no break in this chain, from eternity past to eternity future, forever and ever, amen. To the ordinary person determinism does not appear to be the case. We generally perceive ourselves as free agents. But our perception is an illusion. We just do not know what "caused" us to decide. Something did, of course, but we feel it was our free choice. Such perceived freedom—if one does not think much about its implications—is quite sufficient, at least according to some.[6]

In a closed universe, in other words, *freedom* must be a *determinacy unrecognized*, and, for those who work out its implications, this is not enough to allow for self-determinacy or moral responsibility. For, if I robbed a bank, that would ultimately be due to inexorable (though unperceived) forces triggering my decisions in such a way that I could no longer consider these decisions mine. If these decisions are not mine, I cannot be held responsible. And such would be the case for every act of every person.

A human being is thus a mere piece of machinery, a toy—complicated, very complicated—but a toy of impersonal cosmic forces. A person's self-consciousness is only an epiphenomenon; it is just part of the machinery looking at itself. But consciousness is only part of the machinery; there is no "self" apart from that machinery. There is no "ego" that can "stand over against" the system and manipulate it at its own will. Its "will" is the will of the cosmos. In this picture, by the way, we have a rather good description of human beings as seen by B. F. Skinner. To change people, says Skinner, change their environment, the contingencies under which they act, the forces acting on them. A person must respond in kind, for in Skinner's view every person is only a reactor: "A person does not act on the world, the world acts on him."[7]

The nihilists follow this argument, which can now be stated briefly: Human beings are conscious machines without the ability to effect their own destiny or do anything significant; therefore, human beings (as valuable beings) are dead. Their life is Beckett's "breath," not the life God "breathed" into the first person in the Garden (Gen 2:7).

But perhaps the course of our argument has moved too fast. Have we missed something? Some naturalists would certainly say so. They would say that we went wrong when we said that the only explanation for change is the continuity of cause and effect. Jacques Monod, for example, attributes all basic change—certainly the appearance of anything genuinely new—to chance. And naturalists admit that new things have come into being by the uncountable trillions: every step on the evolutionary scale from hydrogen, carbon, oxygen, nitrogen and so forth in free association to the formation of complex amino acids and other basic building blocks of life.

At every turn—and these are beyond count—chance introduced the new thing. Then necessity, or what Monod calls "the machinery of invariance," took over and duplicated the chance-produced pattern. Slowly over eons of time through the cooperation of chance and necessity, cellular life, multicellular life, the plant and animal kingdoms and human beings emerged.[8] So chance is offered as the trigger for humanity's emergence. As G. G. Simpson says, "Plan, purpose, goal, all absent in evolution to this point, enter with the coming of man and are inherent in the new evolution, which is confined to him."[9]

But what is chance? Chance is either the inexorable proclivity of reality to happen like it does appearing to be chance because we do not know the reason for what happens (making chance another name for our ignorance of the forces of determinism) or it is absolutely irrational. In the first case, chance is just unknown determinism and not freedom at all. In the second case, chance is not an explanation but the absence of an explanation. An event occurs. No cause can be assigned. It is a chance event. Such an event not only might have not happened, it could never have been expected to happen. So while chance produces the appearance of freedom, it actually introduces absurdity. Chance is causeless, purposeless, directionless. It is sudden givenness—gratuity incarnated in time and space.

But as Monod says, chance introduced into time and space a push in a new direction. A chance event is causeless, but it itself is a cause and is now an intimate part of the closed universe. Chance opens the universe not to reason, meaning and purpose, but to absurdity. Suddenly we don't know where we are. We are no longer a flower in the seamless fabric of the universe, but a chance wart on the smooth skin of the impersonal.

Chance, then, does not supply a naturalist with what is necessary for a person to be both self-conscious and free. It only allows one to be self-conscious and subject to caprice. Capricious action is not a free expression of a person with character. It is simply gratuitous, un-caused. Capricious action is by definition not a response to self-de-termination, and thus we are still left without a basis for morality. Such action simply is.

To summarize: The first reason why naturalism turns into nihilism is that naturalism does not supply a basis on which a person can act significantly. Rather, it denies the possibility of a self-determining being who can choose on the basis of an innate self-conscious char-acter. We are machines—determined or capricious. We are not per-sons with self-consciousness and self-determination.

The Second Bridge: The Great Cloud of Unknowing

The metaphysical presupposition that the cosmos is a closed system has implications not only for metaphysics but also for epistemology. The argument in brief is this: If any given person is the result of impersonal forces—whether working haphazardly or by inexorable law—that person has no way of knowing whether what he or she seems to know is illusion or truth. Let us see how that is so.

Naturalism holds that perception and knowledge are either iden-tical with or a byproduct of the brain; they arise from the functioning of matter. Without matter's functioning there would be no thought. But matter functions by a nature of its own. There is no reason to think that matter has any interest in leading a conscious being to true perception or to logical (that is, correct) conclusions based on accu-rate observation and true presuppositions. The only beings in the universe who *care* about such matters are humans.

But people are bound to their bodies. Their consciousness arises from a complex interrelation of highly "ordered" matter. Why should whatever that matter is conscious of be in any way related to what actually is the case? Is there a test for distinguishing illusion from reality? Naturalists point to the methods of scientific inquiry, pragmatic tests and so forth. But all these utilize the brain they are testing. Each test could well be a futile exercise in spinning out the consistency of an illusion.

For naturalism nothing exists outside the system itself. There is no God—deceiving or nondeceiving, perfect or imperfect, personal or impersonal. There is only the cosmos, and humans are the only conscious beings. But they are latecomers. They "arose," but how far? Can they trust their minds, their reason?

Charles Darwin himself once said, "The horrid doubt always arises whether the convictions of man's mind, which has developed from the mind of the lower animals, are of any value or at all trustworthy. Would anyone trust the conviction of a monkey's mind, if there are any convictions in such a mind?"[10] In other words, if my brain is no more than that of a superior monkey, I cannot even be sure that my own theory of my origin is to be trusted.

Here is a curious case: If Darwin's naturalism is true, there is no way of even establishing its credibility, let alone proving it. Confidence in logic is ruled out. Darwin's own theory of human origins must therefore be accepted by an act of faith. One must hold that a brain, a device that came to be through natural selection and chance-sponsored mutations, can actually *know* a proposition or set of propositions to be true.

C. S. Lewis puts the case this way:

If all that exists is Nature, the great mindless interlocking event, if our own deepest convictions are merely the by-products of an irrational process, then clearly there is not the slightest ground for supposing that our sense of fitness and our consequent faith in uniformity tell us anything about a reality external to ourselves.

Our convictions are simply *a fact about us*—like the colour of our hair. If Naturalism is true we have no reason to trust our conviction that Nature is uniform.[11]

What we need for such certainty is the existence of some "Rational Spirit" outside both ourselves and nature from which our own rationality could derive. Theism assumes such a ground; naturalism does not.

We are not only boxed in by the past—our origin in inanimate, unconscious matter. We are also boxed in by our present situation as thinkers. Let us say that I have just completed an argument on the level of All men are mortal; Aristotle Onassis is a man; Aristotle Onassis is mortal. That's a proven conclusion. Right?

Well, how do you know it's right? Simple. I have obeyed the laws of logic. *What laws? How do you know them to be true?* They are self-evident. After all, would any thought or communication be possible without them? *No.* So aren't they true? *Not necessarily.*

Any argument we construct implies such laws—the classical ones of identity, noncontradiction and the excluded middle. But that fact does not guarantee the "truthfulness" of these laws in the sense that anything we think or say that obeys them necessarily relates to what is so in the objective, external universe. Moreover, any argument to check the validity of an argument is itself an argument which might be mistaken. When we begin to think like this, we are not far from an infinite regress; our argument chases its tail down the ever-receding corridors of the mind. Or, to change the image, we lose our bearings in a sea of infinity.

But haven't we gone astray in arguing against the possibility of knowledge? We do *seem* to be able to test our knowledge in such a way that it generally satisfies us. Some things we think we know can be proven false or at least highly unlikely, for example, that microbes are spontaneously generated from totally inorganic mud. And all of us *know* how to boil water, scratch our itches, recognize our friends and distinguish them from others in a crowd.

Virtually no one is a full-fledged epistemological nihilist. Yet naturalism does not allow a person to have any solid reason for confidence in human reason. We thus end in an ironic paradox. Naturalism, born in the Age of Enlightenment, was launched on a firm acceptance of the human ability to know. Now naturalists find that they can place no confidence in their knowing.

The whole point of this argument can be summarized briefly: Naturalism places us as human beings in a box. But for us to have any confidence that our knowing we are in a box is true, we need to stand outside the box or to have some other being outside the box provide us with information (theologians call this "revelation"). But there is *nothing* or *no one* outside the box to give us revelation, and we cannot ourselves transcend the box. Ergo: epistemological nihilism.

A naturalist who fails to perceive this is like the man in Stephen Crane's poem:

I saw a man pursuing the horizon;
Round and round they sped.
I was disturbed at this;
I accosted the man.
"It is futile," I said,
"You can never—"
"You lie," he cried,
And ran on.[12]

In the naturalistic framework, people pursue a knowledge which forever recedes before them. We can never *know*.

One of the most awful consequences of taking epistemological nihilism seriously is that it has led some people to question the very existence and reality of the universe itself. To some people, nothing is real, not even themselves. People who reach this state are in deep trouble, for they can no longer function as human beings. Or, as we often say, they cannot cope.

We usually do not recognize this situation as metaphysical or epistemological nihilism. Rather, we call it schizophrenia, hallucination, fantasizing, daydreaming or living in a dream world. And we "treat" the person as a "case," the problem as a "disease." I have no particular quarrel with doing this, for I do believe in the reality of an external world, one I hold in common with others in my space-time frame. Those who cannot recognize this are beyond coping.

But while we think of such situations primarily in psychological terms and while we commit such people to institutions where someone will keep them alive and others will help them return from their inner trip and get back to waking reality, we should realize that some of these far-out cases may be perfect examples of what happens when a person no longer *knows* in the common-sense way of knowing. It is the "proper" state, the logical result, of epistemological nihilism. If I cannot *know*, then any perception or dream or image or fantasy becomes equally real or unreal. Life in the ordinary world is based on our ability to make distinctions. Ask the man who has just swallowed colorless liquid which he thought was water but which was actually wood alcohol.

Most of us never see the far-out cases. They are quickly committed. But they exist and I have met some whose stories are frightening. Most full epistemological nihilists, however, fall in the class described by Robert Farrar Capon, who simply has no time for such nonsense:

> The skeptic is never for real. There he stands, cocktail in hand, left arm draped languorously on one end of the mantelpiece, telling you that he can't be sure of anything, not even of his own existence. I'll give you my secret method of demolishing universal skepticism in four words. Whisper to him: "Your fly is open." If he thinks knowledge is so all-fired impossible, why does he always look?[13]

As we noted above, there is just too much evidence that knowledge is possible. What we need is a way to explain why we have it. This naturalism does not do. So the one who remains a consistent naturalist must be a nihilist.

The Third Bridge: Is and Ought

Many naturalists—most, so far as I know—are very moral people. They are not thieves; they do not tend to be libertines. Many are faithful husbands and wives. Some are scandalized by the immorality of the twentieth century. The problem is not that moral values are not recognized but that they have no basis. Summing up the position reached by Nietzsche and Max Weber, Allan Bloom remarks, "Reason cannot establish values, and its belief that it can is the stupidest and most pernicious illusion."[14]

Remember that for a naturalist the world is merely there. It does not provide humanity with a sense of *oughtness*. It only *is*. Ethics, however, is about what ought to be whether it is or not. Where, then, does one go for a basis for morality? Where is *oughtness* found?

As we have noted, every person has moral values. There is no tribe without taboos. But these are merely facts of a social nature, and the specific values vary widely. In fact, many of these values conflict with each other. Thus we are forced to ask, Which values are the true values, or the higher values?

Cultural anthropologists, recognizing that this situation prevails, answer clearly: Moral values are relative to one's culture. What the tribe, nation, social unit says is valuable is valuable. But there is a serious flaw here. It is only another way of saying that *is* (the fact of a specific value) equals *ought* (what should be so). Moreover, it does not account for the situation of cultural rebels whose moral values are not those of their neighbors. The cultural rebel's *is* is not considered *ought*. Why? The answer of cultural relativism is that the rebel's moral values cannot be allowed if they upset social cohesiveness and jeopardize cultural survival. So we discover that *is* is not *ought* after all.

The cultural relativist has affirmed a value—the preservation of a culture at its current state—as more valuable than its destruction or transformation by one or more rebels within it. Once more, we are forced to ask *why*.

Cultural relativism, it turns out, is not forever relative. It rests on a primary value affirmed by cultural relativists themselves: that cultures should be preserved. So cultural relativism does not rely only on *is* but on what its adherents think *ought* to be the case. The trouble here is that some anthropologists are not cultural relativists. Some think certain values are so important that cultures that do not recognize them *should* recognize them. So cultural relativists must, if they are to convince their colleagues, show why their values are the true values.[15] Again we approach the infinite corridor down which we chase our arguments.

But let's look again. We must be sure we see what is implied by the fact that values do really vary widely. Between neighboring tribes values conflict. One tribe may conduct "religious wars" to spread its values. Such wars *are*. *Ought* they to be? Perhaps, but only if there is indeed a nonrelative standard by which to measure the values in conflict. But a naturalist has no way of determining which values among the ones in existence are the basic ones that give meaning to the specific tribal variations. A naturalist can only point to the fact of value, never to an absolute standard.

This situation is not so critical so long as sufficient space separates peoples of radically differing values. But in the global community of the twentieth century this luxury is no longer ours. We are continually forced to deal with values in conflict, and we have as naturalists no standard, no way of knowing when peace is more important than preserving another value. We may perhaps give up our property to avoid doing violence to a robber. But what shall we say to the white racists who own rental property in the city? Whose values are to govern their actions when a black person attempts to rent their property?

Who shall be the judge? How shall we decide?

The argument can again be summarized like that above: Naturalism places us as human beings in an ethically relative box. For us to know what values within that box are true values, we need a measure imposed on from outside the box. We need a moral plumb line by which we can evaluate the conflicting moral values we observe in ourselves and others. But there is nothing outside the box. There is no moral plumb line, no ultimate, nonchanging standard of value. Ergo: ethical nihilism.

But nihilism is a feeling, not just a philosophy. And on the level of human perception, Franz Kafka catches in a brief parable the feeling of life in a universe without a moral plumb line.

> I ran past the first watchman. Then I was horrified, ran back again and said to the watchman: "I ran through here while you were looking the other way." The watchman gazed ahead of him and said nothing. "I suppose I really oughtn't to have done it," I said. The watchman still said nothing. "Does your silence indicate permission to pass?"[16]

When people were conscious of a God whose character was moral law, when their consciences were informed by a sense of rightness, their watchmen would shout halt when they trespassed the law. Now their watchmen are silent. They serve no king and protect no kingdom. The wall is a fact without a meaning. One scales it, crosses it, breaches it, and no watchman ever complains. One is left not with the fact but with the feeling of guilt.[17]

In a haunting dream sequence in Ingmar Bergman's film *Wild Strawberries*, an old professor is arraigned before the bar of justice. When he asks the charge, the judge replies, "You are guilty of guilt."

"Is that serious?" the professor asks.

"Very serious," says the judge.

But that is all that is said on the subject of guilt. In a universe where God is dead, people are not guilty of violating a moral law; they are only guilty of guilt, and that is very serious for nothing can be done about it. If one had sinned, there might be atonement. If one had broken a law, the lawmaker might forgive the criminal. But if one is only guilty of guilt, there is no way to solve the very personal problem.[18]

And that states the case for a nihilist, for no one can avoid acting as if moral values exist and as if there is some bar of justice that measures guilt by objective standards. But there is no bar of justice and we are left, not in sin, but in guilt. Very serious indeed.

The Loss of Meaning

The strands of epistemological, metaphysical and ethical nihilism weave together to make a rope long enough and strong enough to hang a whole culture. The name of the rope is Loss of Meaning. We end in a total despair of ever seeing ourselves, the world and others as in any way significant. Nothing has meaning.

Kurt Vonnegut, Jr., in a parody of Genesis 1 captures this modern dilemma:

In the beginning God created the earth, and he looked upon it in His cosmic loneliness.

And God said, "Let Us make creatures out of mud, so mud can see what We have done." And God created every living creature that now moveth, and one was man. Mud as man alone could speak. God leaned close as mud as man sat up, looked around and spoke. Man blinked. "What is the purpose of all this?" he asked politely.

"Everything must have a purpose?" asked God.

"Certainly," said man.

"Then I leave it to you to think of one for all this," said God. And he went away.[19]

This may first appear to be a satire on theism's notion of the origin of the universe and human beings, but it is quite the contrary. It is a satire on the naturalist's view, for it shows our human dilemma. We have been thrown up by an impersonal universe. The moment a self-conscious, self-determining being appears on the scene, that person asks the big question: What is the meaning of all this? What is the purpose of the cosmos? But the person's own creator—the impersonal forces of bedrock matter—cannot respond. If the cosmos is to have meaning, we must manufacture it for ourselves.

As Stephen Crane put it in the poem quoted in the opening of the first chapter, the existence of people has not created in the universe "a sense of obligation." Precisely: We exist. Period. Our maker has no sense of value, no sense of obligation. We alone make values. Are our values valuable? By what standard? Only our own. Whose own? Each person's own. Each of us is king and bishop of our own realm, but our realm is pointland. For the moment we meet another person, we study another king and bishop. There is no way to arbitrate between two free value makers. There is no king to whom both give obeisance. There are values, but no Value. Society is only a bunch of windowless monads, a collection of points, not an organic body obeying a superior, all-encompassing form that arbitrates the values of its separate arms, legs, warts and wrinkles. Society is not a body at all. It is only a bunch.

Thus does naturalism lead to nihilism. If we take seriously the implications of the death of God, the disappearance of the transcendent, the closedness of the universe, we end right there.

Why, then, aren't most naturalists nihilists? The obvious answer is the best one: Most naturalists do not take their naturalism seriously. They are inconsistent. They affirm a set of values. They have friends who affirm a similar set. They appear to know, and they don't bother to ask how they know they know. They seem to be able to choose and don't ask themselves whether their apparent freedom is really caprice or determinism. Socrates said that the unexamined life is not worth living, but for a naturalist he is wrong. For a naturalist it is the examined life that is not worth living.

Inner Tensions in Nihilism

The trouble is that no one can live the examined life, if examination leads to nihilism, for nobody can live a life consistent with nihilism. At every step, at every moment, nihilists think, and they think their thinking has substance, and thus they cheat on their philosophy. There are, I believe, at least five reasons why nihilism is unlivable.

First, from meaninglessness, nothing at all follows, or rather, anything follows. If the universe is meaningless and a person cannot know and nothing is immoral, any course of action is open. One can respond to meaninglessness by any act whatsoever, for none is more or less appropriate. Suicide is one act, but it does not "follow" as any more appropriate than going to a Walt Disney movie.

Yet whenever we set ourselves on a course of action, putting one foot in front of the other in other than a haphazard way, we are affirming a goal. We are affirming the value of a course of action, even if to no one other than ourselves. Thus we are not living by nihilism. We are creating value by choice. From this type of argument comes Jean-Paul Sartre's attempt to go beyond nihilism to existentialism, which we will consider in the following chapter.[20]

Second, every time nihilists think and trust their thinking, they are inconsistent, for they have denied that thinking is of value or that it can lead to knowledge. But at the heart of a nihilist's one affirmation lies a self-contradiction. *There is no meaning in the universe,* nihilists scream. That means that their only affirmation is meaningless, for if it were to mean anything it would be false.[21] Nihilists are indeed boxed in. They can get absolutely nowhere. They merely are; they merely think; and none of this has any significance whatsoever. Except for those whose actions place them in institutions, no one seems to act out their nihilism. Those who do we "treat" as patients.

Third, while a limited sort of practical nihilism is possible for a while, eventually a limit is reached. The comedy of *Catch-22* rests on just this premise. Captain Yossarian is having a knockdown theological argument with Lt. Scheisskopf's wife, and God is coming in for a good deal of hassling. Yossarian is speaking:

> [God] is not working at all. He's playing. Or else He's forgotten all about us. That's the kind of God you people talk about—a country bumpkin, a clumsy, bungling, brainless, conceited, uncouth hayseed.
>
> Good God, how much reverence can you have for a Supreme Being who finds it necessary to include such phenomena as phlegm and tooth decay in His system of creation?[22]

After several unsuccessful attempts to handle Yossarian's verbal attack, Lt. Scheisskopf's wife turns to violence.

> "Stop it! Stop it!" Lieutenant Scheisskopf's wife screamed suddenly, and began beating him ineffectually about the head with both fists. "Stop it!". . .
>
> "What the hell are you getting so upset about?" he asked her bewilderedly in a tone of contrite amusement. "I thought you didn't believe in God."
>
> "I don't," she sobbed, bursting violently into tears. "But the God I don't believe in is a good God, a just God, a merciful God. He's not the mean and stupid God you make Him out to be."[23]

Here is another paradox: In order to deny God one must have a God to deny. In order to be a *practicing* nihilist, there must be something against which to do battle. A practicing nihilist is a parasite on meaning. He runs out of energy when there is nothing left to deny. The cynic is out of business when he is the last one around.

Fourth, nihilism means the death of art. Here too we find a paradox, for much modern art—literature, painting, drama, film—has nihilism for its ideological core. And much of this literature is excellent by the traditional canons of art. Samuel Beckett's *End Game*, Ingmar Bergman's *Winter Light*, Franz Kafka's *The Trial*, Francis Bacon's various heads of popes spring immediately to mind. The twist is this: To the extent that these artworks display the human implication of a nihilistic world view they are not nihilistic; to the extent that they themselves are meaningless, they are not artworks.

Art is nothing if not formal, that is, endowed with structure by the artist. But structure itself implies meaning. So to the extent that an artwork has structure, it has meaning and thus is not nihilistic. Even Beckett's *Breath* has structure. A junkyard, the garbage in a trash heap, a pile of rocks just blasted from a quarry have no structure. They are not art.

Some contemporary art attempts to be anti-art by being random. Much of John Cage's music is predicated on sheer chance, randomness. But it is both dull and grating, and very few people can listen to it. It's not art. Then there is Kafka's "Hunger Artist," a brilliant though painful story about an artist who tries to make art out of public fasting, that is, out of nothing. But no one looks at him; everyone passes by his display at the circus to see a young leopard pacing in his cage. Even the "nature" of the leopard is more interesting than the "art" of the nihilist. *Breath* too, as minimal as it is, is structured and means something. Even if it means only that human beings are meaningless, it participates in the paradox we examined above. In short, art implies meaning and is ultimately non-nihilistic, despite the ironic attempt of nihilists to display their wares by means of it.

Fifth, and finally, nihilism poses severe psychological problems for a nihilist. People cannot live with it because it denies what every fiber of their waking being calls for—meaning, value, significance, dignity, worth. "Nietzsche," Bloom writes, "replaces easygoing or self-satisfied atheism with agonized atheism, suffering its human consequences. Longing to believe, along with intransigent refusal to satisfy that longing, is, according to him the profound response to our entire spiritual condition."[24]

Nietzsche ended in an asylum. Hemingway affirmed a "lifestyle" and eventually committed suicide. Beckett writes black comedy. Vonnegut and Douglas Adams revel in whimsy. And Kafka—perhaps the greatest artist of them all—lived an almost impossible life of tedium, writing novels and stories that boil down to a sustained cry: "God is dead! God is dead! Isn't he? I mean, surely he is, isn't he? God is dead. Oh, I wish, I wish, I wish he weren't."

It is thus that nihilism forms the hinge for modern people. No one who has not plumbed the despair of the nihilists, heard them out, felt as they felt—if only vicariously through their art—can understand the twentieth century. Nihilism is the foggy bottom land through which we modern people must pass if we are to build a life in Western culture. There are no easy answers to our questions, and none of these answers is worth anything unless it takes seriously the problems raised by the possibility that nothing whatever of value exists.

6
Beyond Nihilism: Existentialism

Every existing thing is born without reason,
prolongs itself out of weakness and dies by
chance. I leaned back and closed my eyes.
The images, forewarned, immediately leaped
up and filled my closed eyes with existences:
existence is a fullness which man can never
abandon. . . . I knew it was the World, the
naked World suddenly revealing itself, and I
choked with rage at this gross absurd being.
Jean-Paul Sartre
Nausea

In an essay published in 1950, Albert Camus wrote, "A literature of despair is a contradiction in terms. . . . In the darkest depths of our nihilism I have sought only for the means to transcend nihilism."[1] Here the essence of existentialism's most important goal is summed up in one phrase—*to transcend nihilism.* In fact, every important world view that has emerged since the turn of our century has had that as a major goal. For nihilism, coming as it does directly from a culturally pervasive world view, is the problem of our age. A world view that ignores this fact has little chance of proving relevant to modern thinking people. Existentialism, especially in its secular form, not only takes nihilism seriously, it is an answer to it.

From the outset it is important to recognize that existentialism takes two basic forms, depending on its relation to previous world views, because existentialism is not a full-fledged world view. Atheistic existentialism is a parasite on naturalism; theistic existentialism is a parasite on theism.[2]

Historically, we have an odd situation. On the one hand, atheistic existentialism developed to solve the problem of a naturalism that led to nihilism, but it did not appear in any fullness till well into the twentieth century, unless we count a few hints in Nietzsche. On the other hand, theistic existentialism was born in the middle of the nineteenth century as Kierkegaard responded to the dead orthodoxy of Danish Lutheranism. Yet it was not until after the First World War that either form of existentialism became culturally significant, for it was only then that nihilism finally gripped the intellectual world and began affecting the lives and attitudes of ordinary men and women.

The First World War had not made the world safe for democracy. The generation of flappers and bathtub gin, the rampant violation of an absurd antiliquor law, the quixotic stock market that promised so much—these prefaced in the United States the dustbowl thirties. With the rise of National Socialism in Germany and its incredible travesty on human dignity, students and intellectuals the world over were ready to conclude that life is absurd and human beings are meaningless. In the soil of such frustration and cultural discontent, existentialism in its atheistic form sank its cultural roots. It was to flower into a significant world view by the 1950s and is now in full bloom.

To some extent all world views have subtle variations. Existentialism is no exception. Albert Camus and Jean-Paul Sartre, both existentialists and once friends, had a falling out over important differences, and Heidegger's existentialism is quite different from Sartre's. But, as with other world views, we will focus on major features and general tendencies. The language of most of the propositions listed below derives from either Sartre or Camus. That is quite intentional because that is the form in which it has been most digested by today's intelligentsia, and it is Sartre and Camus who, through their literary works even more than their philosophic treatises, are still wielding enormous influence. To many modern people the propositions of existentialism appear so obvious that people "do not know what they are assuming because no other way of putting things has ever occurred to them."[3]

Basic Atheistic Existentialism

Atheistic existentialism begins by accepting all of the following propositions of naturalism: *Matter exists eternally; God does not exist. The cosmos exists as a uniformity of natural causes in a closed system. History is a linear stream of events linked by cause and effect but without an overarching purpose. Ethics is related only to human beings.* In other words, atheistic existentialism affirms all propositions of naturalism except those relating to human nature and our relationship to the cosmos. Indeed, existentialism's major interest is in our humanity and how we can be significant in an otherwise insignificant world.

1. The cosmos is composed solely of matter, but to human beings reality appears in two forms—subjective and objective.

The world, it is assumed, existed long before human beings came on the scene. It is structured or chaotic, determined by inexorable law or subject to chance. Whichever it is makes no difference. The world merely is.

Then came a new thing, conscious beings—ones who knew *he* and *she* from *it,* ones who seemed determined to determine their own destiny, to ask questions, to ponder, to wonder, to seek meaning, to endow the external world with special value, to create gods. In short, then came human beings. Now we have—for no one knows what reason—two kinds of being in the universe, the one seemingly having kicked the other out of itself and into separate existence.

The first sort of being is the objective world—the world of material, of inexorable law, of cause and effect, of chronological, clock-ticking time, of flux, of mechanism. The machinery of the universe, the spinning electrons, the whirling galaxies, the falling bodies and rising

gases and flowing waters—each is doing its thing, forever unconscious, forever just being where it is when it is. Here, say the existentialists, science and logic have their day. People know the external,
objective world by virtue of careful observation, recording, hypothe-
sizing, checking hypotheses by experiment, ever refining theories and
proving guesses about the lay of the cosmos we live in.

The second sort of being is the subjective world—the world of
mind, of consciousness, of awareness, of freedom, of stability. Here
the inner awareness of the mind is a conscious present, a constant
now; time has no meaning, for the subject is always present to itself,
never past, never future. Science and logic do not penetrate this
realm; they have nothing to say about subjectivity. Subjectivity is the
self's apprehension of the not-self; subjectivity is making that not-self
part of itself. The subject takes in knowledge not as a bottle takes in
liquid but as an organism takes in food. Knowledge turns into the
knower.

Naturalism had emphasized the unity of the two worlds by seeing
the objective world as the real and the subjective as its shadow. "The
brain secretes thought," said Cabanis, "as the liver secretes bile." The
real is the objective. Sartre says, "The effect of all materialism is to
treat all men, including the one philosophizing, as objects, that is, as
an ensemble of determined reactions in no way distinguished from
the ensemble of qualities and phenomena which constitute a table or
a chair or a stone."[4] By that route, as we saw, lies nihilism. The
existentialists take another path.

Existentialism emphasizes the disunity of the two worlds and opts
strongly in favor of the subjective world, what Sartre calls "an ensemble of values distinct from the material realm."[5] For people are *the*
subjective beings. Unless there are extraterrestrial beings, a possibility
most existentialists do not even consider, we are the only beings in
the universe who are self-conscious and self-determinate. The reason
we have become that way is past finding out. But we perceive ourselves

to be self-conscious and self-determinate, and so we work from these givens.

Science and logic do not penetrate our subjectivity, but that is all right because value and meaning and significance are not tied to science and logic. We *can mean;* we *can be valuable;* or better, *we* can mean and be valuable. Our significance is not up to the facts of the objective world over which we have no control, but up to the consciousness of the subjective world over which we have complete control.

2. *For human beings alone existence precedes essence; people make themselves who they are.*

This sentence derives from Sartre, and is the most famous definition of the core of existentialism. To put it in Sartre's words, "If God does not exist, there is at least one being in whom existence precedes essence, a being who exists before he can be defined by any concept, and . . . this being is man." Sartre continues, "First of all, man exists, turns up, appears on the scene, and, only afterwards, defines himself."[6]

Note again the distinction between the objective and subjective worlds. The objective world is a world of essences. Everything comes bearing its nature. Salt is salt; trees are tree; ants are ant. Only human beings are not human before they make themselves to be so. Each of us makes himself or herself to be human by what we do with our self-consciousness and our self-determinacy. Back to Sartre: "At first he [man] is nothing. Only afterwards will he be something, and he himself will have made him what he will be."[7] The subjective world is completely at the beck and call of every subjective being, that is, of every person.

How does this work out in practice? Let us say a soldier fears he is a coward. Is he a coward? Only if he acts like a coward, and his action will proceed not from a nature defined beforehand but from the choices he makes when the bullets start to fly. We can call the

soldier a coward if and only if he does cowardly deeds, and these will
be deeds he chooses to do. So if the soldier fears he is a coward, let
him do brave deeds when they are called for.[8]

3. Each person is totally free as regards their nature and destiny.

From proposition 2 it follows that each person is totally free. Each
of us is uncoerced, radically capable of doing anything imaginable
with our subjectivity. We can think, will, imagine, dream, project visions, consider, ponder, invent. Each of us is king of our own subjective world.

We run into just such an understanding of human freedom in John
Platt's existential defense of B. F. Skinner's naturalistic behaviorism
referred to in chapter four:

> The objective world, the world of isolated and controlled experi-
> ments, is the world of physics; the subjective world, the world of
> knowledge, values, decisions, and acts—of purposes which these
> experiments are in fact designed to serve—is the world of cyber-
> netics, of our own goal-seeking behavior. Determinism or indeter-
> minism lies on *that* side of the boundary, while the usual idea of
> "free will" lies on *this* side of the boundary. They belong to differ-
> ent universes, and no statement about one has any bearing on the
> other.[9]

So we are free within. And thus we can create our own value by
affirming worth. We are not bound by the objective world of ticking
clocks and falling water and spinning electrons. Value is inner, and
the inner is each person's own.

*4. The highly wrought and tightly organized objective world stands over
against human beings and appears absurd.*

The objective world considered in and of itself is as the naturalist
has said—a world of order and law, perhaps triggered into new structures by chance. It is the world of *thereness.*

To us, however, the facticity, the hard, cold thereness of the world,
appears as alien. As we make ourselves to be by fashioning our sub-

jectivity, we see the objective world as absurd. It does not fit us. Our dreams and visions, our desires, all our inner world of value runs smack up against a universe which is impervious to our wishes. Think all day that you can step off a ten-story building and float safely to the ground. Then try it.

The objective world is orderly; bodies fall if not supported. The subjective world knows no order. What is present to it, what is here and now, *is*.

So we are all strangers in a foreign land. And the sooner we learn to accept that, the sooner we transcend our alienation and pass through the despair.

The toughest fact to transcend is the ultimate absurdity—death. We are free so long as we remain subjects. When we die, each of us is just an object among other objects. So, says Camus, we must ever live in the face of the absurd. We must not forget our bent toward nonexistence, but live out the tension between the love of life and the certainty of death.

5. In full recognition of and against the absurdity of the objective world, the authentic person must revolt and create value.

Here is how an existentialist goes beyond nihilism. Nothing is of value in the objective world in which we become conscious, but while we are conscious we create value. The person who lives an authentic existence is the one who keeps ever aware of the absurdity of the cosmos but who rebels against that absurdity and creates meaning.

Dostoevsky's "underground man" is a paradigm of the rebel without a seemingly reasonable cause. In the story the underground man is challenged:

Two and two do make four. Nature doesn't ask your advice. She isn't interested in your preferences or whether or not you approve of her laws. You must accept nature as she is with all the consequences that that implies. So a wall is a wall, etc., etc.

The walls referred to here are the "laws of nature," "the conclusions of the natural sciences, of mathematics." But the underground man is equal to the challenge:

> But, Good Lord, what do I care about the laws of nature and arithmetic if I have my reasons for disliking them, including the one about two and two making four! Of course, I won't be able to breach this wall with my head if I'm not strong enough. But I don't have to accept a stone wall just because it's there and I don't have the strength to breach it.[10]

It is thus insufficient to pit the objective world against the subjective and to point to its ultimate weapon, death. The person who would be authentic is not impressed. Being a cog in the cosmic machinery is much worse than death. As the underground man says, "The meaning of a man's life consists in proving to himself every minute that he is a man and not a piano key."[11]

Ethics, that is, a system of understanding what is the good, is simply solved for an existentialist. The good action is the consciously chosen action. Sartre writes, "To choose to be this or that is to affirm at the same time the value of what we choose, because we can never choose evil. We always choose the good."[12] So the good is whatever a person chooses; the good is part of subjectivity; it is not measured by a standard outside the human dimension.

The problem with this position is twofold. First, subjectivity leads to solipsism, the affirmation that each person alone is the determiner of values and that there are thus as many centers of value as there are persons in the cosmos at any one time. Sartre recognizes this objection and counters by insisting that every person in meeting other persons encounters a recognizable center of subjectivity.[13] Thus, we see that others like us must be involved in making meaning for themselves. We are all in this absurd world together, and our actions affect each other in such a way that "nothing can be good for us without being good for all."[14] Moreover, as I act and think and effect my subjectivity, I am engaged in a social activity: "I am creating a certain image of man of my own choosing. In choosing myself, I choose man."[15] According to Sartre, therefore, people living the authentic lives create value not only for themselves but for others too.

The second objection Sartre does not address, and it seems more telling. If, as Sartre says, we create value simply by choosing it and thus "can never choose evil," does good have any meaning? The first answer is yes, for evil is "not-choosing." In other words, evil is passivity, living by the direction of others, being blown around by one's society, not recognizing the absurdity of the universe, that is, not keeping the absurd alive. If the good is in choosing, then choose. Sartre once advised a young man who sought his counsel, "You're free, choose, that is, invent."[16]

Does this definition satisfy our human moral sensitivity? Is the good merely any action passionately chosen? Too many of us can think of actions seemingly chosen with eyes open that were dead wrong. In what frame of mind have the Russian pogroms against the Jews been ordered and executed? And the bombing of Vietnamese villages, or the massacre at My Lai? Sartre himself sided with causes that appeared quite moral on grounds many traditional moralists accept. But not every existentialist has acted like Sartre, and the system seems to leave open the possibility for a Charles Manson to claim ethical immunity for mass murder.

Placing the locus of morality in each individual's subjectivity leads to the inability to distinguish a moral from an immoral act on grounds that satisfy our innate sense of right, a sense that says others have the same rights as I do. My choice may not be the desired choice of others, though in my choosing I choose for others, as Sartre says. Some standard external to the "subjects" involved is necessary to shape truly the proper actions and relationships between "subjects."

Still, before we abandon existentialism to the charge of solipsism and a relativism that fails to provide a basis for ethics, we should give more than passing recognition to Albert Camus's noble attempt to show how a good life can be defined and lived. This, it seems to me, is the task Camus sets for himself in *The Plague.*

A Saint without God

In *The Brothers Karamazov* (1880) Dostoevsky has Ivan Karamazov say that if God is dead everything is permitted. In other words, if there is no transcendent standard of the good, then there can ultimately be no way to distinguish right from wrong, good from evil, and there can be no saints or sinners, no good men or bad men. If God is dead, ethics is impossible.

Albert Camus picks up that challenge in *The Plague* (1947), which tells the story of Oran, a city in North Africa, in which a deadly strain of the plague breaks out. The city closes its gates to traffic and thus becomes a symbol of the closed universe, a universe without God. The disease, on the other hand, comes to symbolize the absurdity of this universe: The plague is arbitrary; one cannot predict who will and who will not contract it. It is not "a thing made to man's measure."[17] It is terrible in its effects—painful, physically and mentally. Its origins are not known, and yet it becomes as familiar as daily bread. There is no way to avoid it. Thus the plague comes to stand for death itself, for like death it is unavoidable and its effects are terminal. The plague helps make everyone in Oran live an authentic existence because it makes everyone aware of the absurdity of the world they inhabit. It points up the fact that people are born with a love of life but live in the framework of the certainty of death.

The story begins as rats start to come out from their haunts and die in the streets; it ends a year later as the plague lifts and life in the city returns to normal. During the ensuing months, life in Oran becomes life in the face of total absurdity. Camus's genius is to use that as a setting against which to show the reactions of a cast of characters, each of whom represents in some way a philosophic attitude.

M. Michel, for example, is a concierge in an apartment house. He is outraged at the way the rats are coming out of their holes and dying in his apartment building. At first he denies they exist in his building, but eventually he is forced to admit it. Early in the novel he dies, cursing the rats. M. Michel represents the man who refuses to acknowledge the absurdity of the universe. When he is forced to admit it, he dies. He cannot live in the face of the absurd. He represents those who are able to live only *inauthentic* lives.

The old Spaniard has a very different reaction. He had retired at age 50 and went immediately to bed. Then he measured time, day in and day out, by putting peas from one pan to another. " 'Every fifteen peas,' he said, 'it's feeding time. What could be simpler?' "[18] The old Spaniard never leaves his bed, but he takes a sadistic pleasure in the rats, the heat, and the plague, which he calls "life."[19] He is Camus's nihilist. Nothing in his life—inside or out, objective world or subjective world—has value. So he lives it with a complete absence of meaning.

M. Cottard represents a third stance. Before the plague has gripped the city, he is nervous, for he is a criminal and is subject to arrest if detected. But as the plague becomes severe, all the city employees are committed to alleviating the distress and Cottard is left free to do as he will. And what he wills to do is live off of the plague. The worse conditions get, the richer, happier and friendlier he becomes." Getting worse every day isn't it? Well, anyhow, everyone's in the same boat," he says.[20] Jean Tarrou, one of the chief characters in the novel, explains Cottard's happiness this way: "He's in the same peril of death as everyone else, but that's just the point; he's in it *with the others.* "[21]

When the plague begins to lift, Cottard loses his feeling of community because he again becomes a wanted man. He loses control of himself, shoots up a street and is taken by force into custody. Throughout the plague his actions were criminal. Instead of alleviating the suffering of others, he feasted on it. He is Camus's sinner in a universe without God—proof, if you will, in novelistic form that evil is possible in a closed cosmos.

If evil is possible in a closed cosmos, then perhaps good is too. In two major characters, Jean Tarrou and Dr. Rieux, Camus develops this theme. Jean Tarrou was baptized into the fellowship of nihilists when he visited his father at work, heard him argue as a prosecuting attorney for the death of a criminal, and then saw an execution. This had a profound effect on him. As he puts it, "I learned that I had had an indirect hand in the deaths of thousands of people. . . . We all have the plague."[22] And thus he lost his peace.

From then on, Jean Tarrou made his whole life a search for some way to become "a saint without God."[23] Camus implies that Tarrou succeeded. His method lay in comprehension and sympathy, and ultimately issued in action.[24] He was the one who suggested a volunteer corps of workers to fight the plague and comfort its victims. Tarrou worked ceaselessly in this capacity. Yet there remained a streak of despair in his lifestyle: "Winning the match" for Tarrou meant living "only with what one knows and what one remembers, cut off from what one hopes for!" So, writes Dr. Rieux, the narrator of the novel, Tarrou "realized the black sterility of a life without illusions."[25]

Dr. Rieux himself is another case study of the good man in an absurd world. From the very beginning he set himself with all his strength to fight the plague—to revolt against the absurd. At first, his attitude was passionless, detached, aloof. Later, as his life was deeply touched by the lives and deaths of others, he softened and became compassionate. Philosophically, he came to understand what he was doing. He was totally unable to accept the idea that a good God could be in charge of things. As Baudelaire said, that would make God the devil. Rather, Dr. Rieux took as his task "fighting against creation as he found it."[26] He says, "Since the order of the world is shaped by death, mightn't it be better for God if we refuse to believe in Him and struggle with all our might against death, without raising our eyes toward the heaven where He sits in silence?"[27]

Dr. Rieux did exactly that: He struggled against death. And the story he tells is a record of "what had had to be done, and what assuredly would have to be done again in the never ending fight against terror and its relentless onslaughts, despite their personal afflictions, by all who, while unable to be saints but refusing to bow down to pestilences, strive their utmost to be healers."[28]

I have dwelt at length on *The Plague* (though by no means exhausting its riches either as art or as a lesson in life) because I know of no novel or work of existential philosophy that makes so appealing a case for the possibility of living a good life in a world where God is dead and values are ungrounded in a moral framework outside the human frame. *The Plague* is to me almost convincing. Almost, but not quite. For the same questions occur within the intellectual framework of *The Plague* as within the system of Sartre's "Existentialism."

Why should the affirmation of life as Dr. Rieux and Jean Tarrou see it be good and Cottard's living off the plague be bad? Why should the old Spaniard's nihilistic response be any less right than Dr. Rieux's positive action? True, our human sensibility sides with Rieux and Tarrou. But we recognize that the old Spaniard is not alone in his judgment. Who then is right? Those who side with the old Spaniard will not be convinced by Camus or by any reader who sides with Rieux, for without an external moral referent there is no common ground for discussion. There is but one conviction versus another. *The Plague* is attractive to those whose moral values are traditional, not because Camus offers a base for those values, but because he continues to affirm them even though they have no base. Unfortunately, affirmation is not enough. It can be countered by an opposite affirmation.

How Far beyond Nihilism?

Does atheistic existentialism transcend nihilism? It certainly tries to—

with passion and conviction. Yet it fails to provide a referent for a morality which goes beyond each individual. By grounding human significance in subjectivity, it places it in a realm divorced from reality. The objective world keeps intruding: Death, the ever-present possibility and the ultimate certainty, puts a halt to whatever meaning might otherwise be possible. It forces an existentialist forever to affirm and affirm and affirm; when affirmation ceases, so does authentic existence.

Considering precisely this objection to the possibility of human value, H. J. Blackham agrees to the terms of the argument. Death indeed does end all. But every human life is more than itself, for it stems from a past humanity and it affects humanity's future. Moreover, "there is heaven and there is hell in the economy of every human imagination."[29] That is, says Blackham, "I am the author of my own experience."[30] After all the objections have been raised, Blackham retreats to solipsism. And that seems to me precisely the end of all attempts at ethics from the standpoint of atheistic existentialism.

Atheistic existentialism goes beyond nihilism only to reach solipsism—the lonely self that exists for fourscore and seven (if it doesn't contract the plague earlier) then ceases to exist. Many would say that that is not to go beyond nihilism at all; it is only to don a mask called value, a mask stripped clean away by death.

Basic Theistic Existentialism

As was pointed out above, theistic existentialism arose from philosophic and theological roots quite different from those of its atheistic counterpart. It was Søren Kierkegaard's answer to the challenge of a theological nihilism—the dead orthodoxy of a dead church. As Kierkegaard's themes were picked up two generations after his death, they were the response to a Christianity which had lost its theology completely and had settled for a watered-down gospel of morality and good works. God had been reduced to Jesus, who had been reduced to a man pure and simple. The death of God in liberal theology did not produce among liberals the despair of Kafka but the optimism of one English bishop in 1905 who, when asked what he thought would prevent man from achieving a perfect social union, could think of nothing.

Late in the second decade of the twentieth century, however, Karl Barth in Germany saw what ought to happen when theology became anthropology, and he responded by refurbishing Christianity along existential lines. What he and subsequent theologians such as Emil Brunner and Reinhold Niebuhr affirmed came to be called neo-orthodoxy, for while it was significantly different from orthodoxy, it put God very much back in the picture.[31] It will not be our goal to look specifically at any one form of neo-orthodoxy. Rather, we will try to see those propositions which are common to the theistic existential stance.

Theistic existentialism begins by accepting the following presuppositions of theism: *God is infinite and personal (Triune), transcendent and immanent, omniscient, sovereign and good. God created the cosmos ex nihilo to operate with a uniformity of natural causes in an open system. Human beings are created in the image of God, can know something of God and the cosmos and can act significantly. God can and does communicate with us. We were created good but now are fallen and need to be restored by God through Christ. For human beings death is either the gate to life with God and his people or life forever separated from God. Ethics is transcendent and based on God's character.*

If we compare the above list with that in chapter two on theism itself, we may wonder what is so special about theistic existentialism. Don't we just have theism? I am tempted to say that that is just what we have, but that does an injustice to the special existential variations and emphases. For the existential version of theism is much more a special set of emphases within theism than it is a separate world view.

Still, because of its impact on twentieth-century theology and its confusing relation to atheistic existentialism, it deserves a special treatment. Moreover, some tendencies within the existential version of theism place it at odds with traditional theism. These tendencies will get special mention as they arise in the discussion.

As with atheistic existentialism, theistic existentialism's most characteristic elements are concerned, not with the nature of the cosmos or God, but with human nature and our relation to the cosmos and God.

1. Human beings are personal beings who, when they come to full consciousness, find themselves in an alien universe; whether or not God exists is a tough question to be solved not by reason but by faith.

Theistic existentialism does not start with God. This is its most important variation from theism. With theism God is assumed certainly to be there and of a given character; then people are defined in relationship to God. Theistic existentialism arrives at the same conclusion, but it starts elsewhere.

Theistic existentialism emphasizes the place in which human beings find themselves when they first come to self-awareness. Self-reflect for a moment. Your certainty of your own existence, your own consciousness, your own self-determinacy—these are your starting points. When you look around, check your own desires against the reality you find, look for a meaning to your existence, you are not blessed with certain answers. You find a universe that does not fit you, a social order which scratches where you don't itch and fails to scratch where you do. And, worse luck, you do not immediately perceive God.

The human situation is ambivalent, for the evidence for order in the universe is ambiguous. Some things seem explicable by laws which seem to govern events; other things do not. The fact of human love and compassion gives evidence for a benevolent deity. The fact of hatred and violence, the fact of an impersonal universe, point in the other direction.

It is here that Father Paneloux in *The Plague* images for us an existential Christian stance. Dr. Rieux, you will recall, refused to accept the "created order" because it was "a scheme of things in which children are put to torture."[32] Father Paneloux, on the other hand, says, "But perhaps we should love that which we cannot understand."[33] Father Paneloux has "leaped" to faith in and love for the existence of a good God, even though the immediate evidence is all in the other direction. Rather than accounting for the absurdity of the universe on the basis of the Fall, as a Christian theist would do, Father Paneloux assumes God is immediately responsible for this absurd universe; therefore, he concludes that he must believe in God in spite of the absurdity. Camus elsewhere calls such faith "intellectual suicide," and I am inclined to agree with him. But the point is that while reason may lead us to atheism, we can always refuse to accept reason's conclusions and take a leap toward faith.

To be sure, if the Judeo-Christian God exists, we had better acknowledge that because then our eternal destiny depends on it. But, say the existentialists, the data is not all in and never will be, and so every person who would be a theist must step forth and choose to believe. God will never reveal himself unambiguously. Consequently each person, in the loneliness of his or her own subjectivity, surrounded by a great deal more darkness than light, must choose. And that choice must be a radical act of faith. When a person does choose to believe, a whole panorama opens. Most of the propositions of traditional theism flood in. Yet the subjective, choice-centered basis for the world view colors the style of each Christian existentialist's stance within theism.

2. The personal is the valuable.

As in atheistic existentialism, theistic existentialism emphasizes the disjunction between the objective and the subjective worlds. Martin Buber, a Jewish existentialist, has the terms *I-Thou* and *I-It* to distinguish between the two ways a person relates to reality. In the *I-It* relationship a human being is an objectifier:

> Now with the magnifying glass of peering observation he bends over particulars and objectifies them, or with the field-glass of remote inspection he objectifies them and arranges them as scenery, he isolates them in observation without any feeling of their exclusiveness, or he knits them into a scheme of observation without any feeling of universality.[34]

This is the realm of science and logic, of space and time, of measurability. As Buber says, "Without *It* man cannot live. But he who lives by *It* alone is not man."[35] The *Thou* is necessary.

In the *I-Thou* relationship, a subject encounters a subject: "When *Thou* is spoken [Buber means experienced], the speaker has nothing for his object."[36] Rather, such speakers have a subject like themselves with whom to share a mutual life. In Buber's words, "All real living is meeting."[37]

Buber's statement about the primacy of *I-Thou*, person-to-person relationships is now recognized as a classic. No simple summary can do it justice, and I encourage readers to treat themselves to the book itself. Here we must content ourselves with one more quotation about the personal relationship Buber sees possible between God and people:

> Men do not find God if they stay in the world. They do not find Him if they leave the world. He who goes out with his whole being to meet his *Thou* and carries to it all being that is in the world, finds Him who cannot be sought.
>
> Of course God is the "wholly Other"; but He is also the wholly Same, the Wholly Present. Of course He is the *Mysterium Tremendum* that appears and overthrows; but He is also the mystery of the self-evident, nearer to me than my *I*.[38]

So theistic existentialists emphasize the personal as of primary value. The impersonal is there; it is important; but it is to be lifted up to God, lifted up to the *Thou* of all *Thous*. To do so satisfies the *I* and serves to eradicate the alienation so strongly felt by people when they concentrate on their *I-It* relations with nature and, sadly, with other people as well.

This discussion may seem rather abstract to Christians whose faith in God is a daily reality that they live out rather than reflect on. Perhaps the following chart comparing two ways of looking at some basic elements of Christianity will make the issues clearer. It is adapted from a lecture given by theologian Harold Englund at the University of Wisconsin in the early 1960s. Think of the column on the left as describing a dead orthodoxy contrasted with the column on the right describing a live theistic existentialism.

	Depersonalized	**Personalized**
Sin	Breaking a rule	Betraying a relationship
Repentance	Admitting guilt	Sorrow over personal betrayal
Forgiveness	Cancelling a penalty	Renewing fellowship
Faith	Believing a set of propositions	Commiting one's self to a person
Christian life	Obeying rules	Pleasing the Lord, a Person

When put this way, the existential version is obviously more attractive. Of course, traditional theists may well respond in two ways: First, the second column demands or implies the existence of the first column, and, second, theism has always included the second column in its system. Both responses are well founded. The problem has been that theism's total world view has not always been well understood and churches have tended to stick with column one. It has taken existentialism to restore many theists to a full recognition of the richness of their own system.

3. Knowledge is subjectivity; the whole truth is often paradoxical.

An existentialist's stress on personality and wholeness leads to an equal emphasis on the subjectivity of genuine, human knowledge. Knowledge about objects involves *I-It* relationships; they are necessary but not sufficient. Full knowledge is intimate interrelatedness; it involves the *I-Thou* and is linked firmly to the authentic life of the knower.

In 1835 when Kierkegaard was faced with deciding what should be his life work, he wrote,

> What I really need is to become clear in my own mind *what I must do*, not what I must know—except in so far as a knowing must precede every action. The important thing is to understand what I am destined for, to perceive what the Deity wants *me* to do; the point is to find the truth *for me*, to find *that idea for which I am ready to live and die*. What good would it do me to discover a so-called objective truth, though I were to work my way through the systems of the philosophers and were able, if need be, to pass them in review?[39]

Some readers of Kierkegaard have understood him to abandon the concept of objective truth altogether. Certainly some existentialists have done precisely that, disjoining the objective and subjective so completely that the one has no relation to the other.[40] This has been especially true of atheistic existentialists like John Platt.[41] It is not that the facts have no value but that they must be facts *for* someone, *facts for me*. And that changes their character and inextricably binds knowledge to the knower. Truth in its personal dimension is subjectivity; it is truth digested and lived out on the nerve endings of a human life.

When knowledge becomes so closely related to the knower, it has an edge of passion, of sympathy, and it tends to be hard to divide logically from the knower himself. Buber describes the situation of a person standing before God: "Man's religious situation, his being there in the Presence, is characterized by its essential and indissoluble antinomy." What is one's relation to God as regards freedom or necessity? Kant, says Buber, resolved the problem by assigning necessity to the realm of appearances and freedom to the realm of being.

But if I consider necessity and freedom not in worlds of thought but in the reality of standing before God, if I know that "I am given over for disposal" and know at the same time that "It depends on myself," then I cannot try to escape the paradox that has to be lived by assigning irreconcilable propositions to two separate realms of validity; nor can I be helped to an ideal reconciliation by any theological device: but I am compelled to take both to myself, to be lived together, and in being lived they are one.[42]

The full truth is in the paradox, not in an assertion of only one side of the issue. Presumably this paradox is resolved in the mind of God, but it is not resolved in the human mind. It is to be lived out: "God, I rely completely on you; do your will. I am stepping out to act."

The strength of stating our understanding of our stance before God in such a paradox is at least in part a result of the inability most of us have had in stating our stance nonparadoxically. Most nonparadoxical statements end by denying either God's sovereignty or human significance. That is, they tend either to Pelagianism or to hyper-Calvinism.

The weakness of resting in paradox is the difficulty in knowing where to stop. What sets of seemingly contradictory statements are to be lived out as truth? Surely not every set. "Love your neighbor; hate your neighbor." "Do good to those who persecute you. Call your friends together and do in your enemies." "Don't commit adultery. Have every sexual liaison you can pull off."

So beyond the paradoxical it would seem that there must be some noncontradictory proposition governing which paradoxes we will try to live out. In the Christian form of existentialism the Bible, taken as God's special revelation, has set the bounds. It forbids many paradoxes, and it seems to encourage others. The doctrine of the Trinity, for example, may be an unresolvable paradox, but it does justice to the biblical data.[43]

Among those who have no external objective authority to set the bounds, paradox tends to run rampant. Marjorie Grene comments about Kierkegaard, "But much of Kierkegaard's writing seems to be motivated not so much by an insight into the philosophical or religious appropriateness of paradox to a peculiar problem as by the sheer intellectual delight in the absurd for its own sake."[44] Thus this aspect of theistic existentialism has come in for a great deal of criticism from those holding a traditional theistic world view. The human mind is made in the image of God's mind, and thus, though our mind is finite and incapable of encompassing the whole of knowledge, it is yet able to discern some truth. As Francis Schaeffer puts it, we can have substantial truth but not exhaustive truth, and we can discern truth from foolishness by the use of the principle of noncontradiction.[45]

4. *History as a record of events is uncertain and unimportant, but history as a model or type or myth to be made present and lived is of supreme importance.*

Theistic existentialism took two steps away from traditional theism. The first step was to begin to distrust the accuracy of recorded history; the second step was to lose interest in its facticity and to emphasize its religious implication or meaning.

The first step is associated with the higher criticism of the midnineteenth century. Rather than taking the biblical accounts at face value, accepting miracles and all, the higher critics, such as D. F. Strauss and Ernest Renan, started from the naturalistic assumption that miracles cannot happen. Accounts of them must therefore be false, not necessarily fabricated by writers who wished to deceive, but propounded by credulous people of primitive mindset.

This, of course, tended to undermine the authority of the biblical accounts even where they were not riddled with the miraculous. Other higher critics, most notably Julius Wellhausen, also turned their attention to the inner unity of the Old Testament and discovered, so they were sure, that the Pentateuch was not written by Moses at all. In fact, the texts showed that several hands over several centuries had been at work. This undermined what the Bible says about itself and thus called into question the truth of its whole message.[46]

Rather than change their naturalistic presuppositions to match the data of the Bible, they concluded that the Bible was historically untrustworthy. This could have led to an abandonment of Christian faith in its entirety. Instead it led to a second step—a radical shift in emphasis. The facts the Bible recorded were not important; what was important were its examples of the good life and its timeless truths of morality.

Matthew Arnold wrote in 1875 that Christianity "will live, because it depends upon a true and inexhaustible fruitful idea, the idea of death and resurrection as conceived and worked out by Jesus. . . . The importance of the disciples' belief in their Master's resurrection lay in their believing what was true, although they materialized it. Jesus had died and risen again, but in his own sense not theirs."[47]

History—that is, space-time events—was not important; belief was important. And the death and resurrection came to stand, not for the atonement of humankind by the God-man Jesus Christ, but for a "new life" of human service and sacrifice for others. The great mystery of God's entrance into time and space was changed from fact to myth, a powerful myth, of course, one that could transform ordinary people into moral giants.

These steps took place long before the nihilism of Nietzsche or the despair of Kafka. They were responses to the "assured results of scholarship" (which as those who pursue the matter will find are now not so assured). If objective truth could not be found, no matter. Real truth is poetically contained in the "story," the narrative.

It is interesting to note what soon happened to Matthew Arnold. In 1875 he was saying that we should read the Bible as poetry; if we did, it would teach us the good life. In 1880 he had taken the next step and was advocating that we treat poetry in general in the same way we used to treat the Bible: "More and more mankind will discover that we have to turn to poetry to interpret life for us, to console us, to sustain us. . . . Most of what now passes with us for religion and philosophy will be replaced by poetry."[48] For Arnold, poetry in general had become Scripture.

In any case, when the theistic existentialists (Paul Tillich, Reinhold Niebuhr, Rudolf Bultmann and the like) began appearing on the theological scene, they had a ready-made solution to the problem posed for orthodoxy by the higher critics. So the Bible's history was suspect. What matter? The accounts are "religiously" (that is, poetically) true. So while the doctrine of the neo-orthodox theologians looks more like the orthodoxy of Calvin than like the liberalism of Matthew Arnold, the historical basis for the doctrines was discounted and the doctrines themselves began to be lifted out of history.

The Fall was said not to have taken place back there and then in space and time. Rather, each person reenacts in their own life this story. Each enters the world like Adam, sinless; each one rebels against God. The Fall is existential—a here-and-now proposition. Carnell summarizes the existential view of the Fall as "a mythological description of a universal experience of the race."[49]

Likewise the resurrection of Jesus may or may not have occurred in space and time. Barth believes it did; Bultmann, on the other hand, says,"An historical fact that involves a resurrection from the dead is utterly inconceivable!"[50] Again, no matter. The reality behind the resurrection is the New Life in Christ experienced by the disciples. The "spirit" of Jesus was living in them; their lives were transformed. They were indeed living the "cruciform life style."[51]

Other supernatural doctrines are similarly "demythologized," among them Creation, Redemption, the resurrection of the body, the Second Coming, the Anti-Christ. Each is said to be a symbol of "religious" import. They are either not to be taken literally or, if they are, their meaning is not in their facticity but in what they indicate about human nature and our relationship to God.

It is here—in the understanding of history and of doctrine—that theists most find fault with their existential counterparts. The charge is twofold. First, theists say that the existentialists start with two false or certainly highly suspect presuppositions: (1) that miracles are impossible (Bultmann here, but not Barth) and (2) that the Bible is historically untrustworthy. On the level of presuppositions Bultmann simply buys the naturalist notion of the closed universe; Bultmann, although usually associated with the neo-orthodox theologians, is thus not really a "theistic" existentialist at all. Much recent scholarship has gone a long way toward restoring confidence in the Old Testament as an accurate record of events, but existentialist theologians ignore this scholarship or discount the importance of its results. And that brings us to the second major theistic critique.

Theists charge the existentialists with building theology on the shifting sand of myth and symbol. As a reviewer in the *Times Literary Supplement* said about Lloyd Geering's *Resurrection: A Symbol of Hope,* an existential work, "How can a non-event [a resurrection which did not occur] be regarded as a symbol of hope or indeed of anything else? If something has happened we try to see what it means. If it has not happened the question cannot arise. We are driven back on the need for an Easter event."[52]

There must be an event if there is to be meaning. If Jesus arose from the dead in the traditional way of understanding this, then we have an event to mean something. If he stayed in the tomb or if his body was taken elsewhere, we have another event and it must mean something else. So a theist refuses to give up the historical basis for faith and challenges the existentialist to take more seriously the implications of abandoning historical facticity as religiously important. Such abandonment should lead to doubt and loss of faith. Instead it has led to a leap of faith. Meaning is created in the subjective world, but it has no objective referent.

In this area theistic existentialism comes very close to atheistic existentialism. Perhaps when existentialists abandon facticity as a ground of meaning, they should be encouraged to take the next step and abandon meaning altogether. This would place them back in the trackless wastes of nihilism, and they would have to search for another way out.

Concluding Remarks

The two forms of existentialism are interesting to study, for they are a pair of world views which bear a brotherly relationship but are children of two different fathers. Theistic existentialism arose with Kierkegaard as a response to dead theism, dead orthodoxy, and with Karl Barth as a response to the reduction of Christianity to sheer morality. It took a subjectivist turn, lifted religion from history and focused its attention on inner meaning. Atheistic existentialism came to the fore with Jean-Paul Sartre and Albert Camus as a response to nihilism and the reduction of people to meaningless cogs in the cosmic machinery. It took a subjectivist turn, lifted philosophy from objectivity and created meaning from human affirmation.

Brothers in style though not in content, these two forms of existentialism are still commanding attention and vying for adherents. So long as those who would be believers in God yearn for a faith that does not demand too much belief in the supernatural or the accuracy of the Bible, theistic existentialism will be a live option. So long as naturalists who cannot (or refuse to) believe in God are searching for a way to find meaning in their lives, atheistic existentialism will be of service. I would predict that both forms—in probably ever new and changing versions—will be with us for a long time.

7
Journey to the East: Eastern Pantheistic Monism

And all the voices, all the goals, all the
yearnings, all the sorrows, all the pleasures, all
the good and evil, all of them together was the
world. . . . The great song of a thousand voices
consisted of one word: OM—perfection.
Hermann Hesse
Siddhartha

In the course of Western thought eventually we reach an impasse. Naturalism leads to nihilism, and nihilism is hard to transcend on the terms that the Western world—permeated by naturalism—wishes to accept. Atheistic existentialism, as we have seen, is one attempt, but it has some rather serious problems. Theism is an option, but for a naturalist it is uninviting. How can one accept the existence of an infinite-personal, transcendent God? For over a century that question has posed a serious barrier. Many people today would rather stick with their naturalism, for it still seems to be a decided improvement on the fabulous religion it rejected. Moreover, modern Christendom, with its hypocritical churches and its lack of compassion, is a poor testimony to the viability of theism. No, that way will not do.

Perhaps we should look again at naturalism. Where did we go wrong? Well, for one thing we discover that by following reason our naturalism leads to nihilism. But we need not necessarily abandon our naturalism; we can simply say reason is not to be trusted. Existentialism went part way down this route; perhaps we should now go all the way. Second, since we in the West tend to quarrel over "doctrines," ideas, and so forth, let us call a moratorium not only on quarreling but on distinguishing intellectually at all. Perhaps any "useful" doctrine should be considered true. Third, if all our activism to produce change by manipulating the system of the universe produces pollution and our efforts at social betterment go unrewarded, why not abandon our activism? Let's stop doing and raise our quality of life by simply being. Finally, if Western quarrels turn into armed conflicts, why not retreat completely? Let go and let happen: Can that be any worse than what we have now? Has, perhaps, the East a better way?

On a more sociological level, we can trace the interest in the East to the rejection of middle-class values by the young generation in the 1960s. First, Western technology (that is, reason in its practical application) made possible modern warfare. The Vietnam War (the youth were not personally aware of earlier conflicts) is a result of reason. So let us abandon reason. Second, Western economics has led to gross inequity and economic oppression of masses of people. So let us reject the presuppositions from which such a system developed. Third, Western religion has seemed largely to support those in control of technology and the economic system. So let us not fall into that trap.

The swing to Eastern thought is, therefore, primarily a retreat from Western thought. The West ends in a maze of contradictions, acts of intellectual suicide and a specter of nihilism that haunts the dark edges of all our thought. Is there not another way?

Indeed, there is—a very different way. With its antirationalism, its syncretism, its quietism, its lack of technology, its uncomplicated lifestyle and its radically different religious framework, the East is extremely attractive. Moreover, the East has an even longer tradition than the West. Sitting, as it were, next door to us for centuries have been modes of conceiving and viewing the world that are poles apart from ours. Maybe the East, that quiet land of meditating gurus and simple life, has the answer to our longing for meaning and significance.

For over a century Eastern thought has been flowing west. The Hindu and Buddhist scriptures have been translated and now circulate in inexpensive paperback editions. D. T. Suzuki from the East has poured Eastern lore into Western publications. Alan Watts from the West has imbibed Zen and returned to teach his fellow Westerners. I wonder too just how many Western-minded young readers of Salinger's *Catcher in the Rye* have gone on to *Franny and Zooey* and then to a deeper interest in Zen. In any case, in the 1960s Eastern studies filtered down to the undergraduate level. Indian gurus have been crossing and recrossing the United States and Europe for more than two decades. Knowledge of the East is now easy to obtain, and more and more its view of reality is becoming a live option in the West.[1]

Basic Eastern Pantheistic Monism

The East is, of course, as rich and as hard to label and categorize as the West, as will be obvious to anyone who simply scans the table of contents of a study such as Surendranath Dasgupta's five-volume *History of Indian Philosophy*.[2] In what follows I am limiting the description to the Eastern world view most popular in the West: pantheistic monism. This is the root world view which underlies the Hindu Advaita Vedanta system of Shankara, the Transcendental Meditation of Maharishi Mahesh Yogi, much of the Upanishads, some Buddhist writings (notably those in the Zen tradition) and the views so beautifully captured by Hermann Hesse in his novel *Siddhartha*.

Pantheistic monism is distinguished from other related Eastern world views by its monism (the notion that only one impersonal element constitutes reality). Hare Krishna does not fit in this world view, for while it shares many of the characteristics of Eastern pantheistic monism, it has one major difference. It declares that reality is ultimately personal (and thus shares a relationship to theism totally absent in Advaita Vedanta).

Hopefully, these cryptic remarks will become clearer as we proceed. But first we must be even more cryptic.

1. Atman is Brahman; that is, the soul of each and every human being is the Soul of the cosmos.

Atman (the essence, the soul, of any person) is Brahman (the essence, the Soul of the whole cosmos). What is a human being? That is, what is at the very core of each of us? Each person is the whole shooting match. Each person is (to put it boldly but accurately in Eastern terms) God.

But we must define God in pantheistic terms. God is the one, infinite-impersonal, ultimate reality. That is, God is the cosmos. God is all that exists; nothing exists that is not God. If anything that is not God appears to exist, it is *maya*, illusion, and does not truly exist. In other words, anything that exists as a separate and distinct object—this chair, not that one; this rock, not that tree; me, not you—is an illusion. It is not our separateness that gives us reality, it is our oneness—the fact that we are Brahman and Brahman is One. Yes, Brahman is *the* One.

Ultimate reality is beyond distinction; it *is*. In fact, as we shall see when we discuss epistemology, we cannot express in language the nature of this oneness. We can only "realize" it by becoming it, by seizing our unity, our "godhead," and resting there beyond any distinction whatsoever.

In the West we are not used to this kind of system. To think is to distinguish. The laws of thought demand distinction: A is A; but A is not non-A. To know reality is to distinguish one thing from another, label it, catalog it, recognize its subtle relation to other objects in the cosmos. In the East to "know" reality is to pass beyond distinction, to "realize" the oneness of all by being one with the all. This sort of conception—insofar as it can be understood by the mind—is best expressed indirectly. *The Upanishads* abound in attempts to express the inexpressible indirectly in parables.

"Bring me a fruit from this banyan tree."

"Here it is, father."

"Break it."

"It is broken, Sir."

"What do you see in it?"

"Very small seeds, Sir."

"Break one of them, my son."

"It is broken, Sir."

"What do you see in it?"

"Nothing at all, Sir."

Then his father spoke to him: "My son, from the very essence in the seed which you cannot see comes in truth this vast banyan tree.

"Believe me, my son, an invisible and subtle essence is the Spirit of the whole universe. That is Reality. That is Atman. THOU ART THAT."[3]

So the father, a guru, teaches his son, a novice, that even a novice is ultimate reality. Yet all of us—Eastern and Western alike—perceive distinctions. We do not "realize" our oneness. And that leads us to the second proposition.

2. Some things are more one than others.

Here we seem to be multiplying cryptic remarks and getting nowhere. But we ought not despair. Eastern "thought" is like that.

Some things are more one than others is another way of saying that reality is a hierarchy of appearances. Some "things," some appearances or illusions, are closer than others to being at one with the One. The ordinary Eastern hierarchy looks rather like one Westerners might construct but for a different reason. Matter pure and simple (that is, mineral) is the least real; then vegetable, then animal and finally human life. But humanity too is hierarchical; some people are closer to unity than others. The Perfect Master, the Buddha, the guru are the human beings nearest to pure being.

Partly, consciousness seems to be the principle of hierarchy here. To "realize" oneness would seem to imply consciousness. But, as we shall see, when one is one with the One, consciousness completely disappears and one merely is infinite-impersonal Being. Consciousness, like techniques of meditation, is just one more thing to be discarded when its usefulness is past.[4] Still, pure matter is further from realization of its oneness than is humanity, and that is what counts.

At the furthest reaches of illusion, then, is matter. While its essence is Atman, it is not. Yet it should so *be*. We must be careful here not to attach any notion of "morality" to our understanding of the requirement that all things be at one with the One. Here it means simply that being itself requires unity with the One. The One is ultimate reality and all that is not the One is not really anything. True, it is not anything of value either, but, more importantly, it has no being at all.

So we are back to the original proposition: Some things are more one, that is, more real, than others. The next question is obvious: How does an individual, separate being get to be one with the One?

3. Many (if not all) roads lead to the One.

Getting to oneness with the One is not a matter of finding the one true path. There are many paths from maya to reality. I may take one, you another, a friend a third, ad infinitum. The problem is not to be with one another on the same path but to be headed in the right direction on our own path. That is, we must be oriented correctly.

Orientation is not so much a matter of doctrine as of technique. On this the East is adamant. Ideas are not important.[5] You and I may only occasionally agree on what is true about anything—ourselves, the external world, religion. No matter. Realizing oneness with the One is not a matter of belief but of technique, and even techniques vary.

Some gurus, such as the Maharishi Mahesh Yogi, stress chanting a mantra—a seemingly meaningless Sanskrit word sometimes selected by one's own spiritual master and given in secret to an initiate. Others recommend meditation on a mandala—a highly structured, often fascinatingly ornate and beautiful circular image, symbol of the totality of reality. Others encourage contemplation of Zen koans or haiku poems until the self leaps to satori, the sudden experience of enlightenment, of unity with the One. Others require endless repetition of prayers or acts of obeisance.

Almost all of these techniques, however, require quiet and solitude. They are methods of intellectually contentless meditation. One attempts to get on the vibe level with reality, to turn one's soul to the harmony of the cosmos and ultimately to the one solid, nonharmonic, nondual, Ultimate vibration—Brahman, the One.

Of all the "paths" one of the most common involves chanting the word *Om* or a phrase with that word in it, for example, "Om Mane Padme Hum." Both the word *Om* and the larger phrase are essentially untranslatable because they are intellectually contentless. Some have suggested for *Om* the following: *yes, perfection, ultimate reality, all, the eternal word.* Maharishi Mahesh Yogi says that *Om* is the "sustainer of life," "the beginning and end of all creation," "that hum, which is the first silent sound, first silent wave that starts from that silent ocean of unmanifested life."[6] Christmas Humphreys comments that *Om* is "the first syllable of the Tibetan formula Om Mane Padme Hum, the outer meaning of which is merely 'Hail to the Jewel in the Lotus,' and its inward meaning is the meaning of the Universe."[7]

Obviously, the word *meaning* is not used in this Eastern system in the same way it is used in theism or naturalism. We are not talking here about rational content but metaphysical union. We can only truly "pronounce" *Om* and "understand" its meaning when we are at one with the One, when *Atman is Brahman* is not a statement but a realization.

The Mandukya Upanishad says it this way:
OM. This eternal Word is all: what was, what is and what shall be, and what beyond is in eternity. All is OM.

Brahman is all and Atman is Brahman. Atman, the Self, has four conditions.

The first condition is the waking life of outward-moving consciousness, enjoying the seven outer gross elements.

The second condition is the dreaming life of inner-moving consciousness, enjoying the seven subtle inner elements in its own light and solitude.

The third condition is the sleeping life of silent consciousness when a person has no desires and beholds no dreams. That condition of deep sleep is one of oneness, a mass of silent consciousness made of peace and enjoying peace.

This silent consciousness is all-powerful, all-knowing, the inner ruler, the source of all, the beginning and end of all beings.

The fourth condition is Atman in his own pure state: the awakened life of supreme consciousness. It is neither outer nor inner consciousness, neither semi-consciousness, nor sleeping-consciousness, neither consciousness nor unconsciousness. He is Atman, the Spirit himself, that cannot be seen or touched, that is above all distinction, beyond thought and ineffable. In the union with him is the supreme proof of his reality. He is the end of evolution and non-duality. He is peace and love.

This Atman is the eternal Word OM. Its three sounds, A, U, and M, are the first three states of consciousness, and these three states are the three sounds.

The first sound A is the first state of waking consciousness, common to all men. It is found in the words *Apti*, "attaining," and *Adimatvam*, "being first." Who knows this attains in truth all his desires, and in all things becomes first.

The second sound U is the second state of dreaming consciousness. It is found in the words *Utkarsha,* "uprising," and *Ubhayatvam,* "bothness." Who knows this raises the tradition of knowledge and attains equilibrium. In his family is never born any one who knows not Brahman.

The third sound M is the third state of sleeping consciousness. It is found in the words *Miti,* "measure," and in the root *Mi,* "to end," that gives *Apti,* "final end." Who knows this measures all with his mind and attains the final End.

The word OM as one sound is the fourth state of supreme consciousness. It is beyond the senses and is the end of evolution. It is non-duality and love. He goes with his self to the supreme Self who knows this, who knows this.[8]

I have quoted this Upanishad in its entirety because it contains several key ideas in a relatively short passage. At the moment I am most concerned with the word *Om* and how it represents ultimate reality. To say *Om* is not to convey intellectual content. *Om* means anything and everything; and therefore, being beyond distinction, can just as well be said to *mean* nothing. To say *Om* is rather to become or attempt to become what *Om* symbolizes.

4. To realize one's oneness with the cosmos is to pass beyond personality.

Let us go back for a moment to the first proposition and see where it leads us when we turn our attention to human beings in this world. Atman is Brahman. Brahman is one and impersonal. Therefore, Atman is impersonal. Note the conclusion again: Human beings in their truest, fullest being are impersonal.

This notion in pantheistic monism is at diametrical odds with theism. In theism, personality is the chief thing about God and the chief thing about people. It means an individual has complexity at the essence of his or her being. Personality demands self-consciousness and self-determinacy, and these involve duality—a thinker and a thing thought. Both God and humanity in theism are complex.

In pantheism the chief thing about God is his Oneness, his sheer abstract, undifferentiated, nondual unity. This puts God beyond personality. And since Atman is Brahman, human beings are beyond personality too. For any of us to "realize" our being is for us to enter the undifferentiated One.

Let us return for a moment to a section of the Mandukya Upanishad quoted above. Atman, it proclaims, has "four conditions": waking life, dreaming life, deep sleep and "the awakened life of pure consciousness." The progression is important; the higher state is the state most approaching total oblivion, for one goes from the activity of ordinary life in the external world to the activity of dreaming to the nonactivity, the nonconsciousness, of deep sleep and ends in a condition which in its designation sounds like the reversal of the first three—"pure consciousness."

Then we note that "pure consciousness" has nothing to do with any kind of consciousness with which we are familiar. "Pure consciousness" is, rather, sheer union with the One and not "consciousness" at all, for that demands duality—a subject to be conscious and an object for it to be conscious of. Even self-consciousness demands duality in the self. But this "pure consciousness" is not consciousness; it is pure being.

This explanation may help us understand why Eastern thought so often leads to quietism and inaction. To be is not to do. Meditation is the main route to being, and meditation—whatever the style—is a case study in quietude. The picture of the enigmatically smiling Buddha sitting under the Bo tree in rapt contemplation, unseeing, unhearing, unheeding—this now becomes understandable. The Buddha has entered the One; he is the Enlightened One. He is at rest.

5. To realize one's oneness with the cosmos is to pass beyond knowledge. The principle of noncontradiction does not apply where ultimate reality is concerned.

From the statement Atman is Brahman, it also follows that human beings in their essence are beyond knowledge. Knowledge, like personality, demands duality—a knower and a known. But the One is beyond duality; it is sheer unity. Again as the Mandukya Upanishad says, "He is Atman, the Spirit himself, . . . above all distinction, beyond thought and ineffable." In other words, to *be* is not to know.

In *Siddhartha*, which is perhaps the most Eastern novel ever written by a Westerner, Hermann Hesse has the illumined Siddhartha put it this way:

> Knowledge can be communicated, but not wisdom. . . . In every truth the opposite is equally true. For example, a truth can only be expressed and enveloped in words if it is one-sided. Everything that is thought and expressed in words is one-sided, only half the truth; it lacks totality, completeness, unity.[9]

The argument is simple. Reality is one; language requires duality, several dualities in fact (speaker and listener; subject and predicate); ergo, language cannot convey the truth about reality. Juan Mascaró explains what this means for the doctrine of God:

> When the sage of the *Upanishads* is pressed for a definition of God, he remains silent, meaning God is silence. When asked again to express God in words, he says: "Neti, neti," "Not this, not this"; but when pressed for a positive explanation he utters the sublime words: "TAT TVAM ASI," "Thou art That."[10]

Of course! We have already seen this under proposition 3. Now we see more clearly why Eastern pantheistic monism is nondoctrinal. No doctrine can be true. Perhaps some can be more useful than others in getting a subject to achieve unity with the cosmos, but that is different. In fact, a lie might even be more useful.

But again we go astray. We are back to thinking like a Westerner. If there can be no true statement, neither can there be a lie. Commenting on the esoteric symbolism of the Tantric strand in Hinduism, Alex Comfort says, "Both ancient and modern Hindu explanations differ, and all of them are orthodox."[11] In other words, truth disappears as a category, and the only relevant distinction is usefulness. In short, we are back to technique—the substance of much Eastern concern.

6. To realize one's oneness with the cosmos is to pass beyond good and evil; the cosmos is perfect at every moment.

We come to a rather touchy subject here. It is one of the softest spots in Eastern pantheism because people refuse to deny morality. They continue to act as if some actions were right and others wrong. Moreover, the concept of karma is almost universal in Eastern thought.

Karma is the notion that one's present fate, one's pleasure or pain, one's being a king or a slave or a gnat, is the result of past action, especially in a former existence. It is, then, tied to the notion of reincarnation which follows from the general principle that nothing that is real (that is, no soul) ever passes out of existence. It may take centuries upon centuries to find its way back to the One, but a soul will never not be. All soul is eternal, for all soul is essentially Soul and thus forever the One.

On its way back to the One, however, it goes through whatever series of illusory forms its past action requires. Karma is the Eastern version of "you reap what you sow." But karma implies strict necessity. If you have "sinned," there is no God to cancel the debt and to forgive. Confession is of no avail. The sin must be worked out and will be worked out. Of course, a person can choose his future acts, and thus karma does not imply determinism or fatalism.[12]

This sounds very much like the description of a moral universe. People should do the good. If they do not, they will reap the consequences, if not in this life, in the next, perhaps even by coming back as a being lower in the hierarchy. As popularly conceived, a moral universe is what the East in fact has.

But two things should be noted about this system. First, the basis for doing good is not so that the good will be done or so that you benefit another person. Karma demands that every soul suffer for its past "sins," so there is no value in alleviating suffering. The soul will have to suffer later. So there is no agape-love, giving-love, nor would any such love benefit the recipient. One does good deeds in order to attain unity with the One. Doing good is first and foremost a self-helping way of life.

Second, all actions are merely part of the whole world of illusion. The only "real" reality is ultimate reality, and that is beyond differentiation, beyond good and evil. Brahman is beyond good and evil. Thus Siddhartha eloquently says,

> The world, Govinda, is not imperfect or slowly evolving along a long path to perfection. No, it is perfect at every moment; every sin already carries grace within it, all small children are potential old men, all sucklings have death within them, all dying people—eternal life. . . . Therefore, it seems to me that everything that exists is good—death as well as life, sin as well as holiness, wisdom as well as folly.[13]

So, like true and false, ultimately the category of good and evil fades away. Everything is good (which, of course, is identical to saying, "Nothing is good" or "Everything is evil"). The thief is the saint is the thief is the saint . . .

What then shall we say about all of the evidence that people of the East act as if their actions could be considered right or wrong? First, the East has no fewer naive and inconsistent adherents than the West. Second, theists would say, human beings are human beings; they must act as if they were moral beings, for they are moral beings. Third, their moral-looking actions may be done for purely selfish reasons: Who wants to return as a gnat or a stone? Of course, in a nonmoral system selfishness would not be considered immoral.

Hermann Hesse tips his hand, however, in *Siddhartha* and has his hero seemingly say with ordinary meaning that "love is the most important thing in the world."[14] And Hesse and Christmas Humphreys both introduce value distinction when they say that it is better to be illuminated or Enlightened than to be an ordinary person.[15] It would seem, therefore, that even many of the illuminated have a tendency to act morally rather than to live out the implications of their own system. Perhaps this is a way of saying that some people are "better" than their conscious world view would allow.

7. *Death is the end of individual, personal existence, but it changes nothing essential in an individual's nature.*

We have already discussed death as it relates to karma and reincarnation. But it deserves, as in every world view, a separate treatment. Human death signals the end of an individual embodiment of Atman; it signals as well the end of a person. But the soul, Atman, is indestructible.

When naturalists say that they do not expect to survive their death in any sense whatsoever, they do not mean that the atoms that compose their bodies will pass out of existence when they die. What will pass out of existence is their highly complex and unique configuration. And consistent naturalists are willing to say that when that goes, they go. Something would go on—their atoms—but they would not.

The East, strangely, would go along with this conclusion. No human being in the sense of individual or person survives death. Atman survives, but Atman is impersonal. When Atman is reincarnated, it becomes another person. So, does pantheistic monism teach the immortality of the soul? Yes, but it also echoes naturalism in its rejection of personal and individual immortality.

Of course, through Eastern eyes the personal and individual are illusory anyway. Only Atman is valuable. So death is no big deal. Nothing of value perishes; everything of value is eternal. This may help explain the remark Westerners often make about the cheapness of life in the East. Individual embodiments of life—this man, that woman, you, me—are of no value. But in essence they are all of infinite value; for in essence they are infinite.

The ramifications of this for Westerners who search the East for meaning and significance should not be ignored. For a Westerner who places value on individuality and personality—the unique value of an individual human life—Eastern pantheistic monism will prove a grave disappointment.

8. To realize one's oneness with the One is to pass beyond time. Time is unreal. History is cyclical.

One of the central images in *Siddhartha* is the river. From the river Siddhartha learns more than from all the teachings of the Buddha or from all the contact with his spiritual father, Vasudeva. At the climax of the novel Siddhartha bends down and listens intently to the river:

Siddhartha tried to listen better. The picture of his father, his own picture, and the picture of his son all flowed into each other. Kamala's picture also appeared and flowed on, and the picture of Govinda and others emerged and passed on. They all became part of the river. It was the goal of all of them, yearning, desiring, suffering; and the river's voice was full of longing, full of smarting woe, full of insatiable desire. The river flowed on towards its goal. Siddhartha saw the river hasten, made up of himself and his relatives and all the people he had ever seen. All the waves and water hastened, suffering, towards goals, many goals, to the waterfall, to the sea, to the current, to the ocean and all goals were reached and each one was succeeded by another. The water changed to vapor and rose, became rain and came down again, became spring, brook and river, changed anew, flowed anew. But the yearning voice had altered. It still echoed sorrowfully, searchingly, but other voices accompanied it, voices of pleasure and sorrow, good and evil voices, laughing and lamenting voices, hundreds of voices, thousands of voices.[16]

Finally all the voices, and images, and faces intertwined: "And all the voices, all the goals, all the yearnings, all the sorrows, all the pleasures, all the good and evil, all of them together was the world. . . . The great song of a thousand voices consisted of one word: Om—perfection."[17]

It is at this point that Siddhartha achieves an inner unity with the One, and "the serenity of knowledge" shines in his face.

The river in this long passage—and throughout the book—becomes an image for the cosmos. When looked at from the standpoint of a place along the bank, the river flows (time exists). But when looked at in its entirety—from spring to brook to river to ocean to vapor to rain to spring—the river does not flow (time does not exist). It is an illusion produced by sitting on the bank rather than seeing the river from the heavens. Time likewise is cyclical; history is what is produced by the flow of the water past a point on the shore. It is illusory. History then has no meaning where reality is concerned. In fact our task as people who would realize their godhead is to transcend history.

This should help explain why Western Christians who place so much emphasis on history find their presentation of the historical basis of Christianity almost completely ignored in the East. To the Western mind, whether or not Jesus existed, performed miracles, healed the sick, died and rose from the dead is important. If it happened, there must be a vital meaning to these strange, unnatural events. Perhaps there is a God after all.

To the Eastern mind, the whole argument is superfluous. Yesterday's facts are not meaningful in themselves. They do not bear on me today unless they have a here-and-now meaning; and if they have a here-and-now meaning, then their facticity as history is of no concern. The Eastern scriptures are filled with epigrams, parables, fables, stories, myth, songs, haiku, hymns, epics—but almost no history in the sense of events recorded because they took place in an unrepeatable space-time context.

To be concerned with such stuff would be to invert the whole hierarchical order. The unique is not the real; only the absolute and all-encompassing is real. If history is valuable, it will be so as myth and myth only, for myth takes us out of particularity and lifts us to essence.

One of the images of human life and the quest for unity with the One is closely tied to the images of the cycle, or the wheel, or the great mandala. Siddhartha says, "Whither will my path lead me? This path is stupid, it goes in spirals, perhaps in circles, but whichever way it goes, I will follow it."[18] And Juan Mascaró echoes, "The path of Truth may not be a path of parallel lines but a path that follows one circle: by going to the right and climbing the circle, or by going to the left and climbing the circle we are bound to meet at the top, although we started in apparently contradictory directions."[19]

This symbol is worked out in the novel *Siddhartha;* the paths of the Buddha, Vasudeva, Siddhartha and Govinda meet and cross several times, but all of them arrive at the same place. To change the image, Hesse shows this in the exact identity of the smiles on the face of the radiant Buddha, Vasudeva, Siddhartha.[20] All the Enlightened Ones are one in the All.

East and West: A Problem in Communication

Cyclical history, paths that cross, doctrines that disagree, evil that is good, knowledge that is ignorance, time that is eternal, reality that is unreal: All these are the shifting, paradoxical—even contradictory—masks that veil the One. What can Westerners say? If they point to its irrationality, the Easterner rejects reason as a category. If they point to the disappearance of morality, the Easterner scorns the duality that is required for the distinction. If they point to the inconsistency between the Easterner's moral action and amoral theory, the Easterner says, "Well, consistency is no virtue except by reason, which I have already rejected, and furthermore I'm not yet perfect. When I am rid of this load of karma, I'll cease acting as if I were moral. In fact, I'll cease acting at all and just meditate." If the Westerner says, "But if you don't eat, you'll die," the Easterner responds, "So what? Atman is Brahman. Brahman is eternal. A death to be wished!"

It is, I think, no wonder Western missionaries have made so little headway with committed Hindus and Buddhists. They don't speak the same language, for they hold almost nothing in common. It is painfully difficult to grasp the Eastern world view even when one has some idea that it demands a mode of thought different from the West. It seems to many who would like Easterners to become Christians (and thus to become theists) that Easterners have an even more difficult time understanding that Christianity is somehow unique, that the space-time resurrection of Jesus the Christ is at the heart of the good news of God.

In both cases, it seems to me, an understanding that the East and the West operate on two very different sets of assumptions is the place to start. To begin the dialog, at least one party must know how different their basic assumptions may turn out to be, but for true human communication, both parties must know this before the dialog proceeds very far. Perhaps the difficulties in Eastern thought that seem so obvious to Westerners will at least begin to be recognized by Easterners. If an Easterner can see what knowledge, morality and reality are like as seen from, say, the point of view of Western theism, the attractiveness of the Western way may be obvious.

Generally, however, what the East sees of the West is more ugly than Shiva, the great god of destruction himself. Those who would communicate the beauty of truth in Christ have a tough job, for the mists of ugly Western imperialism, war, violence, greed and gluttony are thick indeed.

Where, then, does all this leave the Westerner who has gone East to search for meaning and significance? Many, of course, drop out along the way, try to take a shortcut to Nirvana through drugs, or cop out, come home and take over their father's corporation, re-entering the West and leaving the East behind with little more than a beard left to show for it. (That gets trimmed before the first board meeting and removed before the second.) Others stay on the path for life. Still others perhaps find Nirvana and remain caught up in contemplation.

But many simply die—by starvation, dysentery, skullduggery and who knows what else. Some shipwreck on the shores of Western communities and are slowly made seaworthy by friends.

For a couple of decades, young and old have been flocking to various gurus. Bookstores are filled with books pointing East, their spines to the West, of course. One even offers advice on "how to choose a guru."[21] Transcendental Meditation and other Eastern spiritual techniques are common, as commuters meditate on the way to work and classes are offered in business corporations.

So Westerners are still trekking East. And so long as the East holds out promise—promise of peace, of meaning, of significance—people are likely to respond. What will they receive? Not just an Eastern Band-Aid for a Western scratch but a whole new world view and lifestyle

8
A Separate Reality: The New Age

We are Creating energy, matter and life at the
interface between the void and all known
creation. We are facing into the known
universe, creating it, filling it. . . . I am "one
of the boys in the engine room pumping
Creation from the void into the known
universe; from the unknown to the known I
am pumping."
John Lilly
The Center of the Cyclone

Eastern mysticism poses one way out for Western people caught in naturalism's nihilistic bind. But Eastern mysticism is foreign. Even a watered-down version like Transcendental Meditation requires an immediate and radical reorientation of the West's normal mode of grasping reality. Such reorientation leads to new states of consciousness and feelings of meaning, as we saw, but the intellectual cost is high. One must die to the West to be born in the East.

Is there a less painful, less costly way to achieve meaning and significance? Why not conduct a search for a new consciousness along more Western lines?

This, I think, is what is being done by a host of young scholars, medical doctors and psychologists. There is an avant garde in a number of academic disciplines from the humanities to the hard sciences, and the spillover into culture at large is more than a trickle.

To change the image, we are beginning to experience a world view in its infancy. Not yet completely formed, the New Age world view contains many rough edges and inner tensions, even flat-out contradictions, but it is taking shape and we can, I believe, visualize it in a series of propositions as we have done with other world views.

When this book was first published, there were very few attempts to bring all these New Age notions together in one place. The schemata which follows was at that time almost unique.[1] Since then there have been several significant attempts, most notably Marilyn Ferguson in *The Aquarian Conspiracy* and Fritjof Capra in *The Turning Point.* The former is the more enthusiastic and popular, the latter the more guarded and scholarly.[2] Both have made an impact on the New Age movement itself, giving it a sense of coherence and focus it had formerly lacked. Moreover, Douglas Groothuis in *Unmasking the New Age,* his survey and critique of the New Age movement, has contributed to a clearer and more comprehensive definition.[3]

By the mid-1970s, articles and cover stories in *Time* magazine and other major popular magazines touted the growing interest in the weird and the wonderful.[4] By the mid-1980s, interest in psychic phenomena had become so widespread as barely to raise an eyebrow. Several magazines such as *New Age Journal, Yoga Journal,* and *East-West Journal,* propagating New Age ideas are now available on newsstands.[5] Even Doonesbury cartoons in the summer of 1987 twitted the New Age movement, especially as the turn of the Mayan Calendar (August 16-17) supposedly heralded a Harmonic Convergence in the heavens and thus the final arrival of the Age of Aquarius, the New Age on earth.

Previously the Age of Aquarius had been announced by the musical group The Fifth Dimension in the late 1960s. Now it is really here, or so is the hope. On August 17, three hours of air time over National Public Radio from studios in Boulder, Colorado, were devoted to conversations with New Age aficionados who phoned in from the Great

Pyramid in Egypt, from Glastonbury in England, and other psychic power spots around the world. By the end of 1987 *Time* magazine again focussed on the New Age with a cover featuring Shirley Mac-Laine and a story surveying "faith healers, channelers, space travelers and crystals galore."[6]

As long ago as 1974, however, a British poll of mainly scientists and technicians indicated that nearly 70% believed in the possibility of ESP.[7] Stanley Krippner, a scientist in the Dream Laboratory of Maimonides Medical Center in New York, says,

> Most who believed parapsychic events were either fact or a distinct possibility were convinced by personal experience, not by research. For some reason, today many people are having experiences that they interpret as paranormal. I suspect this, in turn, is the result of increased interest in altered states of consciousness. More and more people are having experiences with meditation, hypnosis, and psychedelic drugs. More and more people are paying attention to sleep and dreams. All these experiences provide very fertile grounds for paranormal events. Parapsychology is simply an idea whose time has come.[8]

Krippner's prediction has proven true. *The New Age world view itself is a mindset whose time has come.* Today many people are grasping for a handle to reality—something that will give them hope. And the New Age is nothing if not hopeful. Its prime spokesmen are euphoric.

The Radical Transformation of Human Nature

Basing much of their hope on the evolutionary model—a leftover from Western naturalism—a number of avant garde thinkers are prophesying the coming of a New Man and a New Age. Jean Houston of the Foundation for Mind Research in Nyack, New York, says that what this world needs is a "psychenaut program to put the first man on earth." But even if we don't get a psychic counterpart to NASA, our psychenaut is coming: "It's almost as if the species [humanity] were taking a quantum leap into a whole new way of being."[9] She concludes that if we learn "to play upon the vast spectrum of consciousness, . . . we would have access to a humanity of such depth and richness as the world has not yet known, so that our great-great grandchildren may look back upon us as Neanderthals, so different will they be."[10]

Popular sociologist George Leonard, editor of *Look* magazine before it folded, predicts the same radical transformation and looks forward to "the emergence of a new human nature." His faith is unshakable: "This new species *will* evolve."[11] Lest we think ordinary people in business would all be cynical and unwilling to take hope in such a vision, we might consider a letter to the editor of the journal in which Leonard's comments appeared: George Leonard, the reader wrote, "brings fresh mystery—and hope—to the mystery of life." The letter was signed John N. DeBoice, V.P., First National Bank of Chicago.[12] Shirley MacLaine echoes this: Both ordinary technology and "inner technology" have advanced, attesting to the "evolution of the human mind" and "a quantum leap in the progress of mankind."[13]

One major strain of optimism about the New Age has, however, been muted. Those who advocate the use of drugs to induce enhancement of human ability have either changed their minds or kept quieter in the last ten years. In the early 1970s Andrew Weil, M.D., a drug researcher and theoretician, argued for a new, more relaxed approach to psychedelic drug use and to alternate ways of achieving new states of consciousness. The drug revolution, he thought, was the harbinger of a New Age, an age in which humankind—because it wisely uses its drugs and mystical techniques—will finally have achieved full health. He wrote, "One day, when the change has occurred, we will no doubt look back on our drug problem of the 1970s as something to laugh about and shake our heads over: how could we not have seen what it was really all about?"[14] We hear little of this in popular literature today. The hope has been belied.

The Panoramic Sweep of New Age Thought

From the above it should be obvious that the New Age world view is not confined to one narrow band of humanity. We have here more than the current fad of New York intellectuals or West Coast gurus, more than the latest cult theology from Tübingen, Basel or Union Seminary. The following list of disciplines and representatives within those disciplines emphasizes this fact. For the people listed here, New Age thought is as natural as theism is to Christians.

In *psychology* the first theorizer to recognize the validity of altered states of consciousness was William James. Later he was to be followed by C. G. Jung and Abraham Maslow. Now there are Robert Masters and Jean Houston of the Foundation for Mind Research; Oscar Ichazo, who founded the Arica Institute; Michael Murphy at the Esalen Institute.

Concentrating on drug therapy and research generally within the field of psychology and psychiatry have been Aldous Huxley, who, while not a professional psychologist, seems to have inspired the drug cult of the 1960s and prompted young scientists to further research for more than academic reasons; Stanislav Grof at the Maryland Psychiatric Research Center, who experiments with dying patients, giving them LSD to help them to a feeling of cosmic unity and thus to prepare them for death; Andrew Weil, who did his early research at Harvard Medical School; John Lilly, whose early work was with dolphins but who progressed beyond that to drug experimentation with himself as prime subject (he has also studied under Oscar Ichazo); and Timothy Leary, once famous for his bouts with drugs and the law but whose influence is now minimal.

Biofeedback of alpha and theta waves which appears to produce altered states of consciousness has been studied by Barbara Brown of the Veterans Administration Hospital (Sepulveda, California), Elmer Green at the Menninger Foundation and Joseph Kamiya of the Langley Porter Neuropsychiatric Institute.[15] Ken Wilber's "transpersonal synthesis of various schools of psychology makes his work intellectually appealing and places him on the cutting edge of the New Age intelligentsia."[16]

In *sociology* and *cultural history* have been George Leonard, quoted above; Theodore Roszak, especially in *Where the Wasteland Ends* and *Unfinished Animal;* and William Irwin Thompson, whose *At the Edge of History* and *Passages about Earth* trace his own intellectual journey from Catholicism through naturalism and on into an occult version of the New Age. Thompson's work is notable because, as a former history professor at MIT and York University and as a recipient of Woodrow Wilson and Old Dominion fellowships, he was recognized and approved by establishment intellectuals. *Passages about Earth* shows how completely he has moved out of establishment circles.[17]

In *anthropology* has been Carlos Castaneda whose books have been best sellers both on university campuses and in general bookstores. *The Teachings of Don Juan* (1968) set the pace and was quickly followed by *A Separate Reality* (1971) and *Journey to Ixtlan* (1972). Several other books came later but found a less interested public. Castaneda, who began by studying the effect of psychedelic drugs in Indian culture, apprenticed himself to Don Juan, a Yaqui Indian sorcerer. Having completed the initiation rites over several years, Castaneda became a sorcerer whose alleged experience with various kinds of new realities and separate universes makes fascinating, sometimes frightening, reading. Castaneda's works have been, I would hazard, one of the major doorways to the new consciousness.[18]

Even in *natural science* the beginnings of New Age thinking can be found. Physics takes the lead, perhaps because at its most theoretical it is the most speculative and least prone to falsification by fact. The case for a New Age interpretation of physics is most popularly put by physicist Fritjof Capra and popular science writer Gary Zukav.[19] More muted in their espousal of New Age ideas are Lewis Thomas and J. E. Lovelock. Thomas is a biologist and medical doctor whose *Lives of a Cell* has attained a solid status in the field of popular science writing.[20] And Lovelock is a specialist in gas chromatography whose *Gaia: A New Look at Life on Earth* is a seminal work on seeing Earth (Gaia is the ancient Greek Earth goddess) as a single symbiotic system.[21]

In the *health* field the number of nonordinary therapies proposed in what has come to be called *holistic* medicine is legion. Acupuncture, Rolfing, psychic healing, kinesiology, therapeutic touch—these are just a few of the techniques used by New Age health practitioners.[22]

In *politics* organizations like Planetary Citizens, founded in 1972 by Donald Keys, proposals like Mark Satin's New Age Political Platform, and political parties like The Greens in Germany actively advocate the political implementation of New Age goals.[23]

Science fiction as a genre has largely been dominated by naturalists whose hope for humanity's future lies in technology. But a few of its writers have been prophetic. Arthur Clarke, for example, has written two scenarios for the radical human transformation along New Age lines. *Childhood's End* (1953) is one of his most successful works of imagination. His script for *2001* (1968), which in its movie version is as much Stanley Kubrick's as his, ends with the dawning of the New Age in a new dimension with a new "man"—the Star-Child.[24] And Robert A. Heinlein's *Stranger in a Strange Land* (1961), first an underground classic, has become a tract for the New Age. Valentine Michael Smith who *groks* reality in its fullness is a prototype for the new humanity.[25] The final three novels of Philip K. Dick *(Valis, The Divine Invasion* and *The Transfiguration of Timothy Archer)* are fictional attempts by Dick to come to grips with his own encounter with "a beam of pink light."[26]

In *movies,* one of the most effective communications media of the modern world, we should note the work of Steven Spielberg, especially *Close Encounters of the Third Kind,* and George Lucas, especially the *Star Wars* series. The Force, divine power that pervades the world of these movies, is much like the Hindu Brahman incorporating both good and evil, and Yoda, the loveable guru of *The Empire Strikes Back,* spouts pure New Age metaphysics. Not least among films encapsuling New Age thought is the brilliant, surprisingly interesting *My Dinner with André,* an autobiographical excursion into the mindset of André Gregory.[27]

Even in *sports* we are seeing more and more emphasis on meditative techniques. Kung fu, judo, karate, aikido—the latter a form of defense that has interested George Leonard—are martial arts based on Eastern techniques that may involve altered states of consciousness. This seems natural enough, but the characteristics of Eastern physical exercises are now being found in professional football. What could be more American! John Brodie, ex-quarterback of the San Francisco 49ers, says, "You can get into another order of reality when you're playing, a reality that doesn't fit into grids and coordinates that most people lay across life—including the categories coaches, fans and sportswriters lay on the game."[28]

Finally, we should note three *psychic theorists.* Arthur Koestler in *Roots of Coincidence* provides a summary of research into psychic phenomena—which, except for psychokinesis, he is convinced exist and have to be accounted for. His attempt is largely based on the apparent similarity between psychic phenomena and the behavior of subatomic particles. Koestler, in the final analysis, attempts to explain psychic phenomena within the framework of a post-Einsteinian naturalism.[29] Laurence LeShan is likewise impressed with the similarities between mediums, mystics and physicists, although his explanation takes a more philosophical than scientific bent.[30] We will return to LeShan's notions later in this chapter. Finally, psychologist Jon Klimo has issued an extensive study of channeling (a New Age term for mediumship).[31]

It can be easily replied that those whose books and ideas I have just listed are on the fringe of Western society—the lunatic fringe. Their ideas do not represent the mainstream. Of course, that is to a large extent true. Establishment scholars, reviewers and critics—by which is largely meant naturalists whose naturalism is not yet pure nihilism—have been highly critical of Ichazo, Leary, Weil and so forth.[32]

But that is actually a tribute to the power these ideas are beginning to have. No one bothers to refute the manic ravings of the village idiot. Only when he gets a following does any one pay attention. The people whose work I have cited above have an enormous influence—by virtue either of their position in key universities, hospitals and research centers, or of their personal charisma or both. In short, a world view of immense cultural impact and penetration is in the process of being formulated. In the next few years we will have the privilege—and responsibility—of watching it grow and vie for the allegiance of men and women and, because of the great interest in education that some advocates of the New Age have, for the allegiance of our children.[33]

Relationship to Other World Views

The New Age world view is highly syncretistic and eclectic. It borrows from every major world view. Though its weirder ramifications and its stranger dimensions come from Eastern pantheism and ancient animism, its connection with naturalism gives it a better chance to win converts than purer Eastern mysticism.

Like *naturalism* the New Age denies the existence of a transcendent god. There is no Lord of the Universe unless it be each of us. There is only the closed universe. True, it is "peopled" by beings of incredible "personal" intelligence and power, and "human consciousness is not contained by the skull."[34] But these beings and even the consciousness of the cosmos are in no way transcendent in the sense required by theism. Moreover, some language about human beings retains the full force of naturalism. John Lilly calls the brain a "biocomputer" and man a "beautiful mechanism," upsetting fellow New Age buff R. D. Laing.[35] Fritjof Capra, Gary Zukav, Arthur Koestler,

Laurence LeShan, William Irwin Thompson and Shirley MacLaine point to the corollaries between psychic phenomena and twentieth-century physics.[36] Even Timothy Leary's drug-induced mysticism has a naturalistic base. "God is the DNA code," says Leary.[37]

Also borrowed from naturalism is the hope of evolutionary change for humanity. We are poised on the brink of a new being. Evolution will bring about the transformation.

Like both *theism* and *naturalism,* and unlike *Eastern pantheistic monism,* the New Age places great value on the individual person. Theism grounds this in each person being made in the image of God. Naturalism reflecting a memory of its theistic roots continues to maintain the value of individuals, grounding it in the notion that all human beings are alike in their common humanity. If one is valuable, all are.

Like *Eastern pantheistic monism,* New Age thinking centers on a mystical experience in which time, space and morality are transcended. One could define New Age thinking as a Western version of Eastern mysticism in which the metaphysical emphasis of the East (its assertion that Atman is Brahman) is replaced by an emphasis on epistemology (seeing, experiencing or perceiving the unity of reality is what life is all about). Moreover, like the East, New Age thought rejects reason (what Andrew Weil calls "straight thinking") as a guide to reality. The world is really irrational or super-rational, and demands new modes of apprehension ("stoned thinking," for example).[38]

But New Age thought is also related to *animism,* a world view we have not discussed in this book. Animism is the general outlook on life that underlies primal or so-called pagan religions. To say the world view is primal is not to say it is simple. Pagan religions are highly complex interplays of ideas, rituals, liturgies, symbol systems, cult objects and so forth. But pagan religions tend to hold certain notions in common.

Among the notions held in pagan religions the following are reflected by the new consciousness: (1) The natural universe is inhabited by countless spiritual beings, often conceived in a rough hierarchy, the top of which is the Sky God (vaguely like theism's God but without his interest in human beings); (2) thus the universe has a personal dimension but not an infinite-personal Creator-God; (3) these spiritual beings range in temperament from vicious and nasty to comic and beneficent; (4) for people to get by in life the evil spirits must be placated and the good ones wooed by gifts and offerings, ceremonies and incantations; (5) witch doctors, sorcerers and shamans, through long, arduous training, have learned to control the spirit world to some extent and ordinary people are much beholden to their power to cast out spirits of illness, drought and so forth; (6) ultimately there is a unity to all of life; that is, the cosmos is a continuum of spirit and matter; "animals may be ancestors of men, people may change into animals, trees and stones may possess souls."[39]

The new consciousness reflects every aspect of animism, though often giving it a naturalistic twist—or demythologizing it by psychology. That Theodore Roszak should call for a return to the "Old Gnosis" and the visions of William Blake and that Carlos Castaneda should take the long apprenticeship that ended in his becoming a sorcerer are indications that those in the New Age are well aware of its animistic roots.[40]

Can the New Age—with roots in three separate world views—be a unified system? Not really. Or, not yet. We are seeing this world view in formation. Not all of the propositions I will list below fit neatly together. Still there is a large measure of agreement among the avant garde in virtually every area of culture that something like this description is a valid—or at least useful—way of looking at reality.

The Basic Tenets of the New Age

Realizing the tenuousness of this set of propositions as an accurate description of the New Age world view, we may yet begin, as with the other world views, with the notion of prime reality.

1. Whatever the nature of being (idea or matter, energy or particle) the self is the kingpin—the prime reality. As human beings grow in their awareness and grasp of this fact, the human race is on the verge of a radical change in human nature; even now we see harbingers of transformed humanity and prototypes of the New Age.

If the transcendent God is the prime reality in theism and the physical universe the prime reality in naturalism, then in the New Age the self (the soul; the integrated, central essence of each person) is the prime reality.

A comparison (and contrast) with the central proposition of Eastern pantheistic monism is helpful. In essence the East says, "Atman is *Brahman,*" putting the emphasis on Brahman. That is, in the East one loses one's self in the whole; the individuality of a drop of water (symbol of the soul) falling into a pail of water (symbol of the whole of reality) is lost. In the New Age the same sentence reads in reverse: "*Atman* is Brahman." It is the single self that becomes important. Thus we see the influence of theism in which the individual is important (because made in the image of God) and naturalism, especially naturalistic existentialism, in which individuals are important (because they are all that are left to be important).[41]

Just exactly what this self is is problematic. Is it idea, or spirit, or a "psycho-magnetic field," or the unity that binds the diversity of cosmic energy? Proponents of the New Age do not agree, but they do insist that the self—the consciousness-center of the human being— is indeed the center of the universe. Whatever else exists besides the self—if in fact anything else does—exists for the self. The external universe exists not to be manipulated from the outside by a transcendent God but to be manipulated from the inside by the self.

John Lilly gives a long description of what it is like to realize that the self is in fact in control of all of reality. Here are his notes taken after experiencing what he believes to be the highest possible state of consciousness:

> We [he and other personal selves] are creating energy, matter and life at the interface between the void and all known creation. We are facing into the known universe, creating it, filling it. . . . I feel the power of the galaxy pouring through me. . . . I am the creation process itself, incredibly strong, incredibly powerful. . . . I am "one of the boys in the engine room pumping creation from the void into the known universe; from the unknown to the known I am pumping."[42]

When Lilly finally reaches the inner space he calls "+3"—the fullest, deepest penetration of reality—he becomes "God" himself. He becomes, so to speak, both the universe and the universe maker. So, he says, "Why not enjoy bliss and ecstasy while still a passenger in the body, on this spacecraft? Dictate thine own terms as passenger. The transport company has a few rules, but it may be that we dream up the company and its rules too. . . . There are no mountains, no molehills . . . just a central core of me and transcendent bliss."[43] For Lilly imagination is the same as reality: *"All and every thing that one can imagine exists."*[44] For Lilly, therefore, the self is triumphantly in charge. Most people do not know that; it takes a technique of some sort to realize it; but the self is indeed king.

Shirley MacLaine speculates on whether in fact she has created her own reality (something she mentions many times in her books). She writes,

> If I created my own reality, then—on some level and dimension I didn't understand—I had created everything I saw, heard, touched, smelled, tasted; everything I loved, hated, revered, abhorred; everything I responded to or that responded to me. . . . I was therefore responsible for all there was in my reality. If that was true, than [sic] I *was* everything. . . . I was my own universe. Did that also mean I had created God and I had created life and death? . . .

To take responsibility for one's power would be the ultimate expression of what we called the God-force.

Was this what was meant by the statement I AM THAT I AM?[45] She concludes that for all practical purposes that was the case. Most readers will, I presume, find all this to contain more than a touch of megalomania.

We have already heard George Leonard and Jean Houston prophesy the coming of a New Age. And they are not alone. The hope— if not prophecy—is echoed by Marilyn Ferguson, Andrew Weil, Oscar Ichazo and William Irwin Thompson. Ferguson closes her book *The Brain Revolution* (1973) with a triumph of optimism: "We are just beginning to realize that we can truly open the doors of perception and creep out of the cavern."[46] Her later book *The Aquarian Conspiracy* (1980) charts the progress and contributes to it.

By 1982 when over a quarter of a million copies of *The Aquarian Conspiracy* had sold, Ferguson expressed amazement at its acceptance: "There are so *many* people in this society now who are living kind of at the evolutionary edge, who have gone beyond 'normal' and have experimented with, explored, and are beginning to use our full human capacities."[47] What a glorious New Age is dawning: a new world peopled by healthy, well-adjusted, perfectly happy, absolutely blissed-out beings—no disease, no war, no famine, no pollution, just transcendent joy. What more could one want?

Critics of this utopian euphoria want one thing—some reasonable, objective assurance that such a vision is more than an opium pipe dream. But during the moments the self is immersed in subjective certainty, no reasons are necessary; no objectivity is required. As George Leonard, speaking of the virtues of aikido, says, "He who has gained the secret of aikido has the universe in himself and can say, 'I am the universe.' "[48] And that's that. Because of its absolute subjectivity, the I-am-God or I-am-the-universe position remains beyond any criticism external to the subject. It is easy enough for an outsider to be convinced—and on solid evidence—that MacLaine is not the infinite I AM THAT I AM and that Leonard is not the universe. But how does one break in on god-consciousness itself?

Aldous Huxley suggests that such a breakthrough is possible. Not long before he died, he had second thoughts about the validity of the new consciousness. His wife Laura recorded on tape many of his final thoughts. Here is a transcript of his conversation two days before his death:

> It [an inner discovery he had just made] shows . . . the almost boundless nature of the ego ambition. I dreamed, it must have been two nights ago . . . that in some way I was in a position to make an absolute . . . *cosmic* gift to the world. . . . Some *vast* act of benevolence was going to be done, in which I should have the sort of star role. . . . In a way it was absolutely terrifying, showing that when *one thinks one's got beyond one self one hasn't.*[49]

Still, Huxley did not abandon his quest. He died while on a "trip." For at his request his wife administered LSD to him and, after the manner of the *Tibetan Book of the Dead,* talked his spirit into rest on "the other side."

The *danger* of self-deception—theists and naturalists alike would add the *certainty* of self-deception—is the great weakness of the New Age at this point. No theist or naturalist—no one at all—can deny the "experience" of perceiving oneself to be a god, a spirit, a devil or a cockroach. Too many people give such reports. But so long as self alone is king, so long as imagination is presupposed to be reality, so long as seeing is being, the imagining, seeing self remains securely locked in its private universe—the only one there is. So long as the self likes what it imagines and is truly in control of what it imagines, others on the "outside" have nothing to offer.

The trouble is that sometimes the self is not king but prisoner. That's a problem we will take up under proposition 3 below.

2. The cosmos, while unified in the self is manifested in two more dimen-

sions: the visible universe, accessible through ordinary consciousness, and the invisible universe (or Mind at Large), accessible through altered states of consciousness.

In the basic picture of the cosmos, then, the self (in the center) is surrounded first by the visible universe to which it has direct access through the five senses and which obeys the "laws of nature" discovered by natural science, and second by the invisible universe to which it has access through such "doors of perception" as drugs, meditation, trance, biofeedback, acupuncture, ritualized dance, certain kinds of music and so forth.

Such a metaphysical schema leads Aldous Huxley to describe every human group as "a society of island universes."[50] Each self is a universe floating in a sea of universes, but because each island universe is somewhat like each other island universe, communication between them can take place. Moreover, because each universe is in its essence (that is, its self) the center of all universes, genuine comprehension is more than a mere possibility. Quoting C. D. Broad, who was himself relying on Bergson, Huxley writes, "The function of the brain and nervous system and sense organs is in the main eliminative and not productive. Each person is at each moment capable of remembering all that has ever happened to him and of perceiving everything that is happening everywhere in the universe."[51]

But because such perception would overwhelm us and appear chaotic, the brain acts as a "reducing valve" to filter out what at the moment is not useful. As Huxley says, "According to such a theory, each one of us is potentially Mind at Large."[52] In other words, each self is potentially the universe; each Atman is potentially Brahman. And further, says Huxley, what comes through the reducing valve is "a measly trickle of the kind of consciousness which will help us to stay alive on the surface of this particular planet."[53]

The New Age world view is Western to a large degree and never more so than in its insistence that the visible universe—the ordinary external world—is really there. It is no illusion. Moreover, it is an orderly universe. It obeys the laws of reality and these laws can be known, communicated and used. Most new consciousness proponents have a healthy respect for science. Aldous Huxley, Laurence LeShan, William Irwin Thompson, Gopi Krishna are prime examples here.[54] In short, the visible universe is subject to the uniformity of cause and effect. But the system is open to being reordered by the self that ultimately controls it and by beings from Mind at Large which the self may enlist as agents for change.

Mind at Large is a sort of universe next door, alternately called "expanded consciousness" or "alternative consciousness" (MacLaine) "a separate reality" (Castaneda), "Clairvoyant Reality" (LeShan), "other spaces" (Lilly), "other realities" (Leonard), "another order of reality" (Brodie), "supermind" (Rosenfeld) or "Universal Mind" (Klimo).[55] This Mind at Large does not obey the laws of the visible universe. The conscious self can travel across the surface of the earth hundreds of miles and do so in the twinkling of an eye. Time and space are elastic; the universe can turn inside out and time can flow backwards.[56] Extraordinary power and energy can surge through a person and be transmitted to others. Physical healing can be effected and—if we are to include the black art users of psychic abilities—enemies can be struck dead and sent mad or caused physical, emotional or mental suffering.

Shirley MacLaine describes Mind at Large this way:

> I was learning to recognize the invisible dimension where there are no measurements possible. In fact, it is the dimension of no-height, no-width, no-breadth, and no-mass, and as matter of further fact, no-time. It is the dimension of the spirit.[57]

Mind at Large, however, is not totally chaotic. It only appears so to the self that operates as if the laws of the invisible universe were the same as those of the visible universe. But Mind at Large has its own rules, its own order, and it may take a person a long time to learn just what that order is. Shirley MacLaine, for example, writes of her own pilgrimage to understand herself and to control her own reality, occasionally experiencing a breakthrough: "It was God and it was me simultaneously. We were intertwined. I could be whatever I wanted to be if I trusted that music, that song, that vibration of God that was *inside* of me."[58]

To discover that the self itself, in John Lilly's language, has made up the rules which govern the game of reality may take time.[59] But when people have discovered this, they can go on to generate whatever order of reality and whatever universe they want. The sky is not the limit: "In the province of the mind, what is believed to be true is true or becomes true, within limits to be found experientially and experimentally. These limits are further beliefs to be transcended. In the province of the mind, there are no limits."[60] Lilly's *Center of the Cyclone* is his autobiography of inner space. To read it is to journey through the geography of Lilly's mind as he opens various "doors of perception" and moves from space to space, from universe to universe.

Those who have never visited these spaces must rely on reports from those who have. John Lilly records a number of them and his book makes fascinating reading. Many others have visited such spaces as well, and their reports are similar in type though rarely in specific detail. We will take up the "feelings" associated with perceiving Mind at Large under proposition 3 below. Here we will be limited to the metaphysical aspect. What "things" appear in Mind at Large? And what characteristics do these "things" have? Aldous Huxley's report is a classic because his testimony has set the pattern for many others. The first characteristic of Mind at Large is its color and luminosity:

> Everything seen by those who visit the mind's antipodes is brilliantly illuminated and seems to shine from within. All colors are intensified to a pitch far beyond anything seen in the normal state, and at the same time the mind's capacity for recognizing fine dis-

tinctions of tone and hue is notably heightened.[61]
Whether the images in Mind at Large are otherwise ordinary objects such as chairs or desks or men and women or special beings such as ghosts or gods or spirits, luminosity is an almost universal characteristic. John Lilly says, "I saw scintillating things in the air like champagne bubbles. The dirt on the floor looked like gold dust. . . ."[62] In eleven of sixteen separate accounts quoted by Marilyn Ferguson, special mention is made about colors—"golden light," "sparkling lights," "intense white light," "ultra unearthly colors."[63] Oscar Ichazo recounts, "My head became pure light."[64] And Carlos Castaneda sees a man whose head is pure light and in the climactic event in *Journey to Ixtlan* converses with a luminous coyote and sees the "lines of the world":

> The coyote was a fluid, liquid luminous being. Its luminosity was dazzling. . . . [Then, somewhat later] I saw the "lines of the world." I actually perceived the most extraordinary profusion of fluorescent white lines which crisscrossed everything around me.[65]

These experiences of luminosity and color lend force to the feeling that what one is perceiving is more real than anything perceived in the visible universe. As Huxley puts it,

> I was seeing what Adam had seen on the morning of his creation— the miracle, moment by moment, of naked existence. . . . *Istigkeit*— wasn't that the word Meister Eckhart liked to use? "Is-ness." . . . A transience that was yet eternal life, a perpetual perishing that was at the same time pure Being, a bundle of minute particulars in which, by some unspeakable and yet self-evident paradox, was to be seen the divine source of all existence.[66]

For Huxley, Mind at Large was not so much a separate reality as the ordinary reality seen as it really is. But this new perception is so different that it appears as an entirely new thing; it appears as a thing apart.[67]

A second distinctive characteristic of Mind at Large is that special beings seem to populate this realm. In addition to seeing what she takes to be herself and others in her past lives, Shirley MacLaine sees her Higher Self—a person in "the form of a very tall, overpoweringly confident, almost androgynous human being."[68] He becomes her guide and interpreter of her experience. Carlos Castaneda encounters "allies," "helpers," "guardians" and "entities of the night."[69] John Lilly frequently meets two "guardians" who instruct him on how to make the most of his life.[70]

Similarly, in account after account, personal beings—or forces with a personal dimension—keep turning up, call them what you will—demons, devils, spirits or angels. Furthermore, some new consciousness aficionados recount experiences of being changed into a bird or an animal or of being made capable of flight or rapid travel, even interplanetary travel.

Indeed, Mind at Large is a very strange place. Do its inhabitants really exist? Are they figments of the self's imagination, projections of its unconscious fears and hopes? Does one really become a bird or fly? In the New Age world view those questions are not important. Still, to theists and naturalists alike they are the obvious ones. We will, however, deal with them later under proposition 5.

3. The core experience of the New Age is cosmic consciousness, in which ordinary categories of space, time and morality tend to disappear.

This proposition is the epistemological flip side of the metaphysical coin discussed under proposition 2. In a sense, proposition 3 does not much advance our understanding of the New Age, but it does add a needed depth.

Underlying the unity which propositions 2 and 3 share is the presupposition discussed in proposition 1: that seeing (or perceiving) is being; anything that the self sees, perceives, conceives, imagines or believes, exists. It exists because the self is in charge of everything that is: "I believe, therefore it is." Philosophically, the new consciousness offers a radical and simple answer to the problem of distinguishing between appearance and reality. It flatly claims there is no distinction. Appearance is reality. There is no illusion.[71]

Of course, perception takes two forms—one for the visible universe, another for the invisible universe. The first is called ordinary consciousness, waking consciousness or "straight thinking." It is the way ordinary people have ordinarily seen ordinary work-a-day reality. Space is seen stretched out in three dimensions. No two bodies can occupy the same space at the same time. Time is linear; yesterday is gone; here we are now; tomorrow is on the way. Two disparate events cannot happen to the same person at the same time; while I can sit and think at the same time, I cannot sit and stand at the same time. In ordinary consciousness some actions appear good; others less good; others bad; still others downright evil. And, of course, we assume they actually are as we perceive them. With all this we are all familiar.

The second state of consciousness is not so familiar. In fact to most of us in the West it is hardly dreamed of. To make it even more complicated, this second state of consciousness is really composed of many different states of consciousness; some say three, some six, some eight.[72] But before we consider any of its various subdivisions, we should grasp its general characteristics. Some of these characteristics are suggested by the various aliases for cosmic consciousness. They are legion: "oceanic feeling" (Freud), "timeless bliss" (Zaehner), "higher consciousness" (Weil), "peak experience" (Maslow), "nirvana" (Buddhists), "satori" (Japanese Zen), "altered states of consciousness" or ASC (Masters and Houston), and "cosmic vision" (Keen).[73]

Two of these labels seem more apt than the others, one for theoretical, the other for historical reasons. Theoretically *altered state of consciousness* carries the most universally accepted understanding of the phenomenon. The states of consciousness involved are, indeed, not ordinary. The other apt label, *cosmic consciousness,* is often used because it is one of the oldest in modern writing on the subject.

Introduced in 1901 by Canadian psychiatrist R. M. Bucke, it was given popularity by its inclusion in William James's classic study of mysticism:

> The prime characteristic of cosmic consciousness is a consciousness of the cosmos, that is, of the life and order of the universe. Along with the consciousness of the cosmos there occurs an intellectual enlightenment which alone would place the individual on a new plane of existence—would make him a member of a new species. . . . With these come what may be called a sense of immortality, a consciousness of eternal life, not a conviction that he shall have this but the consciousness that he has it already.[74]

The label *cosmic consciousness* comes bearing a metaphysical explanation of the experience, one widely accepted among proponents of the New Age world view. The point is this: When the self perceives itself to be at one with the cosmos, it is at one with it. Self-realization, then, is the realization that the self and the cosmos are not only of a piece but are the same piece. In other words, cosmic consciousness is experiencing Atman as Brahman.

Central to cosmic consciousness is the unitary experience: first, the experience of perceiving the wholeness of the cosmos; second, the experience of becoming one with the whole cosmos; and finally, the experience of going beyond even that oneness with the cosmos to recognize that the self is the generator of all reality and in that sense both is the cosmos and the cosmos-maker.[75] *"Know that you are God; know that you are the universe,"* says Shirley MacLaine.[76]

Still, other "things" appear under the states of cosmic consciousness. Even after reading countless records of these experiences, I can do no better than to quote Marilyn Ferguson's exhaustive list of characteristics:

> Loss of ego boundaries and the sudden identification with all of life (a melting into the universe); lights; altered color perception; thrills; electrical sensations; sense of expanding like a bubble or

bounding upward; banishment of fear, particularly fear of death; roaring sound; wind; feeling of being separated from physical self; bliss; sharp awareness of patterns; a sense of liberation; a blending of the senses (synesthesia), as when colors are heard and sights produce auditory sensations; an oceanic feeling; a belief that one has awakened; that the experience is the only reality and that ordinary consciousness is but its poor shadow; and a sense of transcending time and space.[77]

Ferguson goes on to quote a number of interesting accounts of cosmic consciousness, each one illustrating many, if not all, of these characteristics.

On one aspect of proposition 3, however, there is disagreement. Not all New Age proponents will agree that the category of morality disappears. Theoretically, it must, for cosmic consciousness implies the unity of all reality and that must be a unity beyond moral as well as metaphysical distinctions, as we may recall from the analysis of Eastern pantheistic monism in the preceding chapter.[78]

Shirley MacLaine, for example, argues vigorously for the disappearance of the distinction between good and evil as she finds herself in heated arguments with Vassy (one of her lovers who retains an emotional attachment to Russian Orthodoxy).[79] We will look at this issue below as we examine her views in more detail. R. M. Bucke and William Irwin Thompson would take exception to this, but MacLaine, Lilly and Huxley agree.[80]

Still, like Hesse's Siddhartha and all people who remain perceivably people, MacLaine, Huxley and Lilly speak as if it were better to be enlightened—that is, cosmically conscious—than unenlightened, better to love than to hate and better to help usher in the New Age than merely to watch the old one collapse.

Finally, we must note that not every altered state of consciousness is euphoric. Naive proponents of the New Age world view often lose sight of this grim fact, but accounts of bad trips are readily available.

Huxley himself knew the terrors of a "bummer":

> Confronted by a chair which looked like the Last Judgment—or, to be more accurate, like a Last Judgment which, after a long time and with considerable difficulty, I recognized as a chair—I found myself all at once on the brink of panic. This, I suddenly felt, was going too far. Too far, even though the going was into intenser beauty, deeper significance. The fear, as I analyze it in retrospect, was of being overwhelmed, of disintegrating under a pressure of reality greater than a mind, accustomed to living most of the time in a cosy world of symbols, could possibly bear.[81]

Huxley, though, was convinced that only those who have had "a recent case of jaundice, or who suffer from periodical depressions or a chronic anxiety" need fear the mescalin experience.[82] Few today would agree.

John Lilly's various bouts with the "demonic" along with Carlos Castaneda's experiences document the lows of "hell."[83] Even the ever-optimistic Shirley MacLaine has wrestled with visions she has not liked, at least at first.[84] To avoid the regions of inner hell, Huxley, Lilly and Castaneda (as well as many others) strongly urge the presence of a guide during early attempts to experience cosmic consciousness.[85] This is the New Age counterpart to one of the major functions performed by a guru or a Perfect Master in more fully Eastern forms of mysticism.

There is, of course, a blatant contradiction here. If seeing is being and imagination reality, then an experienced hell is simply reality. Or, to put it another way, if the self is king, it is in control of creation and can create as it wishes. If one experiences hell, let him destroy it and create heaven. God should need a guide?

But, like devotees of the East, New Age proponents may respond that while it is true that the self is "god," the self does not always realize it. It is a sleeping god and needs to awaken, or it is a "fallen" god and needs to arise.[86] Shirley MacLaine's Higher Self explains it to her this way:

> Individual souls became separated from the higher vibration in the
> process of creating various life forms. Seduced by the beauty of
> their own creations they became entrapped in the physical, losing
> their connection with Divine Light. The panic was so severe that
> it created a battlefield known to you now as good and evil.[87]

Our task, then, as human beings is to reverse this "fall." Such a view
fits well with the evolutionary motif of the New Age, but it does not
resolve the basic contradiction. If the self is really god, how could it
not be manifest as god? Still, there is no more contradiction here than
in the Eastern version of pantheistic monism, and that has multitudes
of adherents.

*4. Physical death is not the end of the self; under the experience of cosmic
consciousness, the fear of death is removed.*

Again, I mention this characteristic separately because the notion
of death is so central a concern to all of us. We are not just our
physical bodies, says the New Age. Human beings are a unity beyond
the body. States of cosmic consciousness confirm this over and over,
so much so that Stanislav Grof has experimented with LSD, giving it
to patients before they die so that they can experience cosmic unity
as they breathe their last breath.[88]

Perhaps the most well-known student of death, however, is psychiatrist Elisabeth Kübler-Ross whose *On Death and Dying* (1969) has
attained a deserved acclaim. In the 1970s Kübler-Ross studied near-
death out-of-the-body experiences and acquired her own spirit guides
who have assured her that death is just a transition to another stage
of life.[89] Interest in near-death experiences was fueled by the very
popular *Life after Life* written by medical doctor Raymond J. Moody,
Jr.[90]

Another witness to death as transition to another state is provided
by past-life recall, such as that Shirley MacLaine recounts at considerable length in her books, especially *Dancing in the Light.* Through

acupuncture that triggers past-life recall and through consulting channelers such as Kevin Ryerson—through whom speak the voices of
Tom McPherson (who says he was once a pickpocket in the Elizabe-
than age) and John of Zebedee (who identifies himself as the author
of Revelation and the Gospel of John)—MacLaine says she has either
learned about or "seen" herself in former incarnations.

She claims, for example, to have lived thousands of lives before,
having been a harem dancer, "a Spanish infant wearing diamond
earrings, and in a church, . . . a monk meditating in a cave, . . . a
ballet dancer in Russia, . . . [and] an Inca youth in Peru." She was also
"involved with voodoo" and, as "princess of the elephants" in India,
once saved a village from destruction and taught her people a higher
level of morality.[91] In _It's All in the Playing_ she has a vision of cremation
vases which her Higher Self tells her contain "both child and grandfather." She had been both.[92]

The ultimate basis for the belief that death is just a transition to
another form of life is, however, the notion that "consciousness" is
more than one's physical manifestation. If one is the all or the maker
of the all, and if this is "known" intuitively, then a person surely has
no need to fear death. Past-life recall and most near-death accounts,
so the New Age holds, justify this lack of fear. There is, however,
negative evidence from out-of-the-body experiences that is not considered by New Age proponents, and the idea of reincarnation has
been weighed and found wanting as well.[93]

_5. Three distinct attitudes are taken to the metaphysical question of the
nature of reality under the general framework of the New Age: (1) the occult
version in which the beings and things perceived in states of altered consciousness exist apart from the self that is conscious; (2) the psychedelic version in
which these things and beings are projections of the conscious self and (3) the
conceptual relativist version in which the cosmic consciousness is the conscious
activity of a mind using one of many nonordinary models for reality, none
of which is any "truer" than any other._

This is the final proposition of the New Age world view and takes up the question which has been screaming to be answered from the very beginning: What do all these strange experiences mean? Are they real? I've never had one, some say. So am I missing something?

One thing must be clear: There is no use denying that people have the experiences reported. Experience is private. None of us has anyone else's experience. If a person reports a strange experience, he or she may be lying, misremembering, embellishing, but we will never be able to critique the account. Even if it appears to us to be intrinsically self-contradictory, we can deny its existence only on an a priori basis—that such and such a state of affairs is inherently impossible.

If a person holds to his or her report, say, under cross-examination, then at least for that person the experience remains what it was or is remembered to have been. Monitoring a person's brain with an electrical recording device is of no help whatsoever. It can tell us that electrical activity is or is not going on; it cannot tell us anything about the nature of the existence of the things the self is conscious of.

We can also agree, I believe, that states of altered consciousness have many general details in common—light, timelessness, "magic" beings and so forth. So while each self has a private universe or a set of them when his consciousness is altered, each private universe is at least analogous to others. Huxley's description—"every human group is a society of island universes"—is apt.[94]

The upshot is that we have a host of witnesses to what appears to be a universe next door, a separate reality. The maps of this reality are not well drawn, but if we were to enter it ourselves, I think we would know where we had been—at least when we returned, assuming we remembered. So the question: Where is this separate reality?

Three answers are given. The first is the oldest, but not acceptable to some modern New Agers. Ultimately deriving from animism, this view is that cosmic consciousness lets you see, react to, receive power from and perhaps begin to control spiritual beings that reside in a sort of fifth dimension parallel to our normal four (three of space and one of time). This dimension exists as truly and as "really" as the other four. Altered states of consciousness allow us to perceive that dimension.

This first answer I call the *occult* version because it is the intellectual framework for most, if not all, mediums, witches, warlocks, sorcerers, witch doctors and so forth. The assumption of the ever-present and increasingly popular occultists is that by certain means—trances, crystal balls, tarot cards, Ouija boards and other objects with occult powers—a person can consult "the other side" and enlist its aid. But let the beginner beware, say the occultists. Without initiation into the rites and system of the occult, those who toy with incantation and even Ouija boards may bring down upon themselves the wrath of the spirit world. When that happens, all hell may break loose. William Blatty's book *The Exorcist* and its film counterpart imaginatively illustrate this version of the New Age and its terrors.

This occult version has modern-minded adherents. Aldous Huxley's understanding is clearly occult. He talks about doors of perception opening on Mind at Large and describes how he saw this Mind at Large in its multicolored, multidimensional nature. Moreover, he closes *Heaven and Hell* with these words: "My own guess is that modern spiritualism and ancient tradition are both correct. There *is* a posthumous state of the kind described in Sir Oliver Lodge's book *Raymond* but there is also a heaven of blissful visionary experience; there is also a hell of the same kind of appalling visionary experience suffered here by schizophrenics and some who take mescalin; and there is also an experience, beyond time, of union with the divine Ground."[95] And he and his wife Laura applied their knowledge of the *Tibetan Book of the Dead* at his death, as she "talked" him into peace on the other side. Shirley MacLaine seems to accept it as well.

John Lilly is more attracted by the alternate explanations discussed below, but he considers the occult version a serious option:

In my own far-out experiences in the isolation tank with LSD and in my close brushes with death I have come upon the two guides. . . . They may be entities in other spaces, other universes than our consensus reality. . . . They may be representatives of an esoteric hidden school. . . . They may be members of a civilization a hundred thousand years or so ahead of ours. They may be a tuning in on two networks of communication of a civilization way beyond ours, which is radiating information throughout the galaxy.[96]

So the occult version of the new consciousness is an important alternative. If it is correct, however, it stands in contradiction to the notion that the self is both universe and universe-maker. It means that there are beings other than the self; there are other centers of consciousness that make claim on one's own self. Viewed as less of a challenge, however, the occult version may yet hold that the self is king to the extent that it can—by whatever means—wrest control from the powerful beings that inhabit the separate universe. Occult bondage is nonetheless a frequent problem. Those who would control may themselves become controlled—locked in the jaws of a demonic trap whose strength is as the strength of ten because its heart is evil.

The second answer I call the *psychedelic* version because it is relatively recent and it points to the origin of reality in the psyche of the person who experiences it. The psychedelic version is much more consistent with proposition 1 than is the occult version, for the psychedelic version merely says that the reality perceived under altered states of consciousness is spun out by the self. This reality, in other words, is self-generated. One does not so much open doors of perception as create a new reality to perceive.

We have seen this view described in various ways above, but Lilly's description of his own bad trip is instructive. Early in his work with drugs, Lilly became so confident that he could handle his inner experience, he took LSD without the careful controls of an external and trustworthy guide. As a result, he had a delayed reaction, collapsed in an elevator and almost died. He attributes this collapse to a failure to control his aggressive instincts. On LSD, he turned against himself and, after the manner of Freud's death wish, almost wished himself out of existence.

Lilly's death would never have been ruled a suicide by doctors, but as far as Lilly is concerned it was indeed his own internal programming that put him in this fix. For Lilly both heaven and hell are inner constructs. Whether one sees himself as the freaked-out edges of the universe (hell) or as "one of the boys in the engine room pumping creation from the void" (heaven), it is one's self that is the creator of the vision.

The third answer to the question of the nature of reality involves *conceptual relativism.* Essentially this is the view that there is a radical disjunction between objective reality (reality as it really is) and perceived reality (the way we understand that reality by virtue of our symbol system). That is, reality is what it is; the symbols we use to describe it are arbitrary.

An example is in order. In our Western society we generally conceive of time as "a smooth flowing continuum in which everything in the universe proceeds at an equal rate, out of a future, through a present, into a past."[97] The Hopi Indian has no such general notion, for his language has "no reference to 'time,' either explicit or implicit."[98] Not that reality is really different, but our Western language system with its overlay of cultural conceptions does not allow us to see otherwise. This has led Benjamin Whorf to the hypothesis which in linguistics is now associated with his name: "The structure of the language one habitually uses influences the manner in which one understands his environment. The picture of the universe shifts from tongue to tongue."[99]

How does conceptual relativism work out in a practical situation? Robert Masters gives an illustration: "There are peoples who live in close surroundings, like a dense forest, and who therefore believe it's impossible to see beyond a few thousand yards. And if you take them out into the open, they still can only see that far. But if you persuade them that there's more to see, why then the scales fall away and great vistas are opened." So Masters concludes, "All perception is a kind of symbolic system. . . . There is no direct awareness of reality at all."[100]

In modern philosophy Ernst Cassirer describes this skeptical view of language and its implication as "the complete dissolution of any alleged truth content of language, and the realization that this content is nothing but a sort of phantasmagoria of the spirit."[101] In such a system concepts are creations of thought and "instead of giving us the true forms of objects, show us rather the forms of thought itself." As a result "knowledge, as well as myth, language, and art, has been reduced to a kind of fiction—to a fiction that recommends itself by its usefulness, but must not be measured by any strict standard of truth, if it is not to melt away into nothingness."[102] On the other hand, while objective truth may be unattainable, this idea has a more positive counterpart: Each symbol system "produces and posits a world of its own."[103] To have a new world, one need have only a new symbol system.

At this point, the relevance of our excursion into philosophy and language analysis should be obvious. The conceptual relativist version of the New Age world view simply claims that altered states of consciousness allow people to substitute one symbol system for another symbol system, that is, one vision of reality for another.

The Western world's symbol system has dominated our vision for centuries. It has claimed to be not only *a* symbol system but *the* symbol system—the one leading to objective truth, the truth of correspondence. What a proposition asserts is or is not true, does or does not correspond to reality. Theism and naturalism have insisted that there is no other way to think. So cosmic consciousness—the seeing of the world in a different symbol system—has had a hard time coming. But with theism and naturalism losing their grip, other conceptual orders are now possible.

Many of the proponents of the conceptual relativist version of the new consciousness are well aware of its philosophic roots and its counterpart in modern theories of physics. Laurence LeShan's "general theory of the paranormal" is a specific version of conceptual relativism. When mediums perform the mediumistic task, says LeShan, they assume the following basic, mystical world view: "1. That there is a better way of gaining information than through the senses. 2. That there is a fundamental unity to all things. 3. That time is an illusion. 4. That all evil is mere appearance."[104] At other times when they are ordinary inhabitants of the visible universe they accept more common-sense notions of reality. LeShan quotes liberally from modern scientists, especially physicists who call on the notion of complementarity to explain why an electron appears to be sometimes a particle and at other times a wave, depending on the instrument they are using to "observe" it.[105] All the time, the assumption is, it remains the same as it was. But what that is, no one knows. We know only that it appears in some of our equations as one thing and in other formulations as another.

Andrew Weil, for example, says that a major point of his book *The Natural Mind* is that "reality as we experience it is a product of our conceptual models and that we are free to choose among various conceptual models available to us."[106] You pay your symbol system, and you take your choice.

But Erwin Schrödinger raises an important consequence of assuming that symbol systems can be so easily put on and cast off. He points out that that means no true model of reality exists: "We can think it, but however we think it, it is wrong."[107] The only category left to help us distinguish between the value of two symbol systems is the purely practical issue: Does it get you what you want?

As there are no true models of reality in science, according to some versions of the notion of complementarity, so there are no true models of reality for humanity in general.[108] And just as the value of a scientific model is measured by its practicality, so pragmatic value is the measure of the worth of a particular altered state of consciousness or a particular theory about it. On this there is a chorus of agreement among New Age theorists and practitioners alike.[109] LeShan states the view succinctly: "If the application of a theory produces results in the predicted direction, its fruitfulness has been demonstrated."[110] So much for the theories about cosmic consciousness. Weil applies the pragmatic test to the experience itself: "It would seem obvious that the only meaningful criterion for the genuineness of any spiritual experience . . . is the effect it has on a person's life."[111]

The practical consequence of the conceptual relativist view of the new consciousness is that it frees a person to believe anything that will bring the desired results. Lilly's life has been devoted to the working out of such a theory: "In the province of the mind, what is believed to be true is or becomes true, within limits to be found experientially and experimentally. These limits are further beliefs to be transcended. In the province of the mind there are no limits."[112] And Stanislav Grof comments, "In an altered state of consciousness you can experience any number of infinities, curvatures of space or parallel universes."

So where do you want to go? What do you want to do? When Lilly accepted the naturalist's notion of the universe, he took a journey to hell. When he accepted the notion that there were civilizations beyond ours, he was "precipitated into such spaces."[113] Believing was being. No vision of reality is more real than another. Schizophrenia is one way of seeing things; normality is another, says R. D. Laing. "But who is to say which is the madness, especially considering the results of normality have been so disastrous in the West."[114]

Moreover, it may be that some of our *normal* distinctions and ways of perceiving give us personal as well as social and environmental problems: "Suppose someone gets a feeling, and then he makes some distinction about that feeling. Say he calls it anxiety to distinguish it from other feelings. Then that first feeling is followed by a second which he distinguishes as shame."[115] In a spiraling cycle he feels both more anxious and more depressed. So Laing concludes, "Now, in a sense it's his distinctions that are making him unhappy. Sometimes I think a great deal of people's suffering wouldn't exist if they didn't have names for it."[116]

The solution is obvious: Get rid of distinctions or symbol systems which have them. Imagine a world view in which you could not tell the difference between pain and pleasure, for example. The consequences of doing this might be severe, but why not figure out a way of adopting such a world view when one is ill in an ordinary state of consciousness? Different world views have different values at different times. So why not employ them as needed? Play the sexton—different chimes for different times.

Sam Keen suggests, for example, "It is better to have a dozen contradictory theories and visions than to give up either the hard certainties of the earth or the brilliant intrusions of wandering comets. I would hate to be condemned to live without efficiency or ecstasy. I even suspect they belong together so long as the splendor of human life is entwined with time and deadlines."[117]

This brings us to the end of the description of the five basic propositions defining the new consciousness. These propositions have been explained and illustrated from a dozen different sources. That, I hope, has been acceptable for a definition, but it hardly conveys the feel of the world view. For this is a world view heavily dependent on subjectivity—the self's experience of reality. In the following section we will look at a single proponent of the new consciousness in the hope of giving more spirit and life to the definition. Then we will analyze the New Age world view in the light of naturalism and theism.

Shirley MacLaine: A New Age Exemplar

At this point in the previous edition of this book I selected Carlos Castaneda as a prime example of New Age thinking. With four books in print whose sales totalled some three million copies, Castaneda was in the midseventies one of the major doorways to the strange world of cosmic consciousness. But Castaneda has fallen from popular favor, perhaps because the public soon tires of even the most weird and wonderful, perhaps because it gradually became apparent that Castaneda was not to be taken quite at his word. It became apparent, for example, that he had invented his chief informant, Don Juan (supposedly a Yaqui Indian sorcerer) and had not so much based his books on field research as he had written cleverly devised fiction.[118]

By the early eighties two other New Age proponents had emerged as major spokespersons: Marilyn Ferguson in *The Aquarian Conspiracy* and Fritjof Capra in *The Turning Point*. Their influence is still great, at least in part because of the sweep of their presentations, surveying, as they do, a wide variety of New Age thought and phenomena. Still, to see the New Age in its most personal dimension, we can today do no better than to examine the most recent three books by Shirley MacLaine. In the late eighties she has become the popular focus of the New Age movement. As Jon Klimo says, "Critics and fans alike concur that MacLaine has done more than any other single person in recent times to soften the ground for people to believe and participate in things they once avoided for fear of being thought 'flaky.' "[119] MacLaine herself recognizes this and speculates that the reason she may have this position is that she abused her powers in an early incarnation. As she puts it,

> Perhaps this was why I had created a role for myself this time around whereby I would be at the forefront of the New Age spiritual movement, heralding *the* giant truth that one individual is his or her own best teacher, and that no other idol or false image should be worshipped or adored because the God we are all seek-

ing lies inside one's self, not outside."[120]
Certainly her books have sold as well as those of Castaneda. By the fall of 1987, nearly three million copies of *Out on a Limb* were in print and *Dancing in the Light* had been on the *New York Times* best-seller list for thirty weeks. *It's All in the Playing* was then released in hardback with a first printing of 550,000 copies. Moreover, *Out on a Limb* was turned into a five-hour television miniseries and broadcast in prime time in early 1987 on the ABC network. "Though the ratings were low in TV terms," comments David Tuller in *Publishers Weekly,* "the numbers were huge for the publishing industry. . . . Sales of *Out on a Limb* and its sequel, *Dancing in the Light* exploded, but the event provided a dramatic shot in the arm to the entire New Age publishing community."[121] Tuller goes on to document the dramatic increase in the sales of New Age books in both regular bookshops and stores specializing in the occult and Eastern mysticism.

Shirley MacLaine Beaty (she dropped her final name as inappropriate for the stage) was born and raised in a middle-class family in Virginia; her younger brother is actor Warren Beatty (he apparently changed the spelling). Her first interest was dancing, and in 1954 she broke into the theatrical world as a chorus girl suddenly thrust into the limelight when the star of *Pajama Game* broke her ankle. She quickly pleased audiences and rose rapidly as a star herself, moving to acting first in Alfred Hitchcock's *The Trouble with Harry.* Though she calls this delightful film a failure, she has moved from success to success in singing, dancing and acting. She worked for McGovern in the 1972 presidential campaign and has been an active feminist. She has lived in Japan with her husband Steve (married in 1954 but soon separated and later divorced) and traveled around the world.

Evidence of her religious concerns emerges as she travels the world over, notably Africa, the Himalayas of Bhutan and the Andes of Peru, looking for spiritual enlightenment. Recently she has held seminars and begun planning a retreat center for others seeking what she now feels she has found. Her odyssey is recounted in *"Don't Fall Off the Mountain"* (where we can see the beginning stirrings of her longing for meaning in life), *You Can Get There from Here* (her least spiritual work) and the three more recent books mentioned above (all of which concentrate on spiritual matters). She is currently working on a book tentatively titled *Going Within* that, she says, compiles "the techniques I have learned to work with over the years."[122] Here we will examine several major sections of her last three books.

Case 1. Perhaps the most striking part of both the book and television version of *Out on a Limb* is MacLaine's out-of-the-body experience, triggered by her friend David while she is meditating on the flame of a candle in a mineral spring bath high in the Peruvian Andes. David has been telling her about the spiritual implications of the ultimate make-up of the universe, how atoms at their foundation are energy and how the soul is made up of that energy. She reasons, then, that since energy cannot be destroyed but only transformed, the soul must exist beyond its current incarnation. David concludes: "Hence what we call reincarnation. Hence life after death. Hence life before birth."[123] What follows then I will quote at length:

> I was silent. I wanted to think. I wanted not to think. I wanted, above all, to rest. I breathed deeply. A kind of bile rose to my throat. I stared at the flickering candle. My head felt light. . . . The flame of the candle slowly melted into the space of my mind. Once again I felt myself *become* the flame. I had no arms, no legs, no body, no physical form. I became the space in my mind. I felt myself flow into the space, fill it, and float off, rising out of my body until I began to soar. I was aware that my body remained in the water. I looked down and saw it. David stood next to it. My spirit or mind or soul, or whatever it was, climbed higher into space. Right through the ceiling of the pool house and upward over the twilight river I literally felt I was flying. . . .
>
> And attached to my spirit was a thin, thin silver cord that re-

mained stretched though attached to my body in the pool of water. I wasn't in a dream. No, I was conscious of everything, it seemed. I was even conscious that I didn't want to soar too high. I was conscious that I didn't want to soar too far away from my body. I definitely felt connected. What was certain to me was that I felt two forms . . . my body form below and my spirit form that soared. I was in two places at once, and I accepted it completely. . . .

I watched the silver cord attached to my body. I had read about the silver cord in metaphysical literature. It glistened in the air. It felt limitless in length . . . totally elastic, always attached to my body. My sight came from some kind of spiritual eye. It wasn't like seeing with real eyes. I soared higher and wondered how far the cord would stretch without snapping. The moment I thought about hesitation, my soaring stopped. I stopped my flight, consciously, in space. I didn't want to go any higher. As it was I could see the curvature of the Earth, and darkness on the other side of the globe. The space surrounding my spirit was soothing and gentle and pure. I began to perceive waves of energy connections and undulating thought energy patterns. The silver cord wasn't taut or stretched. It only floated gently.

I directed myself downward, back to my body. . . . The energy vibrations subsided . . . the rolling sensation of the undulating thought waves disappeared above me and with a soft fusion of contact that felt like a puff, I melded [sic] back into my body. My body felt comfortable, familiar, but it also felt restricting and cumbersome and limiting. . . . I was glad to be back, but knew that I would want to go out again.[124]

This kind of experience is reported countless times in the literature of the New Age—the feeling of flying, the sense of leaving and returning to one's body, the triggering of the experience by concentration on a single point, the longing to repeat the experience. Fueling New Age practices is the desire for movement into Huxley's Mind at

Large—that realm outside the one we access through our five senses, the one we enter through "doors of perception." Often when people enter this realm they contact and talk to entities who pass on to them answers to their questions or information about the spirit world or those who have preceded them in death. MacLaine does not report such an experience here, but she does later on.

Case 2. In *Dancing in the Light* MacLaine continues her search for understanding, especially self-understanding which she is continuing to see as the key to her own life and to the life of the whole planet, for that matter. Through acupuncture techniques employed by spiritual advisor Chris Griscom, MacLaine again enters Mind at Large (Huxley's term, not MacLaine's), meets her own Higher Self and learns to converse with "it," as she refers to the entity, and take him as the interpreter of the meaning of her life today and in earlier incarnations. She writes:

> I breathed deeply into the center of myself as though I were getting my psychic balance. Then a picture swam into my mind, at first diffused, but then very clear. It was absolutely astonishing. I saw the form of a very tall, overpoweringly confident almost androgynous human being. . . . And I had the intuitive feeling that it was extremely protective, full of patience, yet capable of great wrath. It was simple, but so powerful that it seemed to "know" all there was to know. I was flabbergasted at what I saw, *and* what I felt about it.
>
> "Who are you?" I asked. . . .
>
> "I am your higher unlimited self," it said.[125]

After her initial shock MacLaine asks H.S. (as she calls it) a number of questions, learning, for example, that there is no morality to *being-ness,* ultimate reality, that there is no difference between H.S. and God and her. Then MacLaine asks, "Then how did we get separated?" This is the great conundrum of any pantheistic system. If all reality used to be unified, then how did it ever become multiple. That is, how if

One is all there ultimately is did it ever become Two (and many more)? Here is H.S.'s answer.

Basically, we are [one great unified energy]. But individual souls became separated from the higher vibration in the process of creating various life forms. Seduced by the beauty of their own creations they became entrapped in the physical, losing their connection with Divine Light. The panic was so severe that it created a battlefield known to you now as good and evil. Karma, that is, cause and effect, came into being as a path, a means, a method, to eventually eliminate the artificial concepts of good and evil. Eventually, too, souls lodged in evolved primates that later became Homo sapiens. Reincarnation is as necessary to karma as karma is to reincarnation. This is the process which allows each soul to experience *every* human condition as the path back to full spirituality and eventual reuniting with the God force.[126]

This answer is, of course, not very satisfactory. If higher being (the "higher vibration") becomes confused by its own actions, why should anyone want to become reunited with it? This kind of ultimate reality constitutes an exceptionally weak divinity. MacLaine's spirituality seems to be more a counsel of despair than an offer of hope. She, however, draws no such conclusions.

Case 3. During further sessions with Griscom, MacLaine also sees visions of many of her past lives, most of which are recounted only briefly. On one she dwells in some detail since it is the account of what happened during five hours of acupuncture-induced "recall" and was both vivid and significant.

I saw myself with a herd of elephants in the bush jungles of the subcontinent of India. . . . It was a time period thousands of years ago. . . . I was living with the elephants. Immediately I understood that I could communicate with them telepathically. I was so well acquainted with their habits and feelings that on command they obeyed me. I was about twelve years old with dark eyes painted with

tree bark that I had crushed, powdered, and mixed with water.[127]
As the vision or dream or imaginary experience or altered state of
consciousness or head trip—one has difficulty in knowing what to call
it—continues, LacLaine describes how she played games with the
elephants. "On my command they would pass me from one trunk to
another while I laughed with delight." Totally carefree she trusts them
and they her. Wondering how she came to be in this situation, she
is told that her father who had once befriended the elephants had
died and the elephants, fearing for her life, had taken her away from
the village to live with them.

In the midst of this story about her past life, MacLaine recounts
how at another level she reflected on her current interest in elephants. This earlier life, she observes, seems to account for the many
pictures and wooden elephants that decorate her apartment and for
the great empathy she feels for "those gentle giants."

Returning to the story, she describes how the elephants in her past
life would occasionally return her to the village so she could enjoy
human company. Nevertheless, she lives most of her life with the
elephants, learning to communicate telepathically with them
"hundreds of miles away," taking care over their births, nursing them
to health when they become ill and eventually becoming known as
the "princess of the elephants." They in turn protect her.

One day, however, a friend in the village is murdered. Asana, Mac-
Laine's name in this incarnation, cries for the first time, and her
hysterics baffle the elephants so much that the bull elephants almost
destroy the whole village. Eventually, she and the female elephants
calm the bull elephants, and they merely surround the house of the
man who had committed the murder and terrify him. From this the
village learns that they had better keep the peace or be destroyed by
the elephants, their "spiritual monitors."

When she asks what this vision means to her now, she is told that
the purpose of this incarnation and its recall is to help her relearn

(1) the "lesson of democracy," (2) "the importance of understanding nature through animals (*They were completely without judgment* and an example of what humans needed to evolve toward") and (3) that, like elephants, humans never forget anything (thus explaining why she can now recall this incarnation of so long ago).[128]

There are a number of interesting elements in this account. First, one notes the interpretative scheme MacLaine employs: She uses the notion that she has had many past lives to interpret her current interest in elephants. A skeptic would reverse the cause-and-effect sequence and suggest that her current interest in elephants (certainly not an unusual one; many people have an interest in elephants) provided the backdrop for an excursion into fantasy. My wife is enamored of whales and loons; we have lots of them around our house. I, on the other hand, have books. Was I once Gutenberg's assistant and she a princess of the whales and loons? I suspect that MacLaine's account stretches the credulity of most readers beyond the breaking point.

Second is MacLaine's supposed status itself. In few of the incarnations she recalls is she anything but a socially, intellectually or religiously important person. Here she is a princess, a moral guardian and teacher. Yet H.S. tells her that in this incarnation she had "learned the lesson of democracy, which required individual respect in a collective environment, and empathy with the complication of human intelligence."[129] She had not yet shown such an understanding in her incarnation as Shirley MacLaine, H.S. tells her, but she will do so if she draws on the memory of this past life. H.S. would seem to be mistaken; MacLaine as princess of elephants is clearly an advanced member of the human race as described in the story. There is, in fact, a hierarchy with MacLaine at the top, the villagers at the bottom and the elephants (first the females, then the males) in between. There is no hint of democracy.

A more serious contradiction is reflected in the internal incoherence of her interpretation of the experience. Animals, she says using italics for emphasis, *"were completely without judgment* and an example of what humans needed to evolve toward in that respect." But, surely, that is not the case with the elephants. They determined that the man who murdered MacLaine's friend was guilty, and they terrorized him. They "understood who the culprit was" and "wanted revenge." Without the restraint of MacLaine and the female elephants, the whole village would have been destroyed.

MacLaine's Higher Self had told her earlier, "The God energy is no judge of persons. In fact, there is no judgment involved with life. There is only experience from incarnation to incarnation until the soul realizes its perfection and that it is total love. . . . Until mankind realizes there is, in truth, no good and there is, in truth, no evil—there will be no peace."[130] But both the story and the explanation fail to cohere. What would perfection mean apart from less than perfection? What would love mean without a distinction from indifference or hatred? Is not love good? What, in fact, would evolution itself mean without there being a judgment as to what was more or less developed, more or less good, more or less complete and so forth?

One can't have it both ways: either we should learn to make no judgments and thus have no way to distinguish between morally good and morally evil actions, between more and less evolved, or we should make these distinctions and thus imply that there is a foundation that can justify them. MacLaine makes distinctions and judgments on every page of her books, apparently not recognizing the internal incoherence involved.

Case 4. Throughout her books, MacLaine lays great stress on her own self-development. For MacLaine the self is, indeed, the kingpin of reality. In her first book she says, "In the last analysis you only have yourself to live with and inside of, and you have no choice but to be true to that inside self."[131] In *Dancing in the Light* she summons catch phrases from a multitude of sources which to her say the same thing: *"The Kingdom of Heaven is within you. Know thyself and that will set you*

free; to thine own self be true; to know self is to know all; know that you are
God; know that you are the universe."[132] Moreover, she frequently mentions the notion that she and the universe are one or that she is
divine. But it is in her fifth book that the theme of the divinity of the
self (her self) reaches its pinnacle, at least so far:

Regardless of how I looked at the riddle of life, it always came
down to one thing: personal identity, personal reality. Having complete dominion and understanding of myself was the answer to
harmony, balance, and peace. . . .

If I created my own reality, then—on some level and dimension
I didn't understand—I had created everything I saw, heard,
touched, smelled, tasted; everything I loved, hated, revered, ab-
horred; everything I responded to or that responded to me. Then,
I created everything I knew. I was therefore responsible for all
there was in my reality. If that was true than [sic] I _was_ everything,
as the ancient texts had taught. I was my own universe. Did that
also mean I had created God and I had created life and death? Was
that why I was all there was? . . .

Was this what the great masters meant when they described the
numbing aloneness that preceded the recognition of one's totally
awesome power? If we could create such negativity as war, then we
could certainly create its polarity. And to take responsibility for
one's power would be the ultimate expression of what we called the
God-force. . . .

Was this what was meant by the statement I AM THAT I AM?

The inevitable wheel tumbled and turned in my head. Had I
created everything or had it created me? How could either be
proved? But if my reality was a question of what I perceived it to
be, then regardless of how I looked at it, I made the choice. _I_ was
the one empowered with the decision-making process of how to
relate to it. So in point of truth, what difference did it make? I was
the one _choosing how_ to experience life.[133]

Here is a clear statement of the essence of New Age thought. Each of us as humans is the center of our own reality and, so it follows, the center of all reality—if not its creator, then the arbiter of what will be real for us. Those who respect the awesome difference between Moses standing before the burning bush and the God of Abraham, Isaac and Jacob who identifies himself as I AM THAT I AM (Ex 3:14) may well see this passage as the ultimate in self-deception. MacLaine from the biblical perspective has taken on herself the name of her own maker, the final stage of blasphemy, the great Lie. For MacLaine, however, it is the "grand truth."

No bolder statement of the options ever confronts a person searching for the truth about reality. Each person is either God or not-God; if God, everything is possible and permitted; if not-God, then everything has to be brought before the bar of God or ultimate reality (which functions as God).

The difficulties of maintaining one's own divinity are severe. We are confronted by indications of the opposite at every turn. We cannot bend either inner or outer reality to our own wishes. MacLaine herself admits her longings are not totally fulfilled by the recognition of her own divinity. She still distinguishes between right and wrong. If she were divine, she would be her own moral arbiter. Everything she thinks would be right; nothing would be wrong. Or, more to the point, the very distinction between right and wrong would disappear.

Vitko Novi, an old Yugoslavian man, who claims to have received this message through contact with extraterrestrials once told her, "You must pursue your truth however you wish."[134] But that, of course, is incoherent. There can be no obligation to do anything "however you wish." Sometimes she seems to see this, as she remarks, "I was beginning to see that we each did whatever we did purely for self, and that was as it should be."[135]

MacLaine often puzzles over these and other implications of what it means to be the universe:

I could legitimately say that I created the Statue of Liberty, chocolate chip cookies, the Beatles, terrorism, and the Vietnam War. I couldn't really say for sure whether anyone else in the world had actually experienced those things separately from me because these people existed as individuals only in my dream. I knew *I* had created the reality of the evening news at night. It was in my reality. But whether anyone else was experiencing the news *separately* from me was unclear, because *they* existed in my reality too. And if they reacted to world events, then I was creating them to react so I would have someone to interact with, thereby enabling myself to know me better.[136]

She then takes as her New Year's resolution "to improve myself—which would in turn improve the world I lived in."[137] But what, as we have questioned above, can self-improvement mean to God? Seldom have the many inconsistencies of New Age thought been so obviously displayed.[138]

Cracks in the New Consciousness

Is the New Age world view a step beyond nihilism? Does it deliver what it promises—a new life, a new person, a new age? One thing is clear: It hasn't yet, and the mañana argument is not reassuring. We have had visionaries before, and they and their followers have not done much to save either the world or themselves. Tomorrow is always on the way. As Alexander Pope said, "Hope springs eternal in the human breast."[139]

We have little assurance now that with cosmic consciousness will come the new society. Far greater is the case for pessimism, for the New Age world view is shot through with inner inconsistencies, and it does not even begin to solve the dilemmas posed by naturalistic nihilism or Eastern mysticism. It simply ignores them.

In other words, the first major difficulty with the New Age world view is shared with naturalism and pantheistic monism. The notion of a closed universe—the absence of a transcendent God—poses the problem. William Irwin Thompson says, "God is to the universe what grammar is to language."[140] God is just the structure of the universe. We have already seen how such a situation makes ethics impossible, for either there is no value at all in the external universe (pure naturalism) or God is inseparable from all its activities and at the level of the cosmos distinctions between good and evil disappear.

New Age proponents have not solved this problem at all. To be sure, many assume that the survival of the human race is a prime value, and they insist that unless humanity evolves, unless people become radically transformed, humanity will disappear. But few discuss ethical issues, and some admit that in the New Age categories of good and evil disappear, just as do categories of time and space and illusion and reality. Even those who opt for moral distinctions are careful not to be fastidious. If human survival means submission to the new elite (the growing group of gurus such as David Spangler), then the finer ethical distinctions may be too costly. To survive people may have to abandon traditional notions of freedom and dignity.[141]

The reason ethical questions receive so little attention is clear from proposition 1. If the self is king, why worry about ethics? The king can do no wrong. If the self is satisfied, that is sufficient. Such a conception allows for the grossest cruelty. In other words, the New Age world view falls prey to all the pitfalls of solipsism and egoism.[142] Yet virtually no proponent of the system pays any attention to that problem. Why? Because, I presume, they buy the consequences and are unconcerned. Let go and let be. Be here now. There is simply no place for ethical distinctions.

A second major difficulty in the New Age world view comes with what it borrows from animism—a host of demigods, demons and guardians who inhabit the separate reality or the inner spaces of the mind. Call them projections of the psyche or spirits of another order of reality. Either way they haunt the New Age and must be placated by rituals or controlled by incantation. The New Age has reopened a door closed since Christianity drove out the demons from the woods, desacralized the natural world and generally took a dim view of excessive interest in the affairs of Satan's kingdom of fallen angels. Now they are back, knocking on university dorm-room doors, sneaking around psychology laboratories and chilling the spines of Ouija players. Modern folk have fled from grandfather's clockwork universe to great-great grandfather's chamber of gothic horrors.

Theism—like animism—affirms the existence of spirits, for the Old and New Testaments alike attest to the reality of the spirit world. There are both angels under the command of God and demons (or fallen angels) under their own command or at the beck and call of the master fallen angel, Satan. But biblical teaching about this spirit world is sketchy, and what there is is often cast in the form of sidelong allusions to pagan religious practices and of warnings not to toy with the realm of spirits.

It may seem strange that Christian theism does not have a well-developed angelology. If there exist dynamic powerful beings whose nature is beneficent, why should we not contact them, employ them as guides and harness their power for our human ends? The major reason is simple: God alone is to be our source of power, of wisdom and of knowledge. How easy it would be for us to worship the angels and forget God!

This is precisely what happened in the early years of the Christian church. The Gnostics, borrowing perhaps from Chaldean astrological lore, taught that God was too exalted, too far away to be personally interested in mere human beings. But other beings exist—"principalities" and "powers"—who are higher than humans but lower than God. We must, so the argument goes, learn to placate the more unfriendly of these beings and to call on the more friendly for help. Vestiges of this idea remain in the Roman church's notion of saints. Beseech Mary, for she is human and knows our need; she will in turn ask God to help us: *Sancte Marie, ora pro nobis.* The challenge to this has been that it tends both to overexalt the departed "saints" and to denigrate God.

Saints and angels play quite a different role in the Bible. The word *saint* simply means church member or Christian, and angels are solely at the command of God. They are not given to human beings for their own manipulation. God's infinite love is manifest in many finite ways, but he alone is our helper. Though he sometimes employs angels to do his bidding, he needs no intermediaries. He himself became human, and he knows us inside out.

So the Bible contains no model—no counterpart to the Lord's Prayer—for enlisting angels in our plans. But it does contain warnings against enlisting the aid of spirits or "other gods." One of the earliest and clearest is in Deuteronomy:

> When you come into the land which the LORD your God gives you, you shall not learn to follow the abominable practices of those nations. There shall not be found among you any one who burns his son or his daughter as an offering, any one who practices divination, a soothsayer, or an augur, or a sorcerer, or a charmer, or a medium, or a wizard, or a necromancer. For whoever does these things is an abomination to the LORD; and because of these abominable practices the LORD your God is driving them out before you. You shall be blameless before the LORD your God. For these nations, which you are about to dispossess, give heed to soothsayers and to diviners; but as for you, the LORD your God has not allowed you so to do. (Deut 18:9-14)

This instruction was given just before Israel entered the Promised Land. Canaan is full of false religion, full of occult practices. So watch out. Have nothing to do with this. Yahweh is God—the one God. Israel needs no other. There is no other. To think so—or to cover all bets by seeking the services of diviners, soothsayers, sorcerers, wizards, charmers, mediums or whatever—is blasphemy. God is God, and Israel is his people.

The New Testament likewise forbids divination and recounts many instances of demon possession.[143] One of the most instructive is the account of Jesus' casting the demons from the Gerasene demoniac (Lk 5:1-21). From this account it is clear that many demons had possessed the man; that they were not a projection of his psychosis since when they left the man they entered a herd of swine; that demons are personal beings who can use language and communicate with people; and that they have the very worst in mind for humanity. It is also clear—and this is most important—that Jesus had complete control over them. It is in this that Christians have hope. Many modern men and women who have become involved in the occult have found freedom in Christ. The apostle Paul himself assures us:

> If God is for us, who is against us? . . . Who shall separate us from the love of Christ? . . . I am sure that neither death, nor life, nor angels, nor principalities, nor things present, nor things to come, nor powers, nor height, nor depth, nor anything else in all creation, will be able to separate us from the love of God in Christ Jesus our Lord. (Rom 8:31, 35, 38-39. See also Col 2:15.)

No natural force, no spiritual being, absolutely nothing can overcome God. God is our refuge, not because we, like some Superstar Magician, can command him to help us, but because he wants to. "God is love," said the apostle John. "In him is no darkness at all" (1 Jn 1:5; 4:8). So the demonic can be overcome and will be overcome.

While spirit activity has been constant in areas where Christianity has barely penetrated, it has been little reported in the West from the time of Jesus. Christ is said to have driven the spirits from field and stream, and when Christianity permeates a society the spirit world seems to disappear or go into hiding. Only in the last few decades have the spirits of the woods and rivers, the air and the darkness been invited back by those who have rejected the claims of Christianity and the God of Abraham, Isaac and Jacob. Perhaps it will be a case of sowing to the wind and reaping the whirlwind.

A third major difficulty with the New Age world view is its understanding of the nature of reality and the nature of truth. Unlike Shirley MacLaine, some of the most sophisticated New Age proponents are not occultists in the usual sense. They do not cast I Ching or consult tarot cards. Rather they accept the languages of all systems of reality—the languages of sorcery and science, of witchcraft and philosophy, of drug experience and waking reality, of psychosis and normality, and they understand them all to be equally valid descriptions of reality.[144] In this version of New Age thought there is no truth of correspondence; only a pattern of inner coherence. So there is no critique of anyone's ideas or of anyone's experience. Every system is equally valid; it must only pass the test of experience; and experience is private.

Taken to its logical conclusion this notion is a form of epistemological nihilism.[145] For we can never know what really is. We can only know what we experience. The flip side is that the self is kingpin—god if you will—and reality is what any god takes it to be or makes it to be.

We are caught in an impasse. The issue is primary: Either the self is god and the New Age is a read-out of the implications of that, or the self is not god and thus is subject to the existence of things other than itself.

To the self that opts for its own godhead, there is no argument. The naturalist's charge that this is megalomania or the theist's accusation that it is blasphemy is beside the point. Theoretically such a self accepts as real only what it decides to accept. It would be theoretically futile (but perhaps not practically so) to try to shock out of their delusion those who suppose themselves to be gods. Pouring a pot of hot tea on their heads should produce no particular response. Still, it might be worth a try!

Perhaps (but how can we know?) this is the situation of psychotics who have totally withdrawn from conversation with others. Are they making their own universe? What is their subjective state? Only if they waken may we find out, and then memory is often dim if present at all. Their reports may be quite useless. If they waken, they waken into our universe of discourse. But perhaps this universe is our made-up universe, and we ourselves are alone in a corner of a hospital ward unwittingly dreaming we are reading this book, which actually we have made up by our unconscious reality-projecting machinery.

Most people do not go that route. To do so is to recede down the corridors of infinite regress. Nausea lies that way, and most of us prefer a less queasy stomach. So we opt for the existence of not only our own self but the selves of others, and thus we require a system that will bring not only unity to our world but knowledge as well. We want to know who and what else inhabits our world.

But if we are not the unity-giver (god), who or what is? If we answer that the cosmos is the unity-giver, we end in naturalistic nihilism. If we say it is God who is the one and all, we end in pantheistic nihilism. So we need, says Samuel McCracken in his brilliant essay on the mindset of the drug world, "a certain simpleminded set of working assumptions: that there is a reality out there, that we can perceive it, that no matter how difficult the perception, the reality is finally an external fact."[146] We also need a basis for thinking that these needs can be met. Where do we go for that?

9
The Examined
Life

> Across my foundering deck shone
> A beacon, an eternal beam. / Flesh fade, and mortal trash
> Fall to the residuary worm; / world's wildfire, leave but ash:
> In a flash, at a trumpet crash,
> I am all at once what Christ is, / since he was what I am, and
> This Jack, joke, poor potsherd, / patch, matchwood, immortal diamond,
> Is immortal diamond.
>
> **Gerard Manley Hopkins**
> **"That Nature Is a Heraclitean Fire and of the Comfort of the Resurrection"**

We have now examined seven basic world views, six if we don't count nihilism, or eight if we count both forms of existentialism separately. Or nine, if we add the briefly mentioned animism. But who is counting? We could multiply world views to fit the number of conscious inhabitants of the universe at any one time—or at all times if we take an Eastern twist or if we see the universe from the aspect of eternity. On the contrary, we could say that there is one basic world view composed of one proposition: Everyone has a world view!

Still, we may ask, Are these the only choices? Where is the Playboy philosophy? And what about the artist who "creates" to bring order out of the chaos of life? These options certainly have adherents. Yet, when we examine each option, we find that each is a subdivision or specific version of one or more of those we have already discussed.

Hedonistic Playboy philosophy is an unsophisticated version of naturalism. People are sex machines; oil them, grease them, set them in motion, feel the thrill. Wow! Pure naturalism in which the good is what makes you feel good and, with any luck, doesn't hurt anyone else.

Aestheticism—the world view of a person who makes art out of life in order to give form to chaos and meaning to absurdity—is considerably more sophisticated and attractive. Its adherents (writers and artists like Walter Pater in the late nineteenth century and Ernest Hemingway, Hermann Hesse, James Joyce, Wallace Stevens, Somerset Maugham, Pablo Picasso, Leonard Bernstein, in our own) are often personally attractive, even charismatic. But aestheticism is a form of existentialism in which the artist makes value, endowing the universe with a certain formality and order.

The code hero of Hemingway is a case in point. His ethical norms are not traditional, but they are consistent. He lives by his own rules, if not the rules of others. The roles Humphrey Bogart played in _Key Largo, Casablanca_ and _The Treasure of the Sierra Madre_ have given this world view a more than professional dimension and have taken aestheticism (life as a certain style) into the marketplace. Nonetheless, aestheticism is just a specific type of atheistic existentialism in which people choose their own values and make their own character by their choices and actions. We have seen in chapter six where that leads.

The fact is that, while world views at first appear to proliferate, they are made up of answers to questions which have only a limited number of answers. For example, to the question of prime reality, only two basic answers can be given: Either it is the universe which is self-existent and has always existed or it is a transcendent God who is self-existent and has always existed. Theism and deism claim the latter; naturalism, Eastern pantheistic monism and the New Age claim the former. As one twentieth-century evangelist puts it, either the present universe of our experience has had a personal origin or it is the product of the impersonal, plus time, plus chance.[1]

Or to take a different example, to the question of whether one can know something truly or not there are only two possibilities: One can either know or not know something about the nature of reality. If a person can know something, then language in which that knowledge is expressed in some way corresponds unequivocally to reality and the principle of noncontradiction operates.

To say that we can know something true does not mean we must know exhaustively what is true. Knowledge is subject to refinement, but if it is true knowledge, there must have been at least a grain of truth in one's unrefined conception. Some aspect of that conception has to remain as it was in the beginning, or it was not knowledge. For example, ancient people observed the sun move in the sky. We know that the sun stands still and the earth turns. But our knowledge includes the truth of the ancients' observation; the sun appears to rise as much to us as it did to them. In any case, if we can know something about reality, this rules out the infinite number of possible explanations suggested by conceptual relativism. In that system we cannot know what is actually the case. We are bound within the borders of our language system. This is essentially nihilism.

There are likewise a limited number of choices regarding the notion of time. Time is either cyclical or linear; it either goes someplace (that is, is nonrepeatable) or it eternally returns (and thus does not exist as a meaningful category). And there are a limited number of choices regarding basic ethics and metaphysics and questions about personal survival at death. And so on.

World views, in other words, are not infinite in number. In a pluralistic society they seem to exist in profusion, but the basic issues and options are actually rather small. The field, as I have narrowed it, contains eight options (or seven, or six—our counting problem!). Our own personal choice lies somewhere on this field, but if the argument of this book is valid, our choice need not be blind.

Choosing a World View

How, then, can we decide among these finite alternatives: What can help us choose between a world view that assumes the existence of a transcendent, personal God and one that does not? Something of my own view of this matter should certainly have become obvious in the descriptions and critiques of the various options. Yet now is the time to make this view explicit.

Unless each of us begins by assuming that we are in our present state the sole maker and meaning-giver of the universe—a position held by few even within the New Age world view—it would be well to accept an attitude of humility as a working frame of reference. Whatever world view we adopt will be limited. Our finitude as human beings, whatever our humanity turns out to be, will keep us both from total accuracy in the way we grasp and express our world view and from completeness or exhaustiveness. Some truths of reality will slip through our finest intellectual nets, and our nets will have some holes we have not even noticed. So the place to start is in humility.

But humility is not skepticism. If we expect to know anything, we must assume we can know something. And with that assumption other elements are entailed, primarily the so-called laws of thought: the laws of identity, noncontradiction and the excluded middle. By following such laws we are able to think clearly and be assured that our reasoning is valid. Such assumptions, then, lead to the first characteristic that our adopted world view should possess—inner intellectual coherence. Professor Keith Yandell of the University of Wisconsin states this succinctly: "If a conceptual system contains as an essential element a (one or more membered) set of propositions which is logically inconsistent, it is false."[2]

On this basis the world views of deism, naturalism, pantheistic monism and so forth were examined in the preceding chapters. Each was found inconsistent at some (or, in the case of the New Age, many) points. Naturalists declare the universe to be closed on the one hand

and yet affirm that human beings can reorder it on the other hand. If our argument is correct, we have seen that for us to be able to reorder or to shape our environment, we must be able to transcend our immediate environment. But since naturalism declares we cannot do this, naturalism is inconsistent and cannot be true, at least as it is normally formulated.[3]

A second characteristic of an adequate world view is that it be able to comprehend the data of reality—data of all types—that which each of us gleans through our conscious experience of daily life, that which is supplied by critical analysis and scientific investigation, that which is reported to us from the experience of others. All this data must, of course, be carefully evaluated on the lowest level first (Is it veridical? Is it illusory?). But if the data stands the test, we must be able to incorporate it into our world view. If a ghost refuses to disappear under investigation, our world view must provide a place for it. If a man is resurrected from the dead, our system must explain why. To the extent that our world view denies or fails to comprehend the data, it is falsified or at least proved inadequate.

Just such a challenge to naturalism has caused some to accept theism as an alternative. Many people have found the historical evidence for the resurrection of Christ and for various other miracles to be so heavy that they have abandoned one conceptual system for another. Conversions to Christianity, especially among twentieth-century intellectuals, are almost always accompanied by changes in world view because sin, as seen by the Bible, has an intellectual as well as a moral dimension.[4]

Third, an adequate world view should explain what it claims to explain. Some naturalists, for example, explain morality by reference to the need to survive. But, as we saw, this is explaining the moral quality *(ought)* solely by reference to the metaphysical quality *(is)*. Perhaps the human species must develop a concept of morality in order to survive, but why should it survive? And it is no good responding with B. F. Skinner, "so much the worse" for us if we do not survive, for that just begs the question.

The crucial questions, then, to ask of a world view are, How does it explain the fact that human beings think but think haltingly, love but hate too, are creative but also destructive, wise but often foolish, and so forth? What explains our longing for truth or personal fulfillment? Why is pleasure as we know it now rarely enough to satisfy completely? Why do we usually want more—more money, more love, more ecstasy? How do we explain our human refusal to operate in an amoral fashion?

These are, of course, huge questions. But that is what a world view is for—to answer such questions or at least provide the framework within which such questions can be answered.

Finally, a world view should be subjectively satisfactory. It must meet our sense of personal need as a bowl of hot oatmeal breaks the fast of a long night's sleep. I mention this last because it is the most ephemeral quality. If it were first, it would suggest that subjectivity is the most important factor and it would also beg the question. To say an adequate world view must satisfy is to talk in circles; the question is, How can a world view satisfy? And the answer, I believe, is clear: A world view satisfies by being true. For if we think or even remotely suspect that something in our grasp of reality is illusory, we have a crack that may widen into a fissure of doubt and split the peace of our world into an intellectual civil war. No, truth is ultimately the only thing that will satisfy. But to determine the truth of a world view, we are cast back on the first three characteristics above—internal consistency, adequate handling of data and ability to explain what is claimed to be explained.

Still, subjective satisfaction is important, and it may be lack of it that causes us to investigate our world view in the first place. The vague, uneasy feeling we have that something doesn't fit causes us to seek satisfaction.[5] Our world view is not quite livable. We bury our doubt, but it rises to the surface. We mask our insecurity, but our mask falls off. We find, in fact, that it is only when we pursue our doubts and search for the truth that we begin to get real satisfaction.

Where, then, are we today? In terms of possible world views, our options are numerous but, as we have seen, limited. Of those we have investigated, all but theism were found to have serious flaws. If our argument has been correct, none of them—deism, naturalism, existentialism, Eastern pantheistic monism or New Age philosophy—can adequately account for the possibility of genuine knowledge, the facticity of the external universe or the existence of ethical distinctions. Each in its own way ends in some form of nihilism.

Christian Theism Revisited

There is, however, one route out of such nihilism—not to go beyond it but to return to an early fork in the intellectual road. It may seem strange to suggest to our modern age that we throw off modern thought and return to the seventeenth century. But we should be reminded that Christian theism, as I have defined it, was abandoned not because of its inner inconsistency or its failure to explain the facts, but because it was inadequately understood, forgotten completely or not applied to the issues at hand. Moreover, not everyone abandoned theism three centuries ago. There remain in every academic discipline—in science and the humanities, in technology and the business world—those who have taken their theism with complete intellectual seriousness and honesty.

Questions and rough edges—indeed theism has those. And there are problems. Finite humanity, it would seem, must be humble enough to recognize that any world view will always have those. But theism explains why we have such questions and problems. Its ground is neither the self nor the cosmos, but the God who transcends all—the infinite-personal God in whom all reason, all goodness, all hope, all love, all reality, all distinctions find their origin. It provides the frame of reference in which we can find meaning and significance. It stands the fourfold test for an adequate world view.

Gerard Manley Hopkins, a nineteenth-century Jesuit poet whose own intellectual journey provides a fascinating study of how a searching mind and heart can find a resting place, has left us a rich vein of poems that embody the Christian world view. None, I think, better captures the tone of Christian theism than "God's Grandeur," and it will put a fitting personal close to our rather intellectual consideration of world views:

> The world is charged with the grandeur of God.
>   It will flame out, like shining from shook foil;
>   It gathers to a greatness, like the ooze of oil
> Crushed. Why do men then now not reck his rod?
> Generations have trod, have trod, have trod;
>   And all is seared with trade; bleared, smeared with toil;
>   And wears man's smudge and shares man's smell: the soil
> Is bare now, nor can foot feel, being shod.
>
> And for all this, nature is never spent;
>   There lives the dearest freshness deep down things;
> And though the last lights off the black West went
>   Oh, morning, at the brown brink eastward, springs—
> Because the Holy Ghost over the bent
>   World broods with warm breast and with ah! bright wings.[6]

Of course, there is much more to be said about the personal and theological dimensions of this way of looking at life.[7] To accept Christian theism only as an intellectual construct is not to accept it fully. There is a deeply personal dimension involved with grasping and living within this world view, for it involves acknowledging our own individual dependence on God as his creatures, our own individual rebellion against God and our own individual reliance on God for restoration to fellowship with him. And it means accepting Christ as both our Liberator from bondage and the Lord of our future.

To be a Christian theist is not just to have an intellectual world view; it is to be personally committed to the infinite-personal Lord of the Universe. And it leads to an examined life that is well worth living.

Notes

Chapter 1: A World of Difference
[1]From *War Is Kind and Other Lines* (1899), frequently anthologized. The Hebrew poem which follows is Psalm 8.

[2]From Alfred Lord Tennyson, *In Memoriam* (1850), poem 54.

[3]See Arthur F. Holmes, "Toward a Christian View of Things," *The Making of a Christian Mind,* ed. Arthur F. Holmes (Downers Grove, Ill.: InterVarsity Press, 1985), p. 17, and chapters one and three of Arthur F. Holmes, *Contours of a Christian World View* (Grand Rapids: Eerdmans, 1983) for a somewhat different but very useful understanding of world views.

[4]Whitehead says that some "assumptions appear so obvious that people do not know what they are assuming because no other way of putting things has ever occurred to them." See A. N. Whitehead, *Science and the Modern World* (New York: Mentor Books, 1948; first published in 1925), p. 49.

Chapter 2: A Universe Charged with the Grandeur of God: Christian Theism
[1]One of the most fascinating studies of this is Jean Seznec, *The Survival of the Pagan Gods* (New York: Harper and Row, 1961), which argues that the Greek gods became "Christianized"; that, as Julian the Apostate said, "Thou hast conquered, O Pale Galilean."

[2]Several books on the Christian world view have been published since the first edition of the present book. Especially notable are Arthur F. Holmes, *Contours of a Christian World View;* Arthur F. Holmes, ed. *The Making of a Christian Mind;* W. Andrew Hoffecker and Gary Scott Smith, eds., *Building a Christian World View,* vol. 1, *God, Man and Knowledge* (Phillipsburg, N. J.: Presbyterian and Reformed Publishing Company, 1986); and Brian Walsh and Richard Middleton, *The Transforming Vision: Shaping a Christian World View* (Downers Grove, Ill.: InterVarsity Press, 1984). The latter contains a useful bibliography of Christianity in relation to the various academic disciplines and professions.

[3]One classic Protestant definition of God is found in the Westminster Confession, II,

1: "There is but one living and true God, who is infinite in being and perfection, a most pure spirit, invisible, without body, parts or passions, immutable, immense, eternal, incomprehensible, almighty; most wise, most holy, most free, most absolute, working all things according to the counsel of his own immutable and most righteous will, for his own glory; most loving, gracious, merciful, long-suffering, abundant in goodness and truth, forgiving iniquity, transgression and sin; the rewarder of them that diligently seek him; and withal most just and terrible in his judgments; hating all sin, and who will by no means clear the guilty."

⁴For a consideration of the theistic concept of God from the standpoint of academic philosophy, see H. P. Owen, *Concepts of Deity* (London: Macmillan, 1971), pp. 1-48. Other metaphysical issues dealt with here are discussed in William Hasker, *Metaphysics* (Downers Grove, Ill.: InterVarsity Press, 1983); and C. Stephen Evans, *Philosophy of Religion* (Downers Grove, Ill.: InterVarsity Press, 1985).

⁵Geoffrey W. Bromiley, "The Trinity," *Baker's Dictionary of Theology* (Grand Rapids: Baker Book House, 1960), p. 531.

⁶The phrase comes from Francis A. Schaeffer, *He Is There and He Is Not Silent* (Wheaton, Ill.: Tyndale House, 1972), p. 43. Chapter eight of C. S. Lewis, *Miracles* (London: Fontana Books, 1960), p. 18, also contains an excellent description of what an open universe involves. Other issues involving a Christian understanding of science are discussed in Del Ratzsch, *Philosophy of Science* (Downers Grove, Ill.: InterVarsity Press, 1986).

⁷Sir Philip Sidney, "The Defense of Poesy," frequently anthologized. See also Dorothy Sayers, *The Mind of the Maker* (New York: Meridian, 1956); and J. R. R. Tolkien, "On Fairy Stories," *The Tolkien Reader* (New York: Ballantine Books, 1966), p. 37.

⁸Helmut Thielicke, *Nihilism*, trans. by John W. Doberstein (London: Routledge and Kegan Paul, 1962), p. 110.

⁹The word *Logos* as used in John and elsewhere has a rich context of meaning. See, for example, J. N. Birdsall, "Logos," *New Bible Dictionary* (Grand Rapids: Eerdmans, 1962), pp. 744-45.

¹⁰For a more extensive treatment of epistemology from a Christian perspective see Arthur F. Holmes, *All Truth Is God's Truth* (Downers Grove, Ill.: InterVarsity Press, 1977); and David L. Wolfe, *Epistemology* (Downers Grove, Ill.: InterVarsity Press, 1982).

¹¹See John Wenham, *Christ and the Bible*, 2nd ed. (Grand Rapids: Baker, 1984).

¹²See, for example, the discussion of the Fall and its effects in Francis A. Schaeffer's *Genesis in Space and Time* (Downers Grove, Ill.: InterVarsity Press, 1972), pp. 69-101.

¹³To pursue the biblical teaching on this subject may see John Wenham, *The Enigma of Evil* (Grand Rapids: Zondervan, 1985), pp. 27-41.

¹⁴"God's Grandeur," *The Poems of Gerard Manley Hopkins*, 4th ed., ed. W. H. Gardner and N. H. MacKenzie (New York: Oxford Univ. Press, 1967), p. 66.

¹⁵Saul Bellow, *Mr. Sammler's Planet* (Greenwich, Conn.: Fawcett, 1970), p.216.

Chapter 3: The Clockwork Universe: Deism

¹John Milton, *Paradise Lost*, II, lines 557-61.

²J. Bronowski, *Science and Human Values* (New York: Harper and Row, 1965), p. 7.

³Peter Medawar, "On 'The Effecting of All Things Possible,' " *The Listener*, October 2,

1969, p. 438.

⁴Frederick Copleston, *A History of Philosophy*, vol. 5 (London: Burns and Oates, 1961), pp. 162-63.

⁵Peter Gay's *Deism: An Anthology* (Princeton: D. Van Nostrand, 1968) is a useful collection of writings from a wide variety of deist writers.

⁶*Ideas and Integrities*, quoted by Sara Sanborn ("Who Is Buckminster Fuller?" *Commentary* [October 1973], p. 60), who comments that "Fuller's Benevolent Intelligence seems compounded out of the Great Watchmaker of the Deists and Emerson's Over-Soul" (p. 66).

⁷*Lettres sur divers sujets, metaphysique et de religion*. Letter 5. Quoted in Émile Bréhier, *The History of Philosophy*, vol. 5, trans. Wade Baskin (Chicago: Univ. of Chicago Press, 1967), p. 14.

⁸Bréhier, *History*, p. 15.

⁹*Essay on Man*, I, lines 17-22.

¹⁰Ibid., lines 23-32; cf. lines 233-58.

¹¹Ibid., lines 289-94.

¹²Ibid., lines 123-26, 129-30.

¹³Ibid., lines 145-46.

¹⁴Induction or inductive reasoning—the attempt to argue from particular details to general principles—A. N. Whitehead called "the despair of philosophy" (Whitehead, *Science and the Modern World*, p. 25).

¹⁵Albert Einstein, *Ideas and Opinions* (New York: Bonanza Books, 1954). See also Robert Jastrow, *God and the Astronomers* (New York: Warner, 1978).

Chapter 4: The Silence of Finite Space: Naturalism

¹La Mettrie, *Man a Machine* (1747) in *Les Philosophes*, ed. Norman L. Torrey (New York: Capricorn Books, 1960), p. 176.

²Whitehead, for example, says, "Of course we find in the eighteenth century Paley's famous argument that mechanism presupposes a God who is the author of nature. But even before Paley put the argument into its final form, Hume had written the retort, that the God whom you will find will be the sort of God who makes that mechanism. In other words, that mechanism can, at most, presuppose a mechanic, and not merely a mechanic but *its* mechanic" (Whitehead, *Science and the Modern World*, p. 77).

³The brash, anti-Christian, anti-clerical tone of La Mettrie's essay is of a piece with its anti-theistic content, exalting, as it does, human reason at the expense of revelation. A sample of this from the conclusion to *Man a Machine* is instructive: "I recognize only scientists as judges of the conclusions which I draw, and I hereby challenge every prejudiced man who is not an anatomist, or acquainted with the only philosophy which is to the purpose, that of the human body. Against such a strong and solid oak, what could the weak reeds of theology, metaphysics and scholasticism, avail; childish weapons, like our foils, which may well afford the pleasure of fencing, but can never wound an adversary. Need I say that I refer to the hollow and trivial notions, to the trite and pitiable arguments that will be urged, as long as the shadow of prejudice or superstition remains on earth, for the supposed incompatibility of two substances

which meet and interact unceasingly [La Mettrie is here alluding to Descartes' division of reality into mind and matter]?" (p. 177).

⁴Strictly speaking there are naturalists who are not materialists, that is, who hold that there may be elements of the universe that are not material, but they have had little impact on Western culture. My definition of naturalism will be limited to those who are materialists.

⁵Carl Sagan, Cosmos (New York: Random House, 1980), p. 4. Sagan goes on to say, "Our feeblest contemplations of the cosmos stir us—there is a tingling in the spine, a catch in the voice, a faint sensation, as if a distant memory, of falling from a height. We know we are approaching the greatest of mysteries." For Sagan, in this book and the television series of the same name, the cosmos assumes the position of God, creating the same kind of awe in Sagan, who tries to trigger in his readers and television audience the same response. So-called science thus becomes religion, some say the religion of scientism. See Jeffrey Marsh, "The Universe and Dr. Sagan," Commentary (May 1981), pp. 64-68.

⁶La Mettrie, Man a Machine, p. 177. On the other hand, to define a human being as "a field of energies moving inside a larger fluctuating system of energies" is equally naturalistic. In neither case is man seen as transcending the cosmos. See Marilyn Ferguson, The Brain Revolution: The Frontiers of Mind Research (New York: Taplinger Publishing Co., 1973), p. 22.

⁷Bréhier, The History of Philosophy, vol. 5, p. 129.

⁸Humanist Manifestos I and II (Buffalo: Prometheus Books, 1973), p. 16. These two manifestos, especially the second (which was drafted by Paul Kurtz), are convenient compilations of naturalist assumptions. Paul Kurtz is a professor of philosophy at the State University of New York at Buffalo, editor of Free Inquiry (a quarterly journal devoted to the propagation of "secular humanism") and editor of Prometheus Books.

⁹The Columbia History of the World, ed. John A. Garraty and Peter Gay (New York: Harper and Row, 1972), p. 14.

¹⁰David Jobling, "How Does Our Twentieth-Century Concept of the Universe Affect Our Understanding of the Bible?" Enquiry (September-November 1972), p. 14. Ernest Nagel, in a helpful essay defining naturalism in a midtwentieth-century form, states this position in more rigorously philosophical terms: "The first [proposition central to naturalism] is the existential and causal primacy of organized matter in the executive order of nature. This is the assumption that the occurrence of events, qualities and processes, and the characteristic behaviors of various individuals, are contingent on the organization of spatiotemporally located bodies, whose internal structures and external relations determine and limit the appearance and disappearance of everything that happens" (Ernest Nagel, "Naturalism Reconsidered" [1954] in Essays in Philosophy, ed. Houston Peterson [New York: Pocket Library, 1959], p. 486).

¹¹La Mettrie, Man a Machine, p. 177.

¹²Copleston, History, vol. 6, p. 51. Among recent proponents of the notion that human beings are machines is John Brierly, The Thinking Machine (London: Heinemann, 1973).

¹³William Barrett, The Death of the Soul: From Descartes to the Computer (New York: Anchor, 1987), p. 154.

[14]The *Humanist Manifesto II* states the situation generally with reference to the whole of nature: "Nature may indeed be broader and deeper than we now know; any new discoveries, however, will but enlarge our knowledge of the natural" (p. 16).

[15]Julian Huxley, "The Uniqueness of Man," in *Man in the Modern World* (New York: Mentor Books, 1948), pp. 7-28. George Gaylord Simpson lists man's "interrelated factors of intelligence, flexibility, individualization and socialization" *(The Meaning of Evolution,* revised and abridged [New York: Mentor Books, 1951], p. 138).

[16]Nagel, "Naturalism Reconsidered," p. 490.

[17]*Humanist Manifestos I and II*, p. 17.

[18]Bertrand Russell, "A Free Man's Worship," *Why I Am Not a Christian* (New York: Simon and Schuster, 1957), p. 107.

[19]A. J. Ayer, ed., *The Humanist Outlook* (London: Pemberton, 1968), p. 9.

[20]Nagel, "Naturalism Reconsidered," p. 496.

[21]*Humanist Manifestos I and II*, p. 17.

[22]John Updike, "Pigeon Feathers," in *Pigeon Feathers and Other Stories* (Greenwich, Conn.: Fawcett, 1959), p. 96.

[23]*The Columbia History of the World*, p. 3.

[24]See, for example, Malcolm Jeeves, *The Scientific Enterprise and Christian Faith* (Downers Grove, Ill.: InterVarsity Press, 1969), pp. 80-117; *Evolution and Christian Thought Today*, ed. Russell L. Mixter (Grand Rapids: Eerdmans, 1959); Charles Hummel, *The Galileo Connection* (Downers Grove, Ill.: InterVarsity Press, 1985); and countless articles in the *Journal of the American Scientific Affiliation*.

[25]Simpson, *Meaning of Evolution*, p. 143. Why Simpson should assign human beings a spiritual nature is not clear. We must not, however, take him to mean that they have a dimension which takes them out of the closed universe.

[26]Ibid.

[27]Jacques Monod, *Chance and Necessity*, trans. Austryn Wainhouse (New York: Alfred A. Knopf, 1971), p, 146.

[28]A few naturalists like Carl Sagan believe that, given the size and age of the universe, other intelligent beings must have evolved elsewhere in the universe. But even Sagan admits that there is no hard evidence for this view. (Sagan, *Cosmos*, pp. 292, 307-15).

[29]This shift in the content of ethical norms can be studied by comparing *Humanist Manifesto I* (1933) with *Humanist Manifesto II* (1973).

[30]La Mettrie, *Man a Machine*, p. 176; emphasis mine.

[31]*Humanist Manifestos I and II*, p. 17.

[32]Simpson, *Meaning of Evolution*, p. 149.

[33]John Platt, *The Center Magazine* (March-April 1972), p. 48.

[34]Walter Lippmann, *A Preface to Morals* (New York: Time Incorporated, 1964), p. 190.

[35]Ibid., p. 307. Allan Bloom's *The Closing of the American Mind* could be described as a sustained cry for the maintenance of some other basis for human values than *commitment* or human *decision*. Without seriously contending with an infinite-personal God who acts as the foundation for these values it is difficult to see just how contemporary values will be able to be grounded in any firm absolute. See Allan Bloom, *The Closing of the American Mind* (New York: Simon and Schuster, 1987), esp. pp. 194-216. See also Alasdair McIntyre, *After Virtue,* 2nd ed. (Notre Dame: Notre Dame

University Press, 1984).

[36]A Christian Humanist Manifesto was published in *Eternity* magazine (January 1982), pp. 16-18. The signers were Donald Bloesch, George Brushaber, Richard Bube, Arthur Holmes, Bruce Lockerbie, J. I. Packer, Bernard Ramm and I.

[37]*Humanist Manifestos I and II.* Another, briefer compilation of secular humanist views, "The Affirmations of Humanism: A Statement of Principles and Values," appears on the back cover of *Free Inquiry* (Summer 1987).

[38]One of the best introductions to the many sides of Marxism is Richard Schmitt, *Introduction to Marx and Engels: Critical Reconstruction* (Boulder, Colo.: Westview Press, 1987). A good introduction from a Christian point of view is David Lyon, *Karl Marx: A Christian Assessment of His Life and Thought* (Downers Grove, Ill.: InterVarsity Press, 1979). There is no substitute, of course, for the actual writings of Marx himself to really understand Marx, as well as the writings of Marx's close friend and collaborator, Friedrich Engels. Many of the most important writings are in Richard Tucker, ed., *The Marx-Engels Reader,* 2nd ed. (New York: W. W. Norton and Company, 1978).

[39]*Humanist Manifestos I and II,* p. 19.

[40]"Contribution to the Critique of Hegel's *Philosophy of Right:* Introduction," in Tucker, *Marx-Engels Reader,* p. 60.

[41]Ibid.

[42]Simpson, *Meaning of Evolution,* p. 139.

[43]Ibid., pp. 166-81. From the early days of Darwin and T. H. Huxley, naturalists have placed much hope in human evolution. Some modern optimists are Arthur C. Clarke, *Profiles of the Future* (New York: Bantam, 1964), pp. 212-27; Peter Medawar, pp. 437-42; Glenn Seaborg, "The Role of Science and Technology," *Washington University Magazine* (Spring 1972), pp. 31-35; Julian Huxley, "Transhumanism," *Knowledge, Morality and Destiny* (New York: Mentor Books, 1960), pp. 13-17.

Chapter 5: Zero Point: Nihilism

[1]Douglas Adams, *The Hitchiker's Guide to the Galaxy* (New York: Pocket Books, 1981); *The Restaurant at the End of the Universe* (New York: Pocket Books, 1982; *Life, the Universe and Everything* (New York: Pocket Books, 1983); *So Long and Thanks for All the Fish* (London: Pan, 1984).

[2]Adams, *Hitchiker's Guide,* p. 173.

[3]Adams, *Restaurant,* p. 2.

[4]Ibid., p. 246.

[5]Adams, *Life,* p. 222. At the end of the fourth novel, which seems not nearly so poignant in its effect, we learn God's final message to us: We apologize for the inconvenience (*So Long,* p. 189).

[6]John Platt, for example, thinks this is the only freedom a person really needs (*Center Magazine,* p. 47).

[7]B. F. Skinner, *Beyond Freedom and Dignity* (New York: Alfred A. Knopf, 1971), p. 211.

[8]Monod, *Chance and Necessity,* pp. 98 and 112.

[9]Simpson, *Meaning of Evolution,* p. 179.

[10]From a letter to W. Graham (July 3, 1881) quoted in *The Autobiography of Charles Darwin and Selected Letters* (New York: Dover Publications, Inc., 1958; originally published in

1892). I am indebted to Francis A. Schaeffer for this observation which he made in a lecture on Charles Darwin. C. S. Lewis in a parallel argument quotes Professor Haldane as follows: "If my mental processes are determined wholly by the motion of atoms in my brain, I have no reason to suppose that my beliefs are true . . . and hence I have no reason for supposing my brain to be composed of atoms." See *Miracles*, p. 18.

[11]Lewis, *Miracles*, p. 109. In another context Lewis remarks, "It is only when you are asked to believe in Reason coming from non-reason that you must cry Halt, for, if you don't, all thought is discredited" (p. 32).

[12]From *The Black Riders and Other Lines* (1895), frequently anthologized.

[13]Robert Farrar Capon, *Hunting the Divine Fox* (New York: Seabury Press, 1974), pp. 17-18.

[14]Allan Bloom, *Closing of the American Mind*, p. 194.

[15]See Allan Bloom's discussion of values (*Closing of the American Mind*, pp. 25-43 and 194-215).

[16]Franz Kafka, "The Watchman," in *Parables and Paradoxes* (New York: Schocken Books, 1961), p. 81.

[17]One of Nietzsche's epigrams in *The Gay Science* echoes Kafka's parable: *"Guilt.* Although the most acute judges of the witches, and even the witches themselves, were convinced of the guilt of witchery, the guilt nevertheless was nonexistent. It is thus with all guilt" (*The Portable Nietzsche*, trans. Walter Kaufmann [New York: Viking Press, 1954], pp. 96-97).

[18]One could reply that it is just such guilt (that is, guilt feelings) that can be removed by Freudian psychoanalysis or other psychotherapy and thus there is something that can be done. But that merely emphasizes the amorality of human beings. It solves a person's problem of feeling guilty by not allowing one any way at all to act morally.

[19]Kurt Vonnegut, Jr., *Cat's Cradle* (New York: Dell, 1970), p. 177.

[20]I am indebted to Helmut Thielicke (*Nihilism*, pp. 148-66; esp., pp. 163-66) for this observation about nihilism.

[21]Another way to put this argument is to point out that constructing sentences is such a fundamental act, such a paradigmatic affirmation of meaning, that to construct sentences to deny meaning is self-contradictory. Keith Yandell in "Religious Experience and Rational Appraisal," *Religious Studies* (June 1974), p. 185, expresses the argument as follows: "If a conceptual system *F* is such that it can be shown that (a) *F is true* and (b) *F is known to be true*, are incompatible, then this fact provides a good (though perhaps not conclusive) reason for supposing that *F is false."*

[22]Joseph Heller, *Catch-22* (New York: Dell, 1962), p. 184.

[23]Ibid., p. 185.

[24]Bloom, *Closing of the American Mind*, p. 196.

Chapter 6: Beyond Nihilism: Existentialism

[1]Albert Camus, *L'Été*, quoted in John Crickshank, *Albert Camus and the Literature of Revolt* (New York: Oxford Univ. Press, 1960), p.3.

[2]I am indebted to C. Stephen Board, general manager of Harold Shaw Publishers, for this observation.

[3]Whitehead, *Science and the Modern World,* p. 49.

[4]Jean-Paul Sartre, "Existentialism," reprinted in *A Casebook on Existentialism,* ed. William V. Spanos (New York: Thomas Y. Crowell, 1966), p. 289.

[5]Ibid.

[6]Ibid., p. 278.

[7]Ibid.

[8]This illustration derives from Sartre, pp. 283-84.

[9]Platt, *Center Magazine,* p. 47.

[10]Fyodor Dostoevsky, *Notes from Underground* and other works, trans. Andrew R. MacAndrew (New York: New American Library, 1961), p. 99.

[11]Ibid., p.115.

[12]Sartre, "Existentialism," p. 279.

[13]Ibid., p. 289.

[14]Ibid., p. 279.

[15]Ibid., p. 280.

[16]Ibid., p. 285.

[17]Albert Camus, *The Plague,* trans. Stuart Gilbert (New York: Random House, 1948), p. 35.

[18]Ibid. p. 108.

[19]Ibid., pp. 9, 29, 277.

[20]Ibid., p. 174.

[21]Ibid., p. 175.

[22]Ibid., pp. 227-28.

[23]Ibid., p. 230.

[24]Ibid. pp. 120, 230.

[25]Ibid., pp. 262-63.

[26]Ibid., p. 116.

[27]Ibid., pp. 117-18.

[28]Ibid., p. 278.

[29]H. J. Blackham, "The Pointlessness of It All," in *Objections to Humanism,* ed. H. J. Blackham (Harmondsworth: Penguin, 1965), p. 123.

[30]Ibid., p. 124.

[31]Edward John Carnell gives an excellent introduction to neo-orthodoxy and how it arose in *The Theology of Reinhold Niebuhr,* rev. ed. (Grand Rapids: Eerdmans, 1960), pp. 13-39.

[32]Camus, *The Plague,* p. 197.

[33]Ibid., p. 196.

[34]Martin Buber, *I and Thou,* trans. Ronald Gregor Smith (New York: Charles Scribner, 1958), pp. 29-30.

[35]Ibid., p. 34.

[36]Ibid., p. 4.

[37]Ibid., p. 11.

[38]Ibid., p. 7.

[39]From a letter quoted by Walter Lowrie in *A Short Life of Kierkegaard* (Princeton: Princeton Univ. Press, 1942), p. 82.

⁴⁰Kierkegaard's own stance regarding this is a matter of scholarly debate. Those emphasizing his rejection of the value of objective truth include Marjorie Grene, *Introduction to Existentialism* (Chicago: University of Chicago Press, 1948), pp. 21-22, 35-39; and Francis A. Schaeffer, *The God Who Is There* (Downers Grove, Ill.: InterVarsity Press, 1968), pp. 51-54. On the other side are C. Stephen Evans, *Subjectivity and Religious Beliefs* (Grand Rapids: Christian University Press, 1978); and John Macquarrie, *Existentialism* (Philadelphia: Westminster Press, 1972), pp. 74-123.

⁴¹See p. 114 above.

⁴²Buber, *I and Thou*, p. 96.

⁴³See R. T. France, *The Living God* (Downers Grove, Ill.: InterVarsity Press, 1970), pp. 97-115.

⁴⁴Grene, *Introduction*, p. 36.

⁴⁵Schaeffer, *He Is There and He Is Not Silent*, pp. 37-88, esp. p. 79. Alasdair MacIntyre writes, "What logic does is to articulate and to make explicit those rules which are in fact embodied in actual discourse and which, being so embodied, enable men both to construct valid arguments and to avoid the penalties of inconsistency. . . . A pupil of Duns Scotus demonstrated that . . . from a contradiction any statement whatsoever can be derived. It follows that to commit ourselves to asserting a contradiction is to commit ourselves to asserting anything whatsoever, to asserting anything whatsoever that it is possible to assert—and of course also to its denial. The man who asserts a contradiction thus succeeds in saying nothing and also in committing himself to everything; both are failures to assert anything determinate, to say that this is the case and *not* this other. We therefore depend upon our ability to utilize and to accord with the laws of logic in order to speak at all, and a large part of formal logic clarifies for us what we have been doing all along" *(Herbert Marcuse: An Exposition and a Polemic* [New York: Viking Press, 1970], pp. 86-87).

⁴⁶For a consideration of the current state of scholarship on the subjects treated by higher criticism see Kenneth Kitchen, *Ancient Orient and Old Testament* (Downers Grove, Ill.: InterVarsity Press, 1966); Donald Guthrie, *Introduction to the New Testament*, 3rd ed. (Downers Grove, Ill.: InterVarsity Press, 1970); George Eldon Ladd, *The New Testament and Criticism* (Grand Rapids: Eerdmans, 1967); and R. K. Harrison, *Biblical Criticism: Historical, Literary, and Textual* (Grand Rapids: Zondervan, 1978).

⁴⁷Matthew Arnold, *God and the Bible*, in *English Prose of the Victorian Era*, ed. Charles Frederick Harrold and William D. Templeman (New York: Oxford Univ. Press, 1938), p. 1211.

⁴⁸Matthew Arnold, "The Study of Poetry," in *English Prose of the Victorian Era*, p. 1248.

⁴⁹Carnell, *Theology of Reinhold Niebuhr*, p. 168.

⁵⁰Rudolf Bultmann, *Kerygma and Myth* (New York: Harper and Brothers, 1961), p. 39.

⁵¹See a more recent presentation of this argument in Theodore J. Weeden, "Is the Resurrection an Offense to Faith?" *The Christian Century* (March 29, 1972), pp. 357-59.

⁵²*Times Literary Supplement* (November 26, 1971), p. 148.

Chapter 7: Journey to the East: Eastern Pantheistic Monism

¹The present account of the recent swing to Eastern thought is painfully superficial.

For more detail see the following: R. C. Zaehner, *Zen, Drugs and Mysticism* (New York: Vintage Books, 1974). Jacob Needleman's *The New Religions*, rev. ed. (New York: Pocket Books, 1972), is a sympathetic treatment of the entire phenomenon and includes a brief description of a number of specific men and movements, including Zen, Maher Baba, Subud and Transcendental Meditation. A more expansive and scholarly examination is found in the essays collected in *Religious Movements in Contemporary America*, ed. Irving I. Zaretsky and Mark P. Leone (Princeton: Princeton Univ. Press, 1974). Stephen Neill in *Christian Faith and Other Faiths* (Downers Grove, Ill.: InterVarsity Press, 1984) surveys and evaluates several religions including Hinduism and Buddhism. A Christian critique of the Western trend toward the East is found in Os Guinness, *The East, No Exit* (Downers Grove, Ill.: InterVarsity Press, 1974), an updated version of a chapter in *The Dust of Death* (1973). The Autumn 1972 edition of *Theology Digest* has several articles evaluating the impact of the East in relation to Christianity. In chapter eleven of *Miracles*, pp. 85-98, C. S. Lewis argues that even in the West pantheism is man's natural religion, and his critique of this form of pantheism is helpful. See also Ernest Becker's highly critical analysis of Zen Buddhism from the standpoint of modern psychoanalysis and psychotherapy theory in *Zen: A Rational Critique* (New York: W. W. Norton, 1961).

[2]Surendranath Dasgupta, *A History of Indian Philosophy*, 5 vols. (Cambridge: Cambridge Univ. Press, 1922-69). For texts of Eastern philosophy and religion see Sarvapalli Radhakrishnan and Charles A. Moore, eds., *A Source Book in Indian Philosophy* (Princeton: Princeton University Press, 1957); Wing-tsit Chan, ed., *A Source Book in Chinese Philosophy* (Princeton: Princeton University Press, 1963); and Lucien Stryk, ed. *World of the Buddha* (New York: Grove Press, 1968). The history and flavor of Zen Buddhism can be gleaned from Robert Linssen, *Zen: The Art of Life* (New York: Pyramid, 1962); and Stewart W. Holmes and Chimyo Horioka, *Zen Art for Meditation* (Tokyo: Charles E. Tuttle, 1973).

[3]From the Chandogya Upanishad, *The Upanishads*, trans. Juan Mascaró (Harmondsworth, England: Penguin, 1965), p. 117.

[4]Christmas Humphreys, *Buddhism*, 3rd ed. (Harmondsworth, England: Penguin, 1962), p. 22.

[5]Humphreys comments, for example, that even intellectual and systematic distinctions between major strains of Buddhism (Hinayana and Mahayana) are essentially insignificant: "All argument as to 'better' and 'worse' must cease. Men and women, day and night, inbreathing and outbreathing, the head and the heart, these are alternates, not alternatives and argument on relative worth is no more than debate on the two sides of a coin" (p. 51).

[6]*Meditations of Maharishi Mahesh Yogi* (New York: Bantam Books, 1968), p. 18.

[7]Humphreys, *Buddhism*, p. 203.

[8]Mascaró, *Upanishads*, pp. 83-84.

[9]Hermann Hesse, *Siddhartha*, trans. Hilda Rosner (New York: New Directions, 1951), p. 115.

[10]Mascaró, *Upanishads*, p. 12.

[11]Alex Comfort, Review of *Erotic Spirituality: The Vision of Konorak* (New York: Macmillan, 1971), in *Book World* (August 29, 1971). Sara Davidson describes a community

designed by Baba Ram Dass, the American (Richard Alpert) convert to Eastern mysticism: "On Sundays they read the Bible, and on Tuesdays they fasted, worshipped Hanuman and read the Ramayana, the story of Ram" ("Baba Ram Dass," *Ramparts* [February 1973], pp. 35-42 and 62-68).

[12]In *Siddhartha*, for example, Siddhartha hurts many people as he goes on the path to unity with the One. But he never apologizes or confesses. Neither have meaning in his system.

[13]Hesse, *Siddhartha*, p. 116.

[14]Ibid., p. 119.

[15]Humphreys, *Buddhism*, p. 23; and Hesse, *Siddhartha*, p. 106.

[16]Hesse, *Siddhartha*, p. 110.

[17]Ibid., p. 110-11.

[18]Ibid., p. 78.

[19]Mascaró, *Upanishads*, p. 23.

[20]Hesse, *Siddhartha*, p. 122.

[21]Rick Chapman, *How to Choose a Guru* (New York: Harper and Row, 1973).

Chapter 8: A Separate Reality: The New Age

[1]Perhaps Sam Keen came as close as any in his brief article, "The Cosmic versus the Rational," *Psychology Today* (July 1974), pp. 56-59.

[2]Marilyn Ferguson, *The Aquarian Conspiracy: Personal and Social Transformation in the 1980s* (Los Angeles: Tarcher, 1980); and Fritjof Capra, *The Turning Point: Science, Society, and the Rising Culture* (New York: Bantam, 1982). See also Capra's *The Tao of Physics* (New York: Bantam, 1977). A survey article "What Is New Age?" in *The 1988 Guide to New Age Living*, published by *New Age Journal*, surveys the current status of the New Age movement from a New Age perspective.

[3]Douglas R. Groothuis, *Unmasking the New Age* (Downers Grove, Ill.: InterVarsity Press, 1986). In addition Evangelical Ministries to New Religions (P.O. Box 10000, Denver, CO 80210) sponsored a conference on the New Age in March 1985, out of which came "A Statement on the New Age Movement" drafted by a group of Christian scholars led by Professor Gordon Lewis of Denver Seminary. This statement, available from EMNR, defined New Age thought in comparison to Christianity and listed representative people and groups who promote New Age thought and practices. Various specialist organizations have been watching the development; among them are the Spiritual Counterfeits Project, P.O. Box 4308, Berkeley, CA 94704; Christian Research Institute, P.O. Box 500, San Juan Capistrano, CA 92693; and CARIS, P.O. Box 2067, Costa Mesa, CA 92626. Each publishes literature evaluating the New Age movement.

[4]See "Boom Times on the Psychic Frontier," *Time* magazine's cover story (March 4, 1974), which charted the current interest in psychic phenomena—ESP, psychokinesis (the mental ability to influence physical objects), Kirlian photography (which supposedly shows the "aura" of living things), psychic healing, acupuncture, clairvoyance, "out-of-the-body" experiences, precognition (foreknowledge of events). A year later *Saturday Review* (February 22, 1975) paralleled *Time*'s coverage on a more sophisticated plane, suggesting that the popularity of the new consciousness runs deeper than

mere cultural fads such as the God-is-dead theology. News of New Age celebrations at the time of the Harmonic Convergence were carried in many American newspapers and news magazines, some written with considerable tongue-in-cheek. The New Age generates public interest but not always public respect.

[5]*New Age Journal* has gone through an interesting metamorphosis since its inception in 1974 when it began as a magazine published by self-confessed idealistic New Agers. Suffering the threat of extinction in 1983, its longtime editor has written (September 1983, p. 5), it got an infusion of funds and began to take not only a new look—more professional design, slick paper, and four-color interior printing—but a new editorial direction, focusing less on the more extreme exponents of New Age thought and more on the borders between the New Age and mainstream American culture. By June 1984 the change was signaled by new names on its masthead at key editorial positions. The magazine now reflects much more the established ground of the New Age than the cutting edge. The number of issues per year has also been reduced. One might interpret this change as signaling either a coming of age of the New Age movement itself, an attempt to reach the average newsstand magazine buyer with the more palatable of New Age ideas or a commercializing of the New Age by middle-class management. Issues in early 1988 have begun again to carry more sophisticated articles.

[6]*Time* magazine (December 7, 1987), pp. 62-72.

[7]Conducted by *The New Scientist* (see *Time,* March 4, 1974, p. 65).

[8]Paul Chance interview with Stanley Krippner, "Parapsychology Is an Idea Whose Time Has Come," *Psychology Today* (October 1973), p. 105.

[9]Jerry Avron interview with Robert Masters and Jean Houston, "The Varieties of Post-psychedelic Experience," *Intellectual Digest* (March 1973), p. 16. See also the articles by Masters and Houston in *Saturday Review* (February 22, 1975).

[10] Avron, "Varieties," p. 18.

[11] George Leonard, "Notes on the Transformation," *Intellectual Digest* (September 1972), pp. 25 and 32.

[12]*Intellectual Digest* (December 1972), p. 19.

[13]Shirley MacLaine, *It's All in the Playing* (New York: Bantam, 1987), p. 334-35.

[14]Andrew Weil, *The Natural Mind: A Mew Way of Looking at Drugs and the Higher Consciousness* (Boston: Houghton Mifflin, 1972), p. 205; abridged in *Psychology Today* (October 1972).

[15]To investigate further the work of these psychologists and brain scientists without getting bogged down in details, see Marilyn Ferguson, *The Brain Revolution,* especially chapters 1, 3, 6-12, 17, 20-23. Her bibliography provides a good start toward an in-depth study. John W. White's survey of the field, "The Consciousness Revolution," *Saturday Review,* February 22, 1975, pp. 15-19, and his accompanying bibliography and list of research centers studying human consciousness (pp. 33-34) are also helpful. From the standpoint of academic psychology the collection of essays brought together by Charles Tart (who teaches in the Department of Psychology, University of California at Davis) is extremely useful: *Altered States of Consciousness: A Book of Readings* (New York: John Wiley and Sons, 1969); it includes a detailed bibliography of research. The work of those listed in the footnoted paragraph can be examined in the

following: William James, *Varieties of Religious Experience* (New York: Mentor Books, 1958; first published in 1902), lectures 16 and 17; C. G. Jung, *Modern Man in Search of a Soul* (New York: Harcourt Brace, 1933), especially chapter ten; Abraham Maslow, *Religious Values and Peak Experiences* (Columbus: Ohio State Univ. Press, 1962); Robert Masters and Jean Houston, *The Varieties of Psychedelic Experience* (New York: Holt, Rinehart and Winston, 1966) and the interview in *Intellectual Digest* (March 1973), pp. 16-18; also see Kenneth Cavander, "Voyage of the Psychenauts," *Harper's* (January 1974), pp. 68-74; Sam Keen's interview with Oscar Ichazo in *Psychology Today* (July 1973), pp. 64-72; Tony Hiss, "The Chic of Araby" (on Ichazo), *Saturday Review/Society* (May 1973), pp. 53-59; Winifred Rosen, "Down the Up Staircase" (on Ichazo), *Harper's* (July 1973), pp. 28-36; Aldous Huxley, *The Doors of Perception* and *Heaven and Hell* (New York: Harper and Row, 1963); Stanislav Grof, "Beyond the Bounds of Psychoanalysis," *Intellectual Digest* (September 1972), pp. 86-88; for Andrew Weil see footnote 10 above; for a summary of the electronic insight of biofeedback see Barbara Brown, *New Mind, New Body: Biofeedback: New Directions for the Mind* (New York: Harper and Row, 1974), and David Rorvik, "The Theta Experience," *Saturday Review of the Sciences* (May 1973), pp. 46-51; John Lilly's most interesting book is *The Center of the Cyclone: An Autobiography of Inner Space* (New York: Julian Press, 1972), but see also Sam Keen's interview with Lilly in *Psychology Today* (December 1971), pp. 74-77, 91-94; Timothy Leary's most influential book is *The Politics of Ecstasy* (New York: G. P. Putnam's Sons, 1968); some of Leary's thinking can be found in his "The Principles and Practice of Hedonic Psychology," *Psychology Today* (January 1973), pp. 53-58.

[16]Groothuis, *Unmasking*, p. 80; see his chapter on New Age psychology, pp. 71-91. Ken Wilber's books include *See No Boundary* (Boulder, Colo.: Shambhala, 1981); *Up from Eden* (Boulder, Colo.: Shambhala, 1983); and *A Sociable God* (New York: McGraw-Hill, 1983).

[17]For George Leonard, see "Notes on the Transformation"; Theodore Roszak, *Where the Wasteland Ends: Politics and Transcendence in Postindustrial Society* (Garden City, N.Y.: Anchor Books, 1973) and *Unfinished Animal: An Adventure in the Evolution of Consciousness* (New York: Harper and Row, 1975); William Irwin Thompson, *At the Edge of History: Speculations on the Transformation of Culture* (New York: Harper and Row, 1971) and *Passages about Earth* (New York: Harper and Row, 1974); see also Thompson's *Darkness and Scattered Light* (Garden City, N.Y.: Anchor Books, 1978); and *The Time Falling Bodies Take to Light* (New York: St. Martin's Press, 1981).

[18]Carlos Castaneda, *The Teachings of Don Juan: A Yaqui Way of Knowledge* (Berkeley: Univ. of California Press, 1968); *A Separate Reality: Further Conversations with Don Juan* (New York: Simon and Schuster, 1971); *Journey to Ixtlan: The Lessons of Don Juan* (New York: Simon and Schuster, 1972); *Tales of Power* (New York: Simon and Schuster, 1974); *The Eagle's Gift* (New York: Pocket Books, 1982); and *The Fire from Within* (New York: Simon and Schuster, 1984). The last three of these books, while occasionally showing up on best-seller lists, have not had nearly the public impact of the first three. It remains to be seen how his most recent book, *The Power of Silence* (New York: Simon and Schuster, 1987) will be received.

[19]Capra, *The Tao of Physics;* and chapter three in *The Turning Point;* and Gary Zukav, *The Dancing Wu Li Masters* (New York: Bantam, 1980).

[20]See, for example, Thomas's speculation about what happens to human consciousness at death in *The Lives of a Cell* (New York: Bantam, 1975), pp. 60-61. His frequent mention of the Gaia hypothesis—the idea that the earth is a single organism—is also common among New Age thinkers.

[21]J. E. Lovelock, *Gaia: A New Look at Life on Earth* (New York: Oxford University Press, 1979.

[22]An excellent discussion and critique of holistic medicine is to be found in Paul C. Reisser, Teri K. Reisser and John Weldon, *New Age Medicine* (Downers Grove, Ill.: InterVarsity Press, 1988). This book contains a useful bibliography for those wishing to pursue the matter in depth.

[23]See Douglas Groothuis's analysis of New Age politics in *Unmasking the New Age*, pp. 111-30.

[24]Shirley MacLaine calls Kubrick a "master metaphysician" in *Dancing in the Light* (New York: Bantam, 1985), p. 262.

[25]Robert A. Heinlein, *Stranger in a Strange Land* (New York: Berkeley, 1968; first edition 1961).

[26]Jay Kinney, "The Mysterious Revelations of Philip K. Dick," *Gnosis Magazine* (Fall/ Winter 1985), pp. 6-11.

[27]The text of this latter movie reads well and has been published. See Wallace Shawn and André Gregory, *My Dinner with André* (New York: Grove Press, 1981).

[28]George B. Leonard, "Aikido and the Mind of the West," *Intellectual Digest* (June 1973), pp. 17-20; Michael Murphy and John Brodie, "I Experience a Kind of Clarity," *Intellectual Digest* (January 1973), pp. 19-22.

[29]Arthur Koestler, *Roots of Coincidence* (New York: Vintage Books, 1973).

[30]Laurence LeShan, *The Medium, the Mystic and the Physicist: Toward a General Theory of the Paranormal* (New York: Viking Press, 1974).

[31]Jon Klimo, *Channeling: Investigations on Receiving Information from Paranormal Sources* (Los Angeles: Tarcher, 1987).

[32]See, for example, Tony Hiss's "The Chic of Araby," and Winifred Rosen's "Down the Up Staircase" on Ichazo, and Harvard Medical School professor Dr. Lester Grinspoon's review of Weil's *The Natural Mind* in *The New York Times Book Review*, October 15, 1972, pp. 27-29. Critical reviews of Castaneda's work are legion. See *Time* magazine's cover story, March 5, 1973, pp. 36-45. Several more wide-ranging analyses of the whole movement toward a new consciousness deserve special mention for their penetrating insight: Os Guinness, *The Dust of Death*, chapters six to eight; R. C. Zaehner, *Zen, Drugs and Mysticism;* Samuel McCracken, "The Drugs of Habit and the Drugs of Belief," *Commentary* (June 1971), pp. 43-52; Marcia Covell, "Visions of a New Religion" Saturday Review, December 19, 1970; and Richard King, "The Eros Ethos: Cult in the Counterculture," *Psychology Today* (August 1972), pp. 35-37, 66-70.

[33]Jean Houston says, "If we could get such techniques into the schools, not only would they go far toward opening man to the extraordinary capacities he has, but they might also prevent what has historically been the next beat in the process, in which the totalitarian group comes in and takes over" *(Intellectual Digest* [March 1973], p. 18).

[34]Thompson, *Passages about Earth*, p. 124.

[35]Lilly, *The Center of the Cyclone*, pp. 4, 17, 29; but also see in contrast p. 109. Jonathan

Cott, "Knots, Tangles, Fangles, and Whirligigs," *Rolling Stone,* August 30, 1973, p. 66.

[36]Capra, *The Tao of Physics;* and chapter three of *The Turning Point;* Gary Zukav, *The Dancing Wu Li Masters,* 1980; MacLaine, *Dancing in the Light,* pp. 323-24, 329, and 351-53.

[37]Leary, *The Politics of Ecstasy,* p. 200.

[38]Weil, *The Natural Mind,* chapters six and seven. Many, if not most, of the new consciousness proponents recognize the close affinity of their notions to those of the East, and some believe this to be a strong indication that they are on the right track—taking the best of both worlds. See, for example, Weil, *The Natural Mind,* pp. 175-77; Cavander, "Voyage of the Psychenauts," pp. 92, 160, 171-74; and Grof, "Beyond the Bounds of Psychoanalysis," pp. 87-88. The syncretist tendency of the East we have already noted in chapter seven above.

[39]Eugene Nida and William A. Smalley, *Introducing Animism* (New York: Friendship Press, 1959), p. 50. This brief pamphlet is a remarkable repository of information on modern pagan animism.

[40]Roszak, *Where the Wasteland Ends,* p. xv.

[41]Robert Bellah's study of individualism in America illuminates one major force behind the New Age emphasis on the self as the kingpin of reality. See Robert N. Bellah and others, *Habits of the Heart* (New York: Harper and Row, 1985).

[42]Lilly, *Center of the Cyclone,* p. 210.

[43]Ibid., p. 110.

[44]Ibid., p. 51; italics Lilly's. LeShan is more modest. He writes concerning the way post-Einsteinian science views reality that "within this view, man does not only discover reality; within limits he invents it" *(The Medium, the Mystic and the Physicist,* p. 155).

[45]MacLaine, *It's All in the Playing,* p. 192. David Spangler, the spiritual leader at Findhorn, goes even further than MacLaine: "I AM now the Life of a new heaven and a new earth. Others must draw upon Me and unite with Me to build its forms. . . . There is always only what I AM, but I have revealed Myself in new Life and new Light and new Truth. . . . It is My function through this centre [Findhorn] to demonstrate what I AM through the medium of group evolution." Spangler is talking the language of the elite. Some people have achieved godhead; others are on the way. But the elite—here it is Spangler alone—must show them the way. This *self* is in the vanguard of a host of selves caught up in the evolution of the race through the calling out of a group set apart, the Findhorn group, of course. See David Spangler, *Revelation: The Birth of a New Age* (Findhorn, 1971), pp. 110, 121, quoted in Thompson, *Passages about Earth,* p. 173. Such writing echoes the words of the God, Krishna, in the Bhagavad Gita (6.29-31). I have long had a theory that the far-out, weird and strange writers who make themselves out to be a god—or the God—capitalize every other word or so. Manuscripts I have received as an editor from such authors as that of the God-Principle bear this out. Thompson himself is hard put to know what to think of this strange elitist language, but he appears to see Spangler as one of the first of the transformed people of the New Age (Thompson, *Passages about Earth,* p. 174).

[46]Marilyn Ferguson, *The Brain Revolution,* p. 344; "Life at the Leading Edge: A *New Age* Interview with Marilyn Ferguson," *New Age* magazine (August 1982); Weil, *The Natural Mind,* pp. 204-5; Keen, *Psychology Today* interview, p. 72, quotes Ichazo as saying.

"Humanity is the Messiah." Weil, by the way, says, "I am almost tempted to call the psychotics the evolutionary vanguard of our species. They possess the secret of changing reality by changing the mind; if they can use that talent for positive ends, there are no limits to what they can accomplish" (p. 182). LeShan would seem to agree *(The Medium, the Mystic and the Physicist*, pp. 211-12). Thompson in *Passages about Earth* is optimistic throughout, but see esp. p. 149; twelve years later in "A Gaian Politics," *Whole Earth Review* (Winter, 1986), p. 4, he expressed some reservations, opining that the spirit of the age had replaced " 'Star Trek' and 'Kung Fu' with 'Dynasty' and 'Dallas,' Joni Mitchell with Madonna, and 'Close Encounters' with 'Rambo.' "

[47]Quoted by Peggy Taylor, "Life at the Leading Edge: A *New Age* Interview with Marilyn Ferguson," *New Age* (August 1982), p. 31.

[48]Leonard, "Aikido and the Mind of the West," p. 20.

[49]Laura Archera Huxley, *This Timeless Moment: A Personal View of Aldous Huxley* (New York: Ballantine Books, 1971; first published 1968), pp. 249-51.

[50]Aldous Huxley, *Doors of Perception*, p. 13.

[51]Ibid., p. 22.

[52]Ibid., p. 23.

[53]Ibid. By the way, some readers will have already picked up an inner contradiction in what Huxley has said. On the one hand, without a new consciousness humanity will not be able to survive on this planet; on the other hand, the self, if it just realized it, is the center of the cosmos. Since the cosmos is eternal (a notion implicit in Huxley's system), the self is eternal. So why worry about life on earth? This why-worry attitude has been the position of the East for centuries; but it seems that when the West goes East for wisdom it cannot slough off all the Western baggage—one piece of which is firmly rooted in the Judeo-Christian notion that this present world (people on earth) counts for something.

[54]Gopi Krishna, for example, has been introduced to Western readers in an article written by astrophysicist and biologist Friedrich von Weizsäcker, director of the Max Planck Institute for the Life Sciences: "Gopi Krishna and the Power of Kundalini," *The New Age Book Review* 2, no. 2 (1983):6-11.

[55]MacLaine, *Out on a Limb*, p. 74 and *It's All in the Playing*, p. 265; Castaneda, *A Separate Reality;* LeShan, *The Medium, the Mystic and the Physicist*, p. 34; Lilly, *Center of the Cyclone*, p. 25; Leonard, "Aikido and the Mind of the West," p. 20; Michael Murphy and John Brodie, "I Experience a Kind of Clarity," p. 22; Albert Rosenfeld, "Mind and Supermind," *Saturday Review*, February 22, 1975, p. 10; Jon Klimo, *Channeling*, pp. 174-76.

[56]MacLaine, *It's All in the Playing*, p. 188.

[57]MacLaine, *Dancing in the Light*, p. 309.

[58]MacLaine, *It's All in the Playing*, p. 331.

[59]Lilly, *Center of the Cyclone*, p. 110.

[60]Ibid., p. 5.

[61]Aldous Huxley, *Doors of Perception*, p. 89.

[62]Lilly, *Center of the Cyclone*, p. 180; also see pp. 10, 54.

[63]Ferguson, *The Brain Revolution*, pp. 61-63.

[64]Quoted by "Adam Smith" in "Alumni Notes—Altered States U," *Psychology Today* (July 1973), p. 79.

[65]Castaneda, *A Separate Reality*, p. 235; *Journey to Ixtlan*, pp. 297-298; and *Tales of Power*, p. 219.

[66]Aldous Huxley, *Doors of Perception*, pp. 17-18.

[67]Others do, however, emphasize the continuity, if not unity, of the self, the visible and the invisible universe. See Ferguson, *The Brain Revolution*, p. 21; Thompson, *Passages about Earth*, pp. 97-103 and 166; Lilly, *Center of the Cyclone*, p. 211 and Koestler, *Roots of Coincidence*, pp. 58-59, 106 and 126.

[68]Allusions to her past lives occur throughout MacLaine's writings, but a sort of litany of them appears in *Dancing in the Light*, pp. 366-84. The account of her meeting with her Higher Self in *Dancing in the Light*, pp. 334-35, is quoted on p. 195 below.

[69]Castaneda, *Teachings of Don Juan*, pp. 32, 136-38; *A Separate Reality* pp. 51, 140, 144, 158-59; *Journey to Ixtlan*, pp. 213-15; *Tales of Power*, p. 46, 87-89, 239, 257.

[70]Lilly, *Center of the Cyclone*, pp. 27, 39, 55-57, 90-91 and 199.

[71]Cavander, "Voyage of the Psychenauts," p. 70. MacLaine demonstrates this in *It's All in the Playing*, pp. 191-93; see p. 200 below.

[72]See Lilly's chart (*Center of the Cyclone*, pp. 148-49) detailing and describing his, Gurdjieff's and Taimni's various levels of consciousness and their labels.

[73]Zaehner, *Zen, Drugs and Mysticism*, p. 42; James, *Varieties of Religious Experience*, p. 306; LeShan, *The Medium, the Mystic and the Physicist*, p. 94; Keen, "The Cosmic Versus the Rational," p. 58.

[74]R. M. Bucke, *Cosmic Consciousness* (Philadelphia, 1901), p. 2, as quoted in James, *Varieties of Religious Experience*, p. 306. Bucke also mentions "a quickening of the moral sense," but this is unusual as we shall see below.

[75]Again, see Lilly's various levels (*Center of the Cyclone*, pp. 148-49).

[76]MacLaine, *Dancing in the Light*, p. 350; italics hers.

[77]Ferguson, *The Brain Revolution*, p. 60. See also the descriptions in Lilly, *Center of the Cyclone*, chapters eleven to eighteen; James, *Varieties of Religious Experience*, pp. 292-328; LeShan, *The Medium, the Mystic and the Physicist*, pp. 86-87, 250; Zaehner, *Zen, Drugs and Mysticism*, pp. 89-94; virtually every discussion of altered states of consciousness will mention many, if not all, of those characteristics. For a more scientific approach to the characteristics of altered states of consciousness, see Arnold M. Ludwig, "Altered States of Consciousness, in Tart, *Altered States of Consciousness*, pp. 9-22.

[78]See pp. 148-50.

[79]MacLaine, *Dancing in the Light*, pp. 202-3, 242-43, 248-49, 269, 341-42, 345, 351, 363-64, 383; and *It's All in the Playing*, pp. 173-75.

[80]James, *Varieties of Religious Experience*, p. 306; Thompson, *Passages about Earth*, pp. 29, 82; Lilly, *Center of the Cyclone*, pp. 20, 171, 180; Huxley, *Doors of Perception*, p. 39.

[81]Aldous Huxley, *Doors of Perception*, p. 55; see also pp. 51, 54-58, 133-40.

[82]Ibid., p. 54.

[83]Lilly, *Center of the Cyclone*, pp. 24-25, 33, 88-90, 169; and Castaneda, throughout his first four books.

[84]MacLaine, *It's All in the Playing*, pp. 162-71.

[85]Lilly, *Center of the Cyclone*, p. 35; Laura Huxley, *This Timeless Moment*, pp. 275-88; Weil, *The Natural Mind*, pp. 83, 95.

[86]Keen recounts Ichazo's notion of the "fall" of man in "A Conversation . . . ," p. 67.

[87]MacLaine, *Dancing in the Light*, p. 339; also see p. 255.

[88]Grof, "Beyond the Bounds of Psychoanalysis," pp. 86-88; Lilly, *Center of the Cyclone*, pp. 17, 35; LeShan, *The Medium, the Mystic and the Physicist*, pp. 232-64; James, *Varieties of Religious Experience*, p. 306; Zaehner, *Zen, Drugs and Mysticism*, p. 44.

[89]Elisabeth Kübler-Ross, *On Death and Dying* (New York: Macmillan, 1969). For an explanation of her views and a critique from a Christian perspective see Phillip J. Swihart, *The Edge of Death* (Downers Grove, Ill.: InterVarsity Press, 1978), pp. 25-31; this book contains a useful bibliography of books on near-death and other out-of-the-body experiences.

[90]Raymond J. Moody, Jr., *Life after Life* (New York: Bantam, 1976).

[91]MacLaine, *Dancing in the Light*, pp. 353-59, 366.

[92]MacLaine, *It's All in the Playing*, p. 166.

[93]See Christian critics Swihart, *Edge of Death*, pp. 41-82, esp. 67-69; and Mark Albrecht, *Reincarnation* (1982; reprint ed., Downers Grove, Ill.: InterVarsity Press, 1987); for a secular humanist perspective see Melvin Harris "Are 'Past-Life' Regressions Evidence of Reincarnation?" *Free Inquiry* (Fall 1986), pp. 18-23; and Paul Edwards's three-part article "The Case against Reincarnation," *Free Inquiry* (Fall 1986), pp. 24-34; (Winter 1986/87), pp. 38-43, 46-48; (Spring 1987), pp. 38-43, 46-49.

[94]Aldous Huxley, *Doors of Perception*, p. 13.

[95]Ibid., p. 140. See also Huxley's novel *Island* where he gives many of these new conscious notions a fuller, imaginative treatment.

[96]Lilly, *Center of the Cyclone*, p. 39. The omitted sentences suggest several nonoccult alternatives, including conceptual relativism.

[97]Benjamin Whorf, *Language, Thought and Reality*, ed. John B. Carroll (Cambridge, Mass.: MIT Press, 1951), p. 57.

[98]Ibid., p, 58.

[99]Stuart Chase, from the Foreword to *Language, Thought and Reality*, p. vi.

[100]*Intellectual Digest* (March 1973), p. 18. That his conclusion does not follow from his illustration is beside the point here.

[101]Ernst Cassirer, *Language and Myth*, trans. Susanne K. Langer (New York: Dover, 1946), p. 7.

[102]Ibid., pp. 7-8.

[103]Ibid., p. 8.

[104]LeShan, *The Medium, the Mystic and the Physicist*, p. 43. He is relying on Bertrand Russell for the list, but he documents from his own experience and that of clairvoyants he has interviewed.

[105]I strongly suspect that there is nothing but a metaphoric relationship between the concept of complementarity as used by the scientists and the version of conceptual relativism advocated by LeShan and other new-consciousness theorizers. But it is always a good rhetorical ploy to appeal to the prestige of science—even while advocating a world view that, if practiced, would destroy scientific initiative.

[106]Weil, *The Natural Mind*, p. 212.

[107]Quoted in Ferguson, *The Brain Revolution*, p. 19. See also Koestler, *Roots of Coincidence*, pp. 54-59. Of course, if there is no way of measuring the truth of a model for reality,

there is no way of measuring its falsity. So the idea that all of our models of reality are wrong is a denial of all meaning and thus a case of ciphered nihilism (see Thielicke, *Nihilism*, pp. 63-65).

[108]For a different view of the notion of complementarity, see Donald MacKay, *The Clockwork Image* (Downers Grove, Ill: InterVarsity Press, 1974), pp. 91-92.

[109]See Ferguson, *The Brain Revolution*, p. 83; Weil, *The Natural Mind*, p. 67; LeShan, *The Medium, the Mystic and the Physicist*, pp. 99, 124, 139, 150; James, *Varieties of Religious Experience*, p. 308; Ichazo quoted by Keen, "A Conversation . . ." p. 70; Lilly, *Center of the Cyclone*, throughout.

[110]LeShan, *The Medium, the Mystic and the Physicist*, p. 125.

[111]Weil, *The Natural Mind*, p. 67. This pragmatic criteria also governs the judgment of Charles Tart and Jon Klimo (Klimo, *Channeling*, pp. xiv and 23).

[112]Lilly, *Center of the Cyclone*, p. 5.

[113]Ibid., pp. 87, 48.

[114]Quoted by Peter Mezan, "After Freud and Jung, Now Comes R. D. Laing: Popshrink, Rebel, Yogi, Philosopher-king? *Esquire* (January 1972), p. 171.

[115]Ibid.

[116]Ibid.

[117]Keen, "The Cosmic versus the Rational," p. 57.

[118]Although early on readers wondered if Castaneda had not created Don Juan out of his own fertile imagination (see the various viewpoints expressed by the critics such as Joyce Carol Oates anthologized in *Seeing Castaneda*, ed. Daniel C. Noel [New York: Putnam's Sons, 1976]), Richard De Mille may be credited with convincingly unmasking the fictional character of Castaneda's books; see his *Castaneda's Journey: The Power and the Allegory* (Santa Barbara, Calif.: Capra, 1976). Nonetheless, in the foreword to *The Power of Silence* Castaneda maintains, "My books are a true account of a teaching method that Juan Matus, a Mexican Indian sorcerer, used in order to help me understand the sorcerers' world" (p. 8).

[119]Jon Klimo, *Channeling*, p. 42.

[120]MacLaine, *It's All in the Playing*, p 172.

[121]David Tuller, "New Age: An Old Subject Surges in the '80s," *Publishers Weekly* (September 25, 1987), p. 30. This issue features several articles on the publication and marketing of New Age books and includes an extensive publisher-by-publisher list of books currently being promoted by New Age publishers.

[122]Quoted by Allene Symons, "Inner Visions," *Publishers Weekly* (September 25, 1987), p. 75.

[123]MacLaine, *Out on a Limb*, p. 327.

[124]Ibid., pp. 327-29.

[125]MacLaine, *Dancing in the Light*, pp. 334-35.

[126]Ibid., pp. 339-40.

[127]Ibid., p. 354. The summary which follows covers MacLaine's account on pp. 354-58.

[128]Ibid., p. 358.

[129]Ibid.

[130]Ibid., pp. 341-42.

[131]MacLaine, *"Don't Fall Off the Mountain,"* p. 253.

[132]*Dancing in the Light,* p. 350. This melange of sayings combines phrases from many sources: *The Kingdom of Heaven is within you* is probably a misquotation of Luke 17:21 where Jesus says (as translated in the King James Version), "The kingdom of *God* is within you" (this verse is more accurately translated as "The kingdom of God is *among* you [plural]," or *"in the midst* of you [plural], emphasizing the communal nature of God's reign among his people), *Know thyself* (the Delphic Oracle quoted by Socrates), *that will set you free* (the words of Jesus in John 8: 32 attached to a very different notion from "know thyself"), *to thine own self be true* (the words of Polonius, the old fool in Shakespeare's *Hamlet*), *know that you are God* (reflective of Psalm 46:10 in which Yahweh is quoted as saying, "Be still and know that *I* am God," a quite opposite notion). After quoting these lines, MacLaine adds that "the spiritual masters had all said the same thing. They had each taught that the soul is eternal. They had each alluded to having lived many times before, even Christ: 'I came before, but you didn't recognize me.' They had each taught that the purpose of life was to work one's way back to the Divine Source of which we were all a part." MacLaine does not give the source of her quotation from Christ, and I am unaware of it anywhere in the Bible. In any case, nothing Jesus says there points to reincarnation or to the notion that we are to work our way back to the Divine Source. Moreover, we are not a part of that Source, according to the Bible, but a creation of that Source. This is only one instance of MacLaine's frequent distortion or misunderstanding of religious texts. See also *Out on a Limb,* pp. 209, 211, 233, 239-40, 242-44; on p. 297 she inaccurately attributes "Know thyself" to Christ. Other instances of misinterpretation are found in *"Don't Fall Off the Mountain,"* p. 216; *Dancing in the Light,* pp. 114, 254-55; and *It's All in the Playing,* pp. 221-22. For a general study of misinterpretation of Scripture see my *Scripture Twisting* (Downers Grove, Ill.: InterVarsity Press, 1980).

[133]MacLaine, *It's All in the Playing,* pp. 191-93.

[134]Ibid., p. 323.

[135]Ibid., p. 175.

[136]Ibid., p. 174.

[137]Ibid.

[138]At least one reviewer of *It's All in the Playing,* Dennis Livingston, in *New Age Journal* (November/December, 1987), p. 79, has noted these problems: "I found the implications of her philosophy cruel and callous. . . . It all sounds like the perfect Yuppie religion, a modern prime-time rerun of nineteenth-century Social Darwinism."

[139]Pope, *Essay on Man,* I, line 95.

[140]Thompson, *Passages about Earth,* p. 99.

[141]At this point there is little difference between B. F. Skinner and William Irwin Thompson; see *Beyond Freedom and Dignity,* pp. 180-82, and *Passages about Earth,* pp. 117-18.

[142]See above, pp. 116-17.

[143]See, for example, Mt 7:21-23; Lk 10:20; Acts 8:9-24; 13:8-11; 19:11-20; Gal 5:19-21; Jas 3:13-18; Rev 21:8. See also "Magic and Sorcery," *New Bible Dictionary* (Grand Rapids: Eerdmans, 1961), pp. 766-71.

[144]The word *valid* goes through some interesting permutations in LeShan, *The Medium,*

the Mystic and the Physicist, pp. 99, 108, 150, 154, 210.

[145]Perhaps Thielicke would call it ciphered nihilism; see Thielicke, *Nihilism,* pp. 36, 63-65.

[146]McCracken, "The Drugs of Habit . . ." p. 49.

Chapter 9: The Examined Life

[1]Schaeffer, *The God Who Is There,* p. 88.

[2]Yandell, "Religious Experience," p. 185.

[3]Each formulation of each world view must be considered on its own merits, of course. But for each of the world views I have weighed and found wanting I know no formulation which does not contain problems of inconsistency.

[4]See, for example, Rom 1:28.

[5]For a full treatment of the nature of doubt and its contribution to the formulation of an adequate world view see Os Guinness, *Doubt* (London: Lion, 1976).

[6]Hopkins, "God's Grandeur," p. 66.

[7]The New Testament is the primary text for Christian theism, but I also recommend John R. W. Stott, *Basic Christianity,* rev. ed. (Downers Grove, Ill.: InterVarsity Press, 1973) and J. I. Packer, *Knowing God* (Downers Grove, Ill.: InterVarsity Press, 1973).

Index